MAY 0 1 2014

COMMON CORE MATHEMATICS

A Story of Units

Grade 5, Module 5: Addition and Multiplication with Volume and Area

COMMON CORE™ *consider the source*

East Meadow Public Library
1886 Front Street, East Meadow, NY 11554
(516) 794-2570
www.eastmeadow.info

JB JOSSEY-BASS™

A Wiley Brand

Cover design by Chris Clary

Copyright © 2014 by Common Core, Inc. All rights reserved.

Published by Jossey-Bass
A Wiley Brand
One Montgomery Street, Suite 1200, San Francisco, CA 94104-4594—www.josseybass.com

No part of this publication may be reproduced, stored in a retrieval system, or transmitted in any form or by any means, electronic, mechanical, photocopying, recording, scanning, or otherwise, except as permitted under Section 107 or 108 of the 1976 United States Copyright Act, without either the prior written permission of the publisher, or authorization through payment of the appropriate per-copy fee to the Copyright Clearance Center, Inc., 222 Rosewood Drive, Danvers, MA 01923, 978-750-8400, fax 978-646-8600, or on the Web at www.copyright.com. Requests to the publisher for permission should be addressed to the Permissions Department, John Wiley & Sons, Inc., 111 River Street, Hoboken, NJ 07030, 201-748-6011, fax 201-748-6008, or online at www.wiley.com/go/permissions.

Permission is given for individual classroom teachers to reproduce the pages and illustrations for classroom use. Reproduction of these materials for an entire school system is strictly forbidden.

Limit of Liability/Disclaimer of Warranty: While the publisher and author have used their best efforts in preparing this book, they make no representations or warranties with respect to the accuracy or completeness of the contents of this book and specifically disclaim any implied warranties of merchantability or fitness for a particular purpose. No warranty may be created or extended by sales representatives or written sales materials. The advice and strategies contained herein may not be suitable for your situation. You should consult with a professional where appropriate. Neither the publisher nor author shall be liable for any loss of profit or any other commercial damages, including but not limited to special, incidental, consequential, or other damages. Readers should be aware that Internet Web sites offered as citations and/or sources for further information may have changed or disappeared between the time this was written and when it is read.

ISBN: 978-1-118-81139-9

Printed in the United States of America
FIRST EDITION
PB Printing   10 9 8 7 6 5 4 3 2 1

WELCOME

Dear Teacher,

Thank you for your interest in Common Core's curriculum in mathematics. Common Core is a non-profit organization based in Washington, DC dedicated to helping K-12 public schoolteachers use the power of high-quality content to improve instruction.[1] We are led by a board of master teachers, scholars, and current and former school, district, and state education leaders. Common Core has responded to the Common Core State Standards' (CCSS) call for "content-rich curriculum"[2] by creating new, CCSS-based curriculum materials in mathematics, English Language Arts, history, and (soon) the arts. All of our materials are written by teachers who are among the nation's foremost experts on the new standards.

In 2012 Common Core won three contracts from the New York State Education Department to create a PreKindergarten–12th grade mathematics curriculum for the teachers of that state, and to conduct associated professional development. The book you hold contains a portion of that work. In order to respond to demand in New York and elsewhere, modules of the curriculum will continue to be published, on a rolling basis, as they are completed. This curriculum is based on New York's version of the CCSS (the CCLS, or Common Core Learning Standards). Common Core will be releasing an enhanced version of the curriculum this summer on our website, commoncore.org. That version also will be published by Jossey-Bass, a Wiley brand.

Common Core's curriculum materials are not merely aligned to the new standards, they take the CCSS as their very foundation. Our work in math takes its shape from the expectations embedded in the new standards— including the instructional shifts and mathematical progressions, and the new expectations for student fluency, deep conceptual understanding, and application to real-life context. Similarly, our ELA and history curricula are deeply informed by the CCSS's new emphasis on close reading, increased use of informational text, and evidence-based writing.

Our curriculum is distinguished not only by its adherence to the CCSS. The math curriculum is based on a theory of teaching math that is proven to work. That theory posits that mathematical knowledge is most coherently and

---

1. Despite the coincidence of name, Common Core and the Common Core State Standards are not affiliated. Common Core was established in 2007, prior to the start of the Common Core State Standards Initiative, which was led by the National Governors Association and the Council for Chief State School Officers.

2. *Common Core State Standards for English Language Arts & Literacy in History/Social Studies, Science, and Technical Subjects* (Washington, DC: Common Core State Standards Initiative), 6.

effectively conveyed when it is taught in a sequence that follows the "story" of mathematics itself. This is why we call the elementary portion of this curriculum "A Story of Units," to be followed by "A Story of Ratios" in middle school, and "A Story of Functions" in high school. Mathematical concepts flow logically, from one to the next, in this curriculum. The sequencing has been joined with methods of instruction that have been proven to work, in this nation and abroad. These methods drive student understanding beyond process, to deep mastery of mathematical concepts. The goal of the curriculum is to produce students who are not merely literate, but fluent, in mathematics.

It is important to note that, as extensive as these curriculum materials are, they are not meant to be prescriptive. Rather, they are intended to provide a basis for teachers to hone their own craft through study, collaboration, training, and the application of their own expertise as professionals. At Common Core we believe deeply in the ability of teachers and in their central and irreplaceable role in shaping the classroom experience. We strive only to support and facilitate their important work.

The teachers and scholars who wrote these materials are listed beginning on the next page. Their deep knowledge of mathematics, of the CCSS, and of what works in classrooms defined this work in every respect. I would like to thank Louisiana State University professor of mathematics Scott Baldridge for the intellectual leadership he provides to this project. Teacher, trainer, and writer Robin Ramos is the most inspired math educator I've ever encountered. It is Robin and Scott's aspirations for what mathematics education in America *should* look like that is spelled out in these pages.

Finally, this work owes a debt to project director Nell McAnelly that is so deep I'm confident it never can be repaid. Nell, who leads LSU's Gordon A. Cain Center for STEM Literacy, oversees all aspects of our work for NYSED. She has spent days, nights, weekends, and many cancelled vacations toiling in her efforts to make it possible for this talented group of teacher-writers to produce their best work against impossible deadlines. I'm confident that in the years to come Scott, Robin, and Nell will be among those who will deserve to be credited with putting math instruction in our nation back on track.

Thank you for taking an interest in our work. Please join us at www.commoncore.org.

Lynne Munson
President and Executive Director
Common Core
Washington, DC
October 25, 2013

Common Core's Trustees

Erik Berg, elementary public school teacher in Boston, Massachusetts
Barbara Byrd-Bennett, Chief Executive Officer of the Chicago Public Schools
Antonia Cortese, former Secretary-Treasurer of the American Federation of Teachers
Pascal Forgione, Jr., Executive Director of the Center on K-12 Assessment and Performance Management at ETS
Lorraine Griffith, elementary public school teacher in Asheville, North Carolina
Jason Griffiths, Principal of the Harlem Village Academy High School
Bill Honig, President of the Consortium on Reading Excellence
Carol Jago, Director of the California Reading and Literature Project at UCLA
Richard Kessler, Dean of Mannes College, The New School for Music
Lynne Munson, President and Executive Director of Common Core
Juan Rangel, Chief Executive Officer of Chicago-based United Neighborhood Organization

Common Core's Washington, D.C., Staff

Lynne Munson, President and Executive Director
Barbara Davidson, Deputy Director
Sandra Elliott, Director of Professional Development
Sarah Woodard, Programs Manager
Rachel Rooney, Programs Manager
Alyson Burgess, Partnerships Manager
Becca Wammack, Development Manager
Lauren Shaw, Programs Assistant
Diego Quiroga, Membership Coordinator
Elisabeth Mox, Executive Assistant to the President

Common Core's K-5 Math Staff

Scott Baldridge, Lead Mathematician and Writer
Robin Ramos, Lead Writer, PreKindergarten-5
Jill Diniz, Lead Writer, 6-12
Ben McCarty, Mathematician

Nell McAnelly, Project Director
Tiah Alphonso, Associate Director
Jennifer Loftin, Associate Director
Catriona Anderson, Curriculum Manager,
  PreKindergarten-5

Sherri Adler, PreKindergarten
Debbie Andorka-Aceves, PreKindergarten

Kate McGill Austin, Kindergarten
Nancy Diorio, Kindergarten
Lacy Endo-Peery, Kindergarten
Melanie Gutierrez, Kindergarten
Nuhad Jamal, Kindergarten
Cecilia Rudzitis, Kindergarten
Shelly Snow, Kindergarten

Beth Barnes, First Grade
Lily Cavanaugh, First Grade
Ana Estela, First Grade
Kelley Isinger, First Grade
Kelly Spinks, First Grade
Marianne Strayton, First Grade
Hae Jung Yang, First Grade

Wendy Keehfus-Jones, Second Grade
Susan Midlarsky, Second Grade
Jenny Petrosino, Second Grade
Colleen Sheeron, Second Grade
Nancy Sommer, Second Grade
Lisa Watts-Lawton, Second Grade
MaryJo Wieland, Second Grade
Jessa Woods, Second Grade

Eric Angel, Third Grade
Greg Gorman, Third Grade
Susan Lee, Third Grade
Cristina Metcalf, Third Grade
Ann Rose Santoro, Third Grade
Kevin Tougher, Third Grade
Victoria Peacock, Third Grade
Saffron VanGalder, Third Grade

Katrina Abdussalaam, Fourth Grade
Kelly Alsup, Fourth Grade
Patti Dieck, Fourth Grade
Mary Jones, Fourth Grade
Soojin Lu, Fourth Grade
Tricia Salerno, Fourth Grade
Gail Smith, Fourth Grade
Eric Welch, Fourth Grade
Sam Wertheim, Fourth Grade
Erin Wheeler, Fourth Grade

Leslie Arceneaux, Fifth Grade
Adam Baker, Fifth Grade
Janice Fan, Fifth Grade
Peggy Golden, Fifth Grade
Halle Kananak, Fifth Grade
Shauntina Kerrison, Fifth Grade
Pat Mohr, Fifth Grade
Chris Sarlo, Fifth Grade

Additional Writers

Bill Davidson, Fluency Specialist
Robin Hecht, UDL Specialist
Simon Pfeil, Mathematician

Document Management Team

Tam Le, Document Manager
Jennifer Merchan, Copy Editor

Mathematics Curriculum

Table of Contents

GRADE 5 • MODULE 5

Addition and Multiplication with Volume and Area

© 2014 Common Core, Inc. All rights reserved. commoncore.org

Grade 5 • Module 5

Addition and Multiplication with Volume and Area

OVERVIEW

In this 25-day module, students work with two- and three-dimensional figures. Volume is introduced to students through concrete exploration of cubic units and culminates with the development of the volume formula for right rectangular prisms. The second half of the module turns to extending students' understanding of two-dimensional figures. Students combine prior knowledge of area with newly acquired knowledge of fraction multiplication to determine the area of rectangular figures with fractional side lengths. They then engage in hands-on construction of two-dimensional shapes, developing a foundation for classifying the shapes by reasoning about their attributes. This module fills a gap between Grade 4's work with two-dimensional figures and Grade 6's work with volume and area.

In Topic A, students extend their spatial structuring to three dimensions through an exploration of volume. Students come to see volume as an attribute of solid figures and understand that cubic units are used to measure it (**5.MD.3**). Using improvised, customary, and metric units, they build three-dimensional shapes, including right rectangular prisms, and count units to find the volume (**5.MD.4**). By developing a systematic approach to counting the unit cubes, students make connections between area and volume. They partition a rectangular prism into layers of unit cubes and reason that the number of unit cubes in a single layer corresponds to the number of unit squares on a face. They begin to conceptualize the layers themselves, oriented in any one of three directions, as iterated units. This understanding allows students to reason about containers formed by nets, reasonably predict the number of cubes required to fill them, and test their prediction by packing the container.

Concrete understanding of volume and multiplicative reasoning (**5.MD.3**) come together in Topic B as the systematic counting from Topic A leads naturally to formulas for finding the volume of a right rectangular prism (**5.MD.5**). Students solidify the connection between volume as *packing* and volume as *filling* by comparing the amount of liquid that fills a container to the number of cubes that can be packed into it. This connection is formalized as students see that 1 cubic centimeter is equal to 1 milliliter. Complexity increases as students use their knowledge that volume is additive to partition and calculate the total volume of solid figures composed of non-overlapping, rectangular prisms. Word problems involving the volume of rectangular prisms with whole number edge lengths solidify understanding and give students opportunity to reason about scaling in the context of volume. This topic concludes with a design project that gives students the opportunity to apply the concepts and formulas they have learned throughout Topics A and B to create a sculpture of a specified volume composed of varied rectangular prisms with parameters given in the project description.

In Topic C, students extend their understanding of area as they use rulers and set squares to construct and measure rectangles with fractional side lengths and find their areas. They apply their extensive knowledge of fraction multiplication to interpret areas of rectangles with fractional side lengths (**5.NF.4b**) and solve real world problems involving these figures (**5.NF.6**), including reasoning about scaling through contexts in which

Module 5:   Addition and Multiplication with Volume and Area
Date: 1/10/14

© 2014 Common Core, Inc. All rights reserved. **commoncore.org**

volumes are compared. Visual models and equations are used to represent the problems through the Read-Draw-Write protocol.

In Topic D, students draw two-dimensional shapes in order to analyze their attributes and use those attributes to classify them. Familiar figures, such as parallelograms, rhombuses, squares, trapezoids, etc., have all been defined in earlier grades, and by Grade 4 students have gained an understanding of shapes beyond the intuitive level. Grade 5 extends this understanding through an in-depth analysis of the properties and defining attributes of quadrilaterals. Grade 4's work with the protractor is applied in order to construct various quadrilaterals. Using measurement tools illuminates the attributes used to define and recognize each quadrilateral (**5.G.3**). Students see, for example, that the same process that they used to construct a parallelogram will also produce a rectangle when all angles are constructed to measure 90°. Students then analyze defining attributes and create a hierarchical classification of quadrilaterals (**5.G.4**).

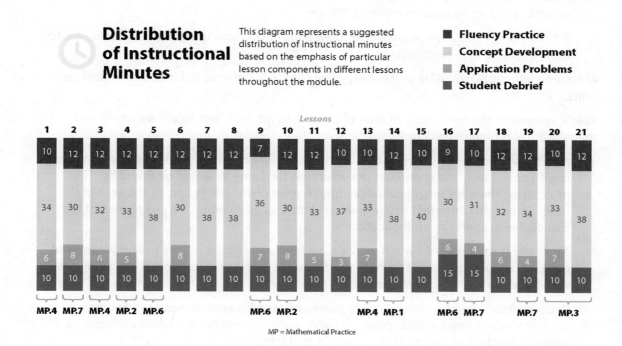

Distribution of Instructional Minutes

This diagram represents a suggested distribution of instructional minutes based on the emphasis of particular lesson components in different lessons throughout the module.

- ■ Fluency Practice
- ■ Concept Development
- ■ Application Problems
- ■ Student Debrief

MP = Mathematical Practice

Focus Grade Level Standards

Apply and extend previous understanding of multiplication and division to multiply and divide fractions.[1]

5.NF.4   Apply and extend previous understandings of multiplication to multiply a fraction or whole number by a fraction.

---
[1] The balance of this cluster is addressed in Module 4.

| | Module 5: | Addition and Multiplication with Volume and Area | |
| Date: | 1/10/14 |

iii

© 2014 Common Core, Inc. All rights reserved. commoncore.org

b. Find the area of a rectangle with fractional side lengths by tiling it with unit squares of the appropriate unit fraction side lengths, and show that the area is the same as would be found by multiplying the side lengths. Multiply fractional side lengths to find areas of rectangles, and represent fraction products as rectangular areas.

5.NF.6 Solve real world problems involving multiplication of fractions and mixed numbers, e.g., by using visual fraction models or equations to represent the problem.

Geometric measurement: understand concepts of volume and relate volume to multiplication and addition.

5.MD.3 Recognize volume as an attribute of solid figures and understand concepts of volume measurement.

a. A cube with side length 1 unit, called a "unit cube," is said to have "one cubic unit" of volume, and can be used to measure volume.

b. A solid figure which can be packed without gaps or overlaps using *n* unit cubes is said to have a volume of *n* cubic units.

5.MD.4 Measure volumes by counting unit cubes, using cubic cm, cubic in, cubic ft, and improvised units.

5.MD.5 Relate volume to the operations of multiplication and addition and solve real world and mathematical problems involving volume.

a. Find the volume of a right rectangular prism with whole-number side lengths by packing it with unit cubes, and show that the volume is the same as would be found by multiplying the edge lengths, equivalently by multiplying the height by the area of the base. Represent threefold whole-number products as volumes, e.g., to represent the associative property of multiplication.

b. Apply the formulas $V = l \times w \times h$ and $V = b \times h$ for rectangular prisms to find volumes of right rectangular prisms with whole-number edge lengths in the context of solving real world and mathematical problems.

c. Recognize volume as additive. Find volumes of solid figures composed of two non-overlapping right rectangular prisms by adding the volumes of the non-overlapping parts, applying this technique to solve real world problems.

Classify two-dimensional figures into categories based on their properties.

5.G.3 Understand that attributes belonging to a category of two-dimensional figures also belong to all subcategories of that category. *For example, all rectangles have four right angles and squares are rectangles, so all squares have four right angles.*

5.G.4 Classify two-dimensional figures in a hierarchy based on properties.

© 2014 Common Core, Inc. All rights reserved. **commoncore.org**

Foundational Standards

3.MD.5   Recognize area as an attribute of plane figures and understand concepts of area measurement.

a.   A square with side length 1 unit, called "a unit square," is said to have "one square unit" of area, and can be used to measure area.

b.   A plane figure which can be covered without gaps or overlaps by *n* unit squares is said to have an area of *n* square units.

4.MD.3   Apply the area and perimeter formulas for rectangles in real world and mathematical problems. *For example, find the width of a rectangular room given the area of the flooring and the length, by viewing the area formula as a multiplication equation with an unknown factor.*

4.MD.5   Recognize angles as geometric shapes that are formed wherever two rays share a common endpoint, and understand concepts of angle measurement:

a.   An angle is measured with reference to a circle with its center at the common endpoint of the rays, by considering the fraction of the circular arc between the points where the two rays intersect the circle. An angle that turns through 1/360 of a circle is called a "one-degree angle," and can be used to measure angles.

b.   An angle that turns through *n* one-degree angles is said to have an angle measure of *n* degrees.

4.MD.6   Measure angles in whole-number degrees using a protractor. Sketch angles of specified measure.

4.MD.7   Recognize angle measure as additive. When an angle is decomposed into non-overlapping parts, the angle measure of the whole is the sum of the angle measures of the parts. Solve addition and subtraction problems to find unknown angles on a diagram in real world and mathematical problems, e.g., by using an equation with a symbol for the unknown angle measure.

3.G.1   Understand that shapes in different categories (e.g., rhombuses, rectangles, and others) may share attributes (e.g., having four sides), and that the shared attributes can define a larger category (e.g., quadrilaterals). Recognize rhombuses, rectangles, and squares as examples of quadrilaterals, and draw examples of quadrilaterals that do not belong to any of these subcategories.

4.G.1   Draw points, lines, line segments, rays, angles (right, acute, obtuse), and perpendicular and parallel lines. Identify these in two-dimensional figures.

4.G.2   Classify two-dimensional figures based on the presence or absence of parallel or perpendicular lines, or the presence or absence of angles of a specified size. Recognize right triangles as a category, and identify right triangles.

5.NF.4   Apply and extend previous understandings of multiplication to multiply a fraction or whole number by a fraction.

a.   Interpret the product *(a/b)* × *q* as *a* parts of a partition of *q* into *b* equal parts;

© 2014 Common Core, Inc. All rights reserved. **commoncore.org**

equivalently, as the result of a sequence of operations $a \times q \div b$. *For example, use a visual fraction model to show* $(2/3) \times 4 = 8/3$, *and create a story context for this equation. Do the same with* $(2/3) \times (4/5) = 8/15$. *(In general,* $(a/b) \times (c/d) = ac/bd$.)

Focus Standards for Mathematical Practice

MP.1   **Make sense of problems and persevere in solving them.** Students work toward a solid understanding of volume through the design and construction of a three-dimensional sculpture within given parameters.

MP.2   **Reason abstractly and quantitatively.** Students make sense of quantities and their relationships when they analyze a geometric shape or real life scenario and identify, represent, and manipulate the relevant measurements. Students decontextualize when they represent geometric figures symbolically and apply formulas.

MP.3   **Construct viable arguments and critique the reasoning of others.** Students analyze shapes, draw conclusions, and recognize and use counter-examples as they classify two-dimensional figures in a hierarchy based on properties.

MP.4   **Model with mathematics.** Students model with mathematics as they make connections between addition and multiplication as applied to volume and area. They represent the area and volume of geometric figures with equations, and vice versa, and represent fraction products with rectangular areas. Students apply concepts of volume and area and their knowledge of fractions to design a sculpture based on given mathematical parameters. Through their work analyzing and classifying two-dimensional shapes, students draw conclusions about their relationships and continuously see how mathematical concepts can be modeled geometrically.

MP.6   **Attend to precision.** Mathematically proficient students try to communicate precisely with others. They endeavor to use clear definitions in discussion with others and in their own reasoning. Students state the meaning of the symbols they choose, including using the equal sign consistently and appropriately. They are careful about specifying units of measure, and labeling axes to clarify the correspondence with quantities in a problem. They calculate accurately and efficiently, express numerical answers with a degree of precision appropriate for the problem context. In the elementary grades, students give carefully formulated explanations to each other. By the time they reach high school, they have learned to examine claims and make explicit use of definitions.

MP.7   **Look for and make use of structure.** Students discern patterns and structures as they apply additive and multiplicative reasoning to determine volumes. They relate multiplying two of the dimensions of a rectangular prism to determining how many cubic units would be in each layer of the prism and relate the third dimension to determining how many layers there are in the prism. This understanding supports students in seeing why volume can be computed as the product of three length measurements or as the product of one area by one length measurement. In addition, recognizing that volume is additive allows students to find the total volume of solid figures composed of more than one non-overlapping right rectangular prism.

© 2014 Common Core, Inc. All rights reserved. **commoncore.org**

Overview of Module Topics and Lesson Objectives

Standards		Topics and Objectives		Days
5.MD.3 **5.MD.4**	A	**Concepts of Volume**		3
		Lesson 1:	Explore volume by building with and counting unit cubes.	
		Lesson 2:	Find the volume of a right rectangular prism by packing with cubic units and counting.	
		Lesson 3:	Compose and decompose right rectangular prisms using layers.	
5.MD.3 **5.MD.5**	B	**Volume and the Operations of Multiplication and Addition**		6
		Lesson 4:	Use multiplication to calculate volume.	
		Lesson 5:	Use multiplication to connect volume as *packing* with volume as *filling*.	
		Lesson 6:	Find the total volume of solid figures composed of two non-overlapping rectangular prisms.	
		Lesson 7:	Solve word problems involving the volume of rectangular prisms with whole number edge lengths.	
		Lessons 8–9:	Apply concepts and formulas of volume to design a sculpture using rectangular prisms within given parameters.	
		Mid-Module Assessment: Topics A–B (assessment 1 day, return ½ day, remediation or further applications ½ day)		2
5.NF.4b **5.NF.6**	C	**Area of Rectangular Figures with Fractional Side Lengths**		6
		Lesson 10:	Find the area of rectangles with whole-by-mixed and whole-by-fractional number side lengths by tiling, record by drawing, and relate to fraction multiplication.	
		Lesson 11:	Find the area of rectangles with mixed-by-mixed and fraction-by-fraction side lengths by tiling, record by drawing, and relate to fraction multiplication.	
		Lesson 12:	Measure to find the area of rectangles with fractional side lengths.	
		Lessons 13:	Multiply mixed number factors, and relate to the distributive property and the area model.	
		Lessons 14–15:	Solve real world problems involving area of figures with fractional side lengths using visual models and/or equations.	
5.G.3 **5.G.4**	D	**Drawing, Analysis, and Classification of Two-Dimensional Shapes**		6
		Lesson 16:	Draw trapezoids to clarify their attributes, and define	

© 2014 Common Core, Inc. All rights reserved. **commoncore.org**

		trapezoids based on those attributes.	
	Lesson 17:	Draw parallelograms to clarify their attributes, and define parallelograms based on those attributes.	
	Lesson 18:	Draw rectangles and rhombuses to clarify their attributes, and define rectangles and rhombuses based on those attributes.	
	Lesson 19:	Draw kites and squares to clarify their attributes, and define kites and squares based on those attributes.	
	Lesson 20:	Classify two-dimensional figures in a hierarchy based on properties.	
	Lesson 21:	Draw and identify varied two-dimensional figures from given attributes.	
	End-of-Module Assessment: Topics A–D (assessment 1 day, return ½ day, remediation or further applications ½ day)		2
Total Number of Instructional Days			**25**

Terminology

New or Recently Introduced Terms

- Base (one face of a three-dimensional solid—often thought of as the surface upon which the solid rests)
- Bisect (divide into two equal parts)
- Cubic units (cubes of the same size used for measuring)
- Height (adjacent layers of the base that form a rectangular prism)
- Hierarchy (series of ordered groupings of shapes)
- Unit cube (cube whose sides all measure 1 unit; cubes of the same size used for measuring volume)
- Volume of a solid (measurement of space or capacity)

Familiar Terms and Symbols[2]

- Angle (the union of two different rays sharing a common vertex)
- Area (the number of square units that covers a two-dimensional shape)
- Attribute (given quality or characteristic)
- Cube (three-dimensional figure with six square sides)
- Degree measure of an angle (subdivide the length around a circle into 360 arcs of equal length; a central angle for any of these arcs is called a *one-degree angle* and is said to have angle measure 1

---

[2] These are terms and symbols students have seen previously.

© 2014 Common Core, Inc. All rights reserved. **commoncore.org**

degree)

- Face (any flat surface of a three-dimensional figure)
- Kite (quadrilateral with two equal sides that are also adjacent; a kite can be a rhombus if all sides are equal)
- Parallel lines (two lines in a plane that do not intersect)
- Parallelogram (four-sided closed figure with opposite sides that are parallel)
- Perpendicular (two lines are *perpendicular* if they intersect, and any of the angles formed between the lines are 90˚ angles)
- Perpendicular bisector (line that cuts a line segment into two equal parts at 90˚)
- Plane (flat surface that extends infinitely in all directions)
- Polygon (closed figure made up of line segments)
- Quadrilateral (closed figure with four sides)
- Rectangle (quadrilateral with four 90˚ angles)
- Rectangular prism (three-dimensional figure with six rectangular sides)
- Rhombus (parallelogram with equal sides)
- Right angle (angle formed by perpendicular lines; angle measuring 90˚)
- Right rectangular prism (rectangular prism with only 90˚ angles)
- Solid figure (three-dimensional figure)
- Square units (squares of the same size, used for measuring)
- Three-dimensional figures (solid figures)
- Trapezoid (quadrilateral with at least one pair of parallel sides)
- Two-dimensional figures (figures on a plane)

Suggested Tools and Representations

- Ruler
- Protractor
- Set square

Scaffolds[3]

The scaffolds integrated into *A Story of Units* give alternatives for how students access information as well as express and demonstrate their learning. Strategically placed margin notes are provided within each lesson elaborating on the use of specific scaffolds at applicable times. They address many needs presented by English language learners, students with disabilities, students performing above grade level, and students performing below grade level. Many of the suggestions are organized by Universal Design for Learning (UDL) principles and are applicable to more than one population. To read more about the approach to

---

[3] Students with disabilities may require Braille, large print, audio, or special digital files. Please visit the website, www.p12.nysed.gov/specialed/aim, for specific information on how to obtain student materials that satisfy the National Instructional Materials Accessibility Standard (NIMAS) format.

© 2014 Common Core, Inc. All rights reserved. **commoncore.org**

differentiated instruction in *A Story of Units,* please refer to "How to Implement *A Story of Units*."

Assessment Summary

Type	Administered	Format	Standards Addressed
Mid-Module Assessment Task	After Topic B	Constructed response with rubric	5.MD.3 5.MD.4 5.MD.5
End-of-Module Assessment Task	After Topic D	Constructed response with rubric	5.NF.4b 5.NF.6 5.MD.3 5.MD.4 5.MD.5 5.G.3 5.G.4

© 2014 Common Core, Inc. All rights reserved. **commoncore.org**

Topic A
Concepts of Volume

5.MD.3, 5.MD.4

Focus Standard:	5.MD.3	Recognize volume as an attribute of solid figures and understand concepts of volume measurement.
		a. A cube with side length 1 unit, called a "unit cube," is said to have "one cubic unit" of volume, and can be used to measure volume.
		b. A solid figure which can be packed without gaps or overlaps using *n* unit cubes is said to have a volume of *n* cubic units.
	5.MD.4	Measure volumes by counting unit cubes, using cubic cm, cubic in, cubic ft, and improvised units.
Instructional Days:	3	
Coherence -Links from:	G2–M8	Time, Shapes, and Fractions as Equal Parts of Shapes
	G3–M4	Multiplication and Area
	G3–M5	Fractions as Numbers on the Number Line
-Links to:	G6–M5	Area, Surface Area, and Volume Problems

In Topic A, students extend their spatial structuring to three dimensions through an exploration of volume. They come to see volume as an attribute of solid figures and understand that cubic units are used to measure it (**5.MD.3**). Using unit cubes, both customary and metric, students build three-dimensional shapes, including right rectangular prisms, and count to find the volume (**5.MD.4**). By developing a systematic approach to counting the unit cubes, they make connections between area and volume.

Next, students pack rectangular prisms made from nets with centimeter cubes. This helps them to visualize the layers of cubic units that compose volumes, an understanding that allows them to reasonably predict the number of cubes required to fill the containers and then test their predictions by packing the containers. Finally, students compose and decompose a rectangular prism from and into layers of unit cubes, and reason that the number of unit cubes in a single layer corresponds to the number of unit squares on a face. They begin to conceptualize the layers themselves, oriented in any one of three directions, as iterated units.

© 2014 Common Core, Inc. All rights reserved. **commoncore.org**

A Teaching Sequence Towards Mastery of the Concepts of Volume

Objective 1: Explore volume by building with and counting unit cubes.
(Lesson 1)

Objective 2: Find the volume of a right rectangular prism by packing with cubic units and counting.
(Lesson 2)

Objective 3: Compose and decompose right rectangular prisms using layers.
(Lesson 3)

© 2014 Common Core, Inc. All rights reserved. **commoncore.org**

Lesson 1

Objective: Explore volume by building with and counting unit cubes.

Suggested Lesson Structure

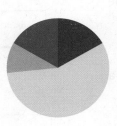

■ Fluency Practice   (10 minutes)
▢ Concept Development   (34 minutes)
▣ Application Problem   (6 minutes)
■ Student Debrief   (10 minutes)

   Total Time   **(60 minutes)**

Fluency Practice (10 minutes)

■ Multiply Whole Numbers Times Fractions Using Two Methods **5.NF.4**   (5 minutes)
■ Find the Area **4.MD.3**   (5 minutes)

Multiply Whole Numbers Times Fractions Using Two Methods (5 minutes)

Materials: (S) Personal white boards

Note: This fluency reviews G5–Module 4 content.

T: (Write $\frac{1}{2} \times 12 = \frac{\quad\times\quad}{2}$.) On your boards, write the complete number sentence.

S: (Write $\frac{1}{2} \times 12 = \frac{1 \times 12}{2}$.)

T: (Write $\frac{1}{2} \times 12 = \frac{1 \times 12}{2} = \frac{}{} =$.) Fill in the missing numbers.

S: (Write $\frac{1}{2} \times 12 = \frac{1 \times 12}{2} = \frac{12}{2} = 6$.)

T: (Write $\frac{1}{2} \times 12 = \frac{1 \times 12}{2}$.) Divide by a common factor and solve.

S: (Write $\frac{1}{2} \times 12 = \frac{1 \times \overset{6}{\cancel{12}}}{\underset{1}{\cancel{2}}} = 6$.)

T: Did you get the same answer using both methods?

S: Yes.

Continue with the following possible suggestions: $16 \times \frac{1}{4}$, $16 \times \frac{3}{4}$, $\frac{2}{3} \times 9$, and $24 \times \frac{5}{6}$.

Lesson 1:	Explore volume by building with and counting unit cubes.	
Date:	1/10/14	**5.A.3**

© 2014 Common Core, Inc. All rights reserved. **commoncore.org**

Find the Area (5 minutes)

Materials: (S) Personal white boards

Note: Reviewing this Grade 4 concept prepares students to explore volume.

T: (Project a 4 inch by 2 inch rectangle.) Name the shape.

S: Rectangle. → Quadrilateral. → Parallelogram.

T: (Write __ in × __ in = __ in².) This shape is a rectangle, though we could also call it a quadrilateral or parallelogram. On your boards, write the area of the rectangle as a multiplication sentence starting with the length of the longest side.

S: (Write 4 in × 2 in = 8 in².)

T: (Project a square with side lengths of 5 cm.) Name the shape.

S: Square. → Rhombus. → Quadrilateral.

T: This shape is a square, but it is also correct to call it a rhombus or quadrilateral. What is the measure of one of the square's sides?

S: 5 centimeters.

T: (Write __ cm × __ cm = __ cm².) On your boards, write the area of the square as a multiplication sentence using the measure of the square's sides.

S: (5 cm × 5 cm = 25 cm².)

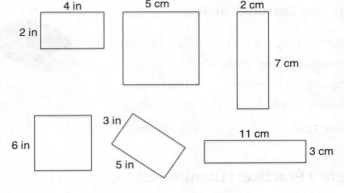

Continue this process for the other squares and rectangles.

Concept Development (34 minutes)

Materials: (T) 20 centimeter cubes, box of cereal or other dry good (S) Ruler, 20 centimeter cubes, centimeter grid paper, isometric dot paper

Problem 1: Build a solid from cubes.

T: Shade a square on your centimeter grid paper with an area of 4 square units. (Pause to allow students to do this.)

T: This is going to be the foundation for our structure. Place 4 cubes directly on top of that square.

S: (Do so.)

T: Think of the first 4 cubes as the ground floor of a building. Make a second floor by putting another 4 cubes on top of them. (Pause.) How many cubes are there now?

 | Lesson 1: Explore volume by building with and counting unit cubes.
Date: 1/10/14

5.A.4

© 2014 Common Core, Inc. All rights reserved. **commoncore.org**

S: 8 cubes.

T: Did we change the ground floor? Why or why not? Turn and talk.

S: No, we just built on top of it. → The second layer of cubes doesn't make it take up more space on the ground. → We built up, not out, so the structure got taller, not longer or wider.

T: Put one more layer of 4. (Pause.) Explain to your partner how you know the total number of cubes.

S: I just counted up from 8 as I put each cube. → Each floor had 4 blocks, so it's 3 fours. → I thought of 3 times 4, 12.

T: What is the total number of cubes in your solid?

S: 12 cubes.

Problem 2: Build solids with a given volume with cubic centimeters.

T: Since this is a cube with each edge measuring 1 centimeter, we call this a **cubic centimeter**.

T: (Hold up a centimeter cube.) These cubes can serve as a unit to measure the **volume** of your solid, the amount of space it takes up. What do we call this unit?

S: A cubic centimeter.

T: Just like we use squares to measure area in square units, we use cubes to measure volume, in cubic units. (Write *cubic unit* and *cubic centimeter* on the board.)

T: (Hold up 2 cubes.) How many cubes?

S: 2 cubes.

T: How many cubic centimeters?

S: 2 cubic centimeters.

T: (Hold up 4 cubes in a square formation.)

T: What is the volume of these 4 units together?

S: 4 cubic centimeters.

T: Work with a partner. On your grid paper, build three different solids with a volume of 4 cubic centimeters

Give the students time to build the structures. Move on to do likewise with five and then six cubes as time allows. As you circulate, encourage students to use the words *volume* and *cubic centimeters* as you ask questions.

NOTES ON
MULTIPLE MEANS OF
REPRESENTATION:

If only 1-inch cubes are available, adapt the lesson to work with 1-inch cubes. Try to obtain 1-inch grid paper from the Internet, or create it on the computer and print it for students to use.

Problem 3: Represent solids on isometric dot paper.

T: We are going to build some other structures, but we want to draw what we build. Let's learn how to use our isometric dot paper to draw our structures.

T: We will start by drawing 1 cube. (Demonstrate while directing the students in each step.)

Explain the process for drawing 1 cubic centimeter using the dot paper.

   Step 1: Connect four dots to make a rhombus. This will represent one square face of the cube, viewed

| Lesson 1: | Explore volume by building with and counting unit cubes. |
| Date: | 1/10/14 |

5.A.5

© 2014 Common Core, Inc. All rights reserved. commoncore.org

at an angle.

Step 2: Draw three straight segments to the right from the two vertices on the top and the one on the bottom right.

Step 3: Draw two segments to represent the missing edges.

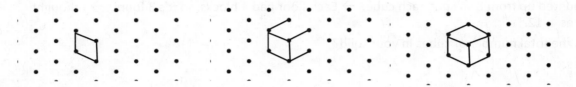

T: Now we will put two cubes next to each other.

Explain the process for drawing 2 cubic centimeters.

Step 1: Connect four dots to make a rhombus.

Step 2: Add another rhombus that shares its right edge, just like your cubes.

Step 3: Draw four straight segments to the right from the three vertices on the top and the one on the bottom right.

Step 4: Draw three segments to represent the missing edges.

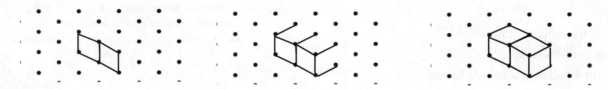

Allow students to practice several times. Then choose examples of several students' work to show the class.

T: With a partner, build a structure with no more than 10 cubes each. Then draw your partner's structure on dot paper. Help each other figure out if it matches what you built.

Circulate and help students draw their figures. When they are comfortable with the process, move them to the Application Problem and Problem Set.

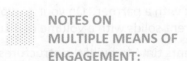

**NOTES ON
MULTIPLE MEANS OF
ENGAGEMENT:**

The spatial reasoning required to draw centimeter cubes on isometric dot paper may be difficult for some students. Pattern block rhombuses may help students orient their drawing. Three rhombuses may be laid on paper (with or without dots) and traced to draw a cube.

Students may also trace the yellow hexagon block and simply add three interior lines to create the cube.

Lesson 1: Explore volume by building with and counting unit cubes.
Date: 1/10/14

5.A.6

© 2014 Common Core, Inc. All rights reserved. **commoncore.org**

Application Problem (6 minutes)

Jackie and Ron both have 12 centimeter cubes. Jackie builds a tower 6 cubes high and 2 cubes wide. Ron builds one 6 cubes long and 2 cubes wide.

Jackie says her structure has the greater volume because it is taller. Ron says that structures have the same volume.

Who is correct? Draw a picture to explain how you know. Use grid paper if you wish.

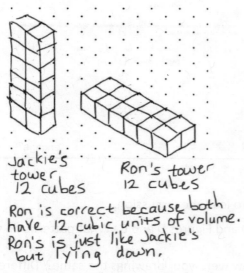

Jackie's tower 12 cubes

Ron's tower 12 cubes

Ron is correct because both have 12 cubic units of volume. Ron's is just like Jackie's but lying down.

NOTES ON MULTIPLE MEANS OF ENGAGEMENT:

Consider what students see written on the board or projected on a screen.

- At different times of the day, walk around the classroom to become aware of light patterns in the room and how sunlight affects the visibility of white boards.

- Take a tip from kindergarten teachers whose handwriting is clear and legible. Students who are trying to process new or challenging information can benefit if the written or projected material is neat and precise.

Note: This problem is intended to help students synthesize the parts they have learned in the lesson and build understanding toward subsequent lessons, where eventually they will learn the formula for volume of a rectangular prism.

Problem Set (10 minutes)

Students should do their personal best to complete the Problem Set within the allotted 10 minutes. All problems do not specify a method for solving. This is an intentional reduction of scaffolding that invokes MP.5, Use Appropriate Tools Strategically. Students should solve these problems using the RDW approach used for Application Problems.

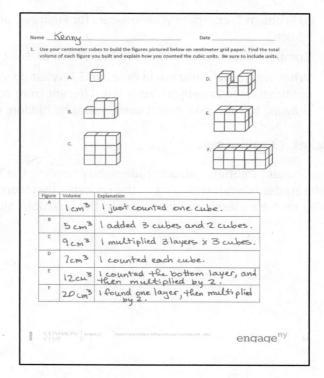

Name __Kenny__   Date _____

1. Use your centimeter cubes to build the figures pictured below on centimeter grid paper. Find the total volume of each figure you built and explain how you counted the cubic units. Be sure to include units.

Figure	Volume	Explanation
A	1 cm^3	I just counted one cube.
B	5 cm^3	I added 3 cubes and 2 cubes.
C	9 cm^3	I multiplied 3 layers x 3 cubes.
D	7 cm^3	I counted each cube.
E	12 cm^3	I counted the bottom layer, and then multiplied by 2.
F	20 cm^3	I found one layer, then multiplied by 2.

engage^{ny}

© 2014 Common Core, Inc. All rights reserved. commoncore.org

For some classes, it may be appropriate to modify the assignment by specifying which problems students should work on first. With this option, let the careful sequencing of the Problem Set guide your selections so that problems continue to be scaffolded. Balance word problems with other problem types to ensure a range of practice. Assign incomplete problems for homework or at another time during the day.

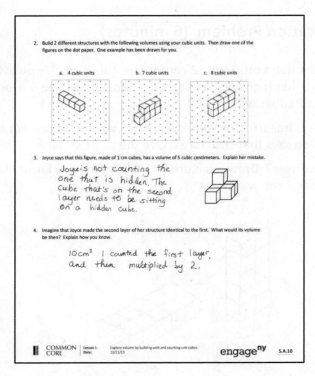

Student Debrief (10 minutes)

Lesson Objective: Explore volume by building with and counting cubic units.

The Student Debrief is intended to invite reflection and active processing of the total lesson experience.

Invite students to review their solutions for the Problem Set. They should check work by comparing answers with a partner before going over answers as a class. Look for misconceptions or misunderstandings that can be addressed in the Debrief. Guide students in a conversation to debrief the Problem Set and process the lesson.

You may choose to use any combination of the questions below to lead the discussion.

- In Problem 1, compare your answers for Figures C and D and Figures D and E. What patterns do you notice?

- Compare your answers to Problem 2 with a partner. How were your drawings the same? Different?

- What was Joyce's mistake in Problem 3? What do you need to think about when counting cubic centimeters in drawings? How is it different from counting them in person? Is it possible for a drawing to fool you? Might some cubes be hidden, or might there be gaps that you cannot see?

Exit Ticket (3 minutes)

After the Student Debrief, instruct students to complete the Exit Ticket. A review of their work will help you assess the students' understanding of the concepts that were presented in the lesson today and plan more effectively for future lessons. You may read the questions aloud to the students.

Lesson 1:   Explore volume by building with and counting unit cubes.
Date: 1/10/14

5.A.8

© 2014 Common Core, Inc. All rights reserved. **commoncore.org**

Name _____ Date _____

1. Use your centimeter cubes to build the figures pictured below on centimeter grid paper. Find the total volume of each figure you built, and explain how you counted the cubic units. Be sure to include units.

A.

B.

C.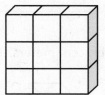

D.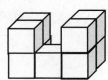

E.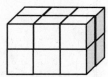

F.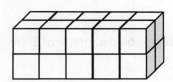

Figure	Volume	Explanation
A		
B		
C		
D		
E		
F		

COMMON CORE

Lesson 1:   Explore volume by building with and counting unit cubes.
Date: 1/10/14

5.A.9

© 2014 Common Core, Inc. All rights reserved. commoncore.org

2. Build 2 different structures with the following volumes using your cubic units. Then draw one of the figures on the dot paper. One example has been drawn for you.

a.   4 cubic units

b. 7 cubic units

c. 8 cubic units

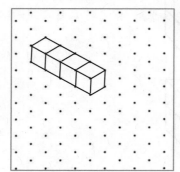
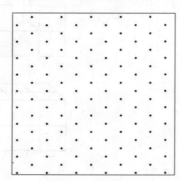
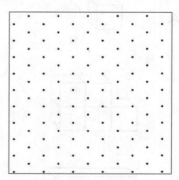

3. Joyce says that the figure below, made of 1-cm cubes, has a volume of 5 cubic centimeters. Explain her mistake.

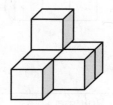

4. Imagine that Joyce made the second layer of her structure identical to the first. What would its volume be then? Explain how you know.

COMMON CORE

Lesson 1:   Explore volume by building with and counting unit cubes.
Date: 1/10/14

5.A

© 2014 Common Core, Inc. All rights reserved. commoncore.org

Name _____   Date _____

1.   What is the volume of the figures pictured below?

A. 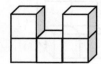   B.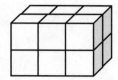

2.   Draw a picture of a figure with a volume of 3 cubic units on the dot paper.

© 2014 Common Core, Inc. All rights reserved. **commoncore.org**

Name _____ Date _____

1. The following solids are made up of 1-cm cubes. Find the total volume of each figure, and write it in the chart below.

A.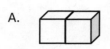

B.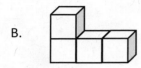

C.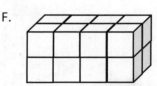

D.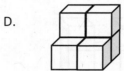

E.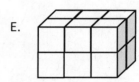

F.

Figure	Volume	Explanation
A		
B		
C		
D		
E		
F		

© 2014 Common Core, Inc. All rights reserved. commoncore.org

5. Draw the figures on the dot paper with the given number of unit cubes.

    a. 3 cubic units   b. 6 cubic units   c. 12 cubic units

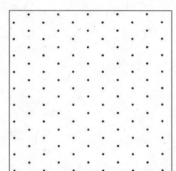 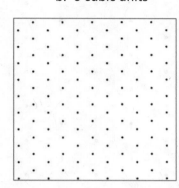 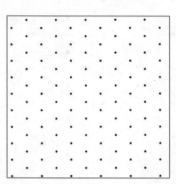

6. John built and drew a structure that has a volume of 5 cubic centimeters. His little brother tells him he made a mistake because he only drew 4 cubes. Help John explain to his brother why his drawing is accurate.

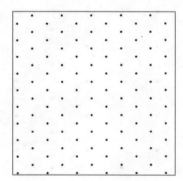

7. Draw another figure below that represents a structure with a volume of 5 cubic centimeters.

© 2014 Common Core, Inc. All rights reserved. **commoncore.org**

Lesson 1:   Explore volume by building with and counting unit cubes.
Date: 1/10/14

5.A

© 2014 Common Core, Inc. All rights reserved. **commoncore.org**

Lesson 2

Objective: Find the volume of a right rectangular prism by packing with cubic units and counting.

Suggested Lesson Structure

- ■ Fluency Practice   (12 minutes)
- ■ Application Problem   (8 minutes)
- ■ Concept Development   (30 minutes)
- ■ Student Debrief   (10 minutes)

  Total Time   **(60 minutes)**

Fluency Practice (12 minutes)

- Multiply a Fraction and a Whole Number **5.NF.3**   (4 minutes)
- Find the Area **4.MD.3**   (4 minutes)
- Find the Volume **5.MD.3**   (4 minutes)

Multiply a Fraction and a Whole Number (4 minutes)

Materials: (S) Personal white boards

Note: This fluency reviews G5–M4–Lessons 6–8.

T: (Write $15 \div 3$.) Say the division sentence.

S: $15 \div 3 = 5$.

T: (Write $\frac{1}{3} \times 15$.) Say the multiplication sentence.

S: $\frac{1}{3} \times 15 = 5$.

T: (Write $\frac{2}{3} \times 15$.) On your boards, write the multiplication sentence.

S: (Write $\frac{2}{3} \times 15 = 10$.)

T: (Write $15 \times \frac{2}{3}$.) On your boards, write the multiplication sentence.

S: (Write $15 \times \frac{2}{3} = 10$.)

Continue with the following possible sequence: $18 \div 6$, $\frac{1}{6} \times 18$, $\frac{5}{6} \times 18$, $18 \times \frac{5}{6}$, $\frac{1}{8} \times 32$, $32 \times \frac{1}{8}$, $32 \times \frac{5}{8}$, $\frac{2}{3} \times 18$, and $24 \times \frac{3}{4}$.

Lesson 2:	Find the volume of a right rectangular prism by packing with cubic units and counting.
Date:	1/10/14

5.A.15

© 2014 Common Core, Inc. All rights reserved. **commoncore.org**

Find the Area (4 minutes)

Materials: (S) Personal white boards

Note: Reviewing this Grade 4 concept prepares students to calculate volume.

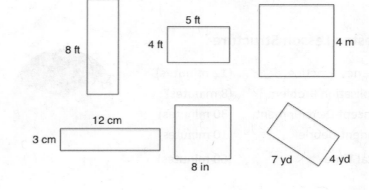

- T: (Project a 2 ft by 8 ft rectangle.) Name the shape.
- S: Rectangle. → Quadrilateral. → Parallelogram.
- T: (Write __ ft × __ ft = __ ft^2.) This shape is a rectangle, though we could also call it a quadrilateral or parallelogram. On your boards, write the area of the rectangle as a multiplication sentence starting with the length of the longest side.
- S: (Write 8 ft × 2 ft = 16 ft^2.)
- T: (Project a square with side lengths 4 m.) Name the shape.
- S: Square. → Rhombus. → Parallelogram. → Quadrilateral. → Rectangle.
- T: (Write __ m × __ m = __ m^2.) On your boards, write the area of the square as a multiplication sentence using the measure of the square's sides.
- S: (Write 4 m × 4 m = 16 m^2.)

Continue process for the other squares and rectangles.

Find the Volume (4 minutes)

Materials: (S) Personal white boards

Note: This fluency reviews G5–M5–Lesson 1.

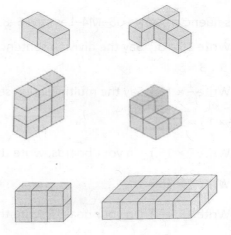

- T: (Project the first of the images to the right.) Each cube is 1 cubic centimeter.
- T: (Write *Volume = ___ cubic cm.*) On your boards, complete the equation.
- S: (Write *Volume = 2 cubic cm.*)

Continue process for the remaining images.

Lesson 2:   Find the volume of a right rectangular prism by packing with cubic
             units and counting.   5.A
Date: 1/10/14

© 2014 Common Core, Inc. All rights reserved. commoncore.org

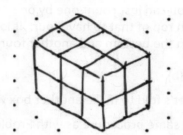

Application Problem (8 minutes)

Mike uses 12 centimeter cubes to build structures. Use centimeter cubes to build at least 3 different structures with the same volume as Mike's. Record one of your structures on dot paper.

Note: This problem is designed to bridge from the previous lesson. Students will work with different factors of 12 to discover different ways of arranging the cubes. This will lead to a better understanding of how rectangular prisms are constructed from identical cubes, towards developing an understanding of volume. Students may work with a partner if desired.

Concept Development (30 minutes)

Materials: (S) Pencil, grid paper (also needed for homework), scissors, tape, 50 centimeter cubes, net template, Problem Set

Note: This lesson uses the Problem Set as part of the lesson.

Problem 1(a)

Project the image from Problem 1(a) from the Problem Set.

T: To make a box, copy this image on grid paper by first shading the bottom of the box and then outline the figure. (If necessary, model how to draw onto grid paper.)

T: Now cut around the outside. The bottom is shaded, so fold up the flaps to make the sides of the box. Crease well and tape to make the edges of the box. (Model cutting and folding as necessary.)

NOTES ON MULTIPLE MEANS OF ENGAGEMENT:

Breaking down a tissue or cereal box to show how the sides form a flat shape and then building it back into a box may be helpful for students to understand the figures used in the lesson to make the boxes.

Be aware that spatial skills and fine motor skills vary widely in fifth-graders. All may require more time to cut, fold, and tape the boxes. Proximity to the teacher and the demonstration can support students whose spatial skills are developing.

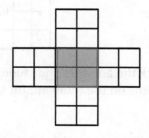

T: Fill the box with cubic centimeters to find how many fill it up.
S: Eight cubes.
T: What is the volume of the box?

© 2014 Common Core, Inc. All rights reserved. commoncore.org

S: 8 cubic centimeters. → 8 centimeters cubed.

T: Talk to your partner about different ways to pack and count the cubic centimeters.

S: You can just count one by one. → You can put in a row of two on the bottom and then another row on top of that to have four. It looks like a slice. Another slice makes four more. → You can put four on the bottom and another four on top of that, 2 × 4 is 8. → You can count by two or by four.

Problem 1(b)

T: Let's fold to make another box with rectangular sides, or a **rectangular prism**.

Follow the same procedure as with Problem 1(a) to have the students make the prism and pack the cubes into the box.

T: What is the volume of this box?

S: 16 cubic centimeters.

T: How does its volume compare with the volume of the first rectangular prism?

MP.7

S: It doubled.

T: Interesting. Why do you think that might be? Turn and talk.

S: It was like two of the first box laid side by side. → The bottom was twice as long, but it had the same number of layers, so it was 16. → The sides of the box were the same height. Just the cubic centimeters on the bottom doubled.

T: Look at the image on the board. Talk to your partner about how you might find the volume without packing it.

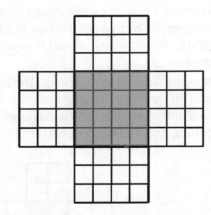

Problem 1(c)

T: (Project or show the next figure.) This time, put in the first layer of cubes on the bottom without cutting to actually make the box. (Pause.) What do you think the volume of this box will be?

S: The flaps show the number of layers. → The bottom has 16 cubes and there are 3 layers. → The bottom is 4 by 4, and it looks like it will be 3 layers, so... 4 × 4 is 16, and double is 32, and another 16 is 48, so 48. → I think it will be 48 cubic centimeters, because 16 × 3 is 48.

Allow students to answer Problems 2(a) and 2(b) independently. Check the answers and student thinking together following the sequence above. Then distribute the box patterns on the template for students to cut out, and have them work independently on Problem 3.

Lesson 2:	Find the volume of a right rectangular prism by packing with cubic units and counting.
Date:	1/10/14

5.A

© 2014 Common Core, Inc. All rights reserved. **commoncore.org**

Student Debrief (10 minutes)

Lesson Objective: Find the volume of a right rectangular prism by packing with cubic units and counting.

The Student Debrief is intended to invite reflection and active processing of the total lesson experience.

Invite students to review their solutions for the Problem Set. They should check work by comparing answers with a partner before going over answers as a class. Look for misconceptions or misunderstandings that can be addressed in the Debrief. Guide students in a conversation to debrief the Problem Set and process the lesson.

You may choose to use any combination of the questions below to lead the discussion.

- How did you pack your boxes in Problems 1(a), (b), and (c)? Cube by cube, row by row, or layer by layer? Did the way you packed your boxes change from problem to problem? If so, how and why did your thinking change?

- In Problem 2, how did you verify your prediction? Did your prediction change between 2(a) and 2(c)? Why or why not?

- What did you discover in Problem 3? Did your discovery match your prediction? Could you have used fewer cubes to make your prediction? Why or why not?

- How has your understanding of the term *volume* changed from yesterday to today?

NOTES ON
MULTIPLE MEANS OF
ENGAGEMENT:

Encourage students who easily grasp this concept and move quickly through the Problem Set to think about the results of the same problems if the units were 2-cm cubes, 3-cm cubes, etc.

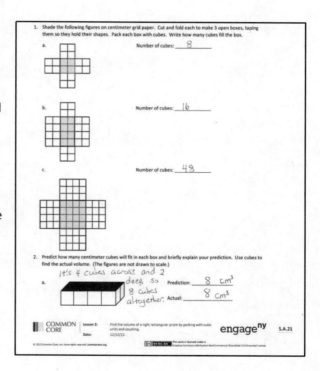

COMMON CORE

Lesson 2:   Find the volume of a right rectangular prism by packing with cubic
              units and counting.

Date: 1/10/14

5.A.19

© 2014 Common Core, Inc. All rights reserved. **commoncore.org**

Exit Ticket (3 minutes)

After the Student Debrief, instruct students to complete the Exit Ticket. A review of their work will help you assess the students' understanding of the concepts that were presented in the lesson today and plan more effectively for future lessons. You may read the questions aloud to the students.

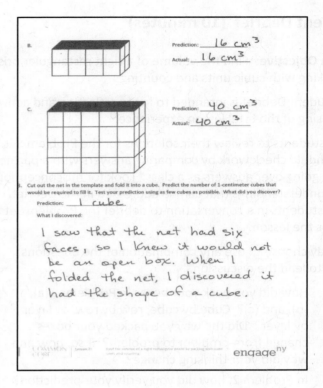

B.
Prediction: 16 cm³
Actual: 16 cm³

C.
Prediction: 40 cm³
Actual: 40 cm³

3. Cut out the net in the template and fold it into a cube. Predict the number of 1-centimeter cubes that would be required to fill it. Test your prediction using as few cubes as possible. What did you discover?

Prediction: 1 cube

What I discovered:

I saw that the net had six faces, so I knew it would not be an open box. When I folded the net, I discovered it had the shape of a cube.

COMMON CORE

Lesson 2:   Find the volume of a right rectangular prism by packing with cubic units and counting.

Date: 1/10/14

5.A

© 2014 Common Core, Inc. All rights reserved. commoncore.org

Name _____ Date _____

1. Shade the following figures on centimeter grid paper. Cut and fold each to make 3 open boxes, taping them so they hold their shapes. Pack each box with cubes. Write how many cubes fill the box.

    a.   Number of cubes: _____

    b.   Number of cubes: _____

    c.   Number of cubes: _____

2. Predict how many centimeter cubes will fit in each box and briefly explain your prediction. Use cubes to find the actual volume. (The figures are not drawn to scale.)

    a.      Prediction: _____

                                                   Actual: _____

COMMON CORE

Lesson 2:   Find the volume of a right rectangular prism by packing with cubic units and counting.

Date: 1/10/14

5.A.21

© 2014 Common Core, Inc. All rights reserved. commoncore.org

b.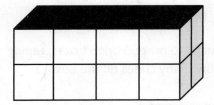

Prediction: _____

Actual: _____

c.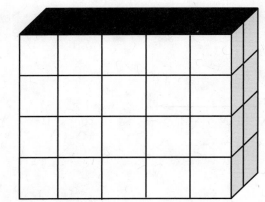

Prediction: _____

Actual: _____

3. Cut out the net in the template and fold it into a cube. Predict the number of 1-centimeter cubes that would be required to fill it. Test your prediction using as few cubes as possible. What did you discover?

Prediction: _____

What I discovered:

Lesson 2:   Find the volume of a right rectangular prism by packing with cubic units and counting.

Date: 1/10/14

5.A

© 2014 Common Core, Inc. All rights reserved. commoncore.org

Name _____   Date _____

1. If this net were to be folded into a box, how many cubes would fill it?

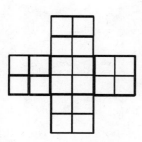

                                    Number of cubes: _____

2. Predict how many centimeter cubes will fit in the box, and briefly explain your prediction. Use cubes to
    find the actual volume. (The figure is not drawn to scale.)

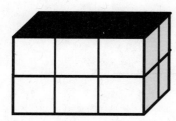

                                    Prediction: _____

                                    Actual: _____

COMMON CORE™   **Lesson 2:**   Find the volume of a right rectangular prism by packing with cubic
                                       units and counting.   **5.A.23**
                      Date: 1/10/14

© 2014 Common Core, Inc. All rights reserved. **commoncore.org**

Name _____   Date _____

1. Make the following boxes on centimeter grid paper. Cut and fold each to make 3 open boxes, taping them so they hold their shapes. How many cubes would fill each box? Explain how you found the number.

a.

Number of cubes: _____

b.

Number of cubes: _____

c.

Number of cubes: _____

COMMON CORE

Lesson 2: Find the volume of a right rectangular prism by packing with cubic units and counting.

Date: 1/10/14

5.A

© 2014 Common Core, Inc. All rights reserved. **commoncore.org**

2. How many centimeter cubes would fit inside each box? Explain your answer using words and diagrams on the box. (The figures are not drawn to scale; the first box is 3 centimeters across and 2 centimeters wide.)

a.

Number of cubes: _____

Explanation:

b.

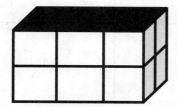

Number of cubes: _____

Explanation:

c.

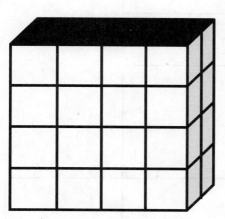

Number of cubes: _____

Explanation:

3. The box pattern below holds 24 1-cm cubes. Draw two different box patterns that would hold the same number of cubes.

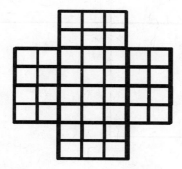

COMMON CORE™

Lesson 2:   Find the volume of a right rectangular prism by packing with cubic units and counting.

Date: 1/10/14

5.A.25

2014 Common Core, Inc. All rights reserved. **commoncore.org**

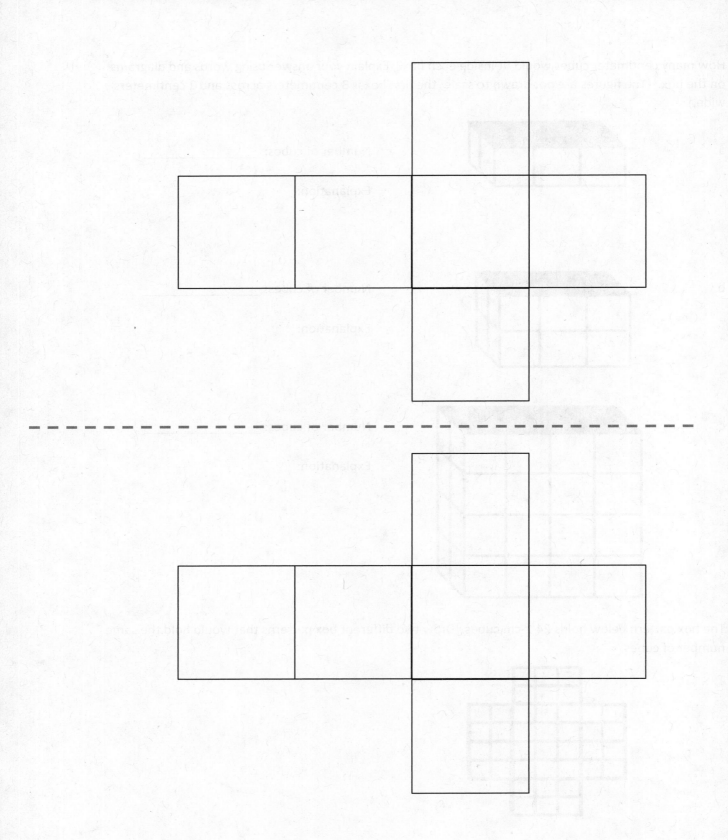

Lesson 2: Find the volume of a right rectangular prism by packing with cubic units and counting.

Date: 1/10/14

5.

© 2014 Common Core, Inc. All rights reserved. **commoncore.org**

Centimeter Grid

Lesson 2:   Find the volume of a right rectangular prism by packing with cubic
              units and counting.

Date: 1/10/14

5.A.27

© 2014 Common Core, Inc. All rights reserved. commoncore.org

Lesson 3

Objective: Compose and decompose right rectangular prisms using layers.

Suggested Lesson Structure

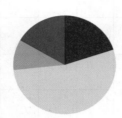

■ Fluency Practice   (12 minutes)
■ Application Problem   (6 minutes)
■ Concept Development   (32 minutes)
■ Student Debrief   (10 minutes)

Total Time   (60 minutes)

Fluency Practice (12 minutes)

▪ Sprint: Multiply a Fraction and a Whole Number **5.NF.3**   (8 minutes)
▪ Find the Volume **5.MD.3**   (4 minutes)

Sprint: Multiply a Fraction and Whole Number (8 minutes)

Materials: (S) Multiply a Fraction and Whole Number Sprint

Note: This Sprint reviews content from G5–M4–Lessons 6–8.

Find the Volume (4 minutes)

Materials: (S) Personal white boards

Note: This fluency reviews G5–M5–Lessons 1–2.

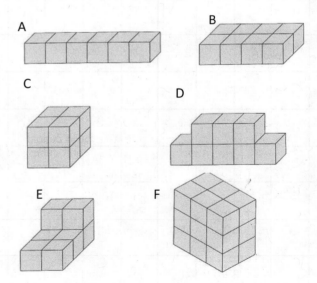

A B C D E F

T: (Project Image A, pictured at right.) Each cube is 1 cubic centimeter. Respond on your board. How many cubes are there?
S: 6.
T: Write the volume on your board with the correct units.
S: 6 cubic centimeters.

Follow this sequence for the other images pictured to the right.

Lesson 3:   Compose and decompose right rectangular prisms using layers.
Date: 1/10/14

5.

© 2014 Common Core, Inc. All rights reserved. commoncore.org

Application Problem (6 minutes)

An ice cube tray has two rows of 8 cubes in each. How many ice cubes are in a stack of 12 ice cube trays? Draw a picture to explain your reasoning.

Note: This problem encourages students to visualize layers in the stack that will be helpful as students refine their understanding of volume in today's lesson.

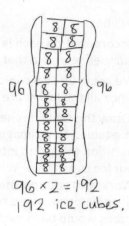

$96 \times 2 = 192$

192 ice cubes.

Concept Development (32 minutes)

Materials: (T) 20 centimeter cubes (S) 20 centimeter cubes, rectangular prism recording sheet

T: Build this with your own cubes. (Show 4 cubes in a square formation stacked vertically—2 layers with 2 cubes in each layer.)

T: What's the volume of this rectangular prism?

S: 4 cubic centimeters.

T: Let's add layers horizontally. Add another layer *next* to the first one.

S: (Work.)

T: What is the volume?

S: 8 cubic centimeters.

T: Add 3 more layers next to the first two. (Pause for students to do this.)

T: What is the volume now?

S: 20 cubic centimeters.

T: How did you figure that out? Turn and talk.

S: I added the first 8 to the 12 more that I added. → I saw 5 along the bottom, and there were 2 layers going back, so that makes 10, and 2 layers going up makes 20. → I knew that I had 20 cubes to start, and I used them all up.

T: (Project a blank rectangular prism from the recording sheet or draw one on the board.) Let's record how we built the layers. Use the first rectangle in the row of your recording sheet.

T: How many layers did we build in all?

S: 5.

T: Let's show that by partitioning the prism into 5 layers. (Partition the prism vertically into 5 equal sections.) Make your prism look like mine. How many cubes were in each layer?

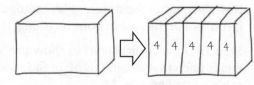

$4 \text{ cm}^3 + 4 \text{ cm}^3 + 4 \text{ cm}^3 + 4 \text{ cm}^3 + 4 \text{ cm}^3 = 20$ cubic cm

5×4 cubic cm = 20 cm^3

© 2014 Common Core, Inc. All rights reserved. commoncore.org

S: 4 cubes.

T: Record that on each layer that we drew. (Write a 4 on each of the horizontal layers.) Write a number sentence that expresses the volume of this prism using these layers. Turn and talk.

S: We could write 4 cubic cm + 4 cubic cm + 4 cubic cm + 4 cubic cm + 4 cubic cm = 20 cubic cm. → Since all the layers are the same, we could write 5 × 4 cubic cm = 20 cubic cm.

T: (Draw the table on the board.) I'll record that in a table. Now, imagine that we could partition this prism into layers like a cake, like our ice cube trays. What might that look like? Work with your partner to show the layers on the next prism in the row and tell how many cubes would be in each. Use your cubes to help you.

MP.4

S: The prism is 2 units high, so we could cut the prism in half horizontally from left to right. That would be 10 cubes in each one. → We could make a top layer of 10 cubes and a bottom layer of 10 cubes.

T: Let's record your thinking. (Draw the figure to the right.) Write a number sentence that expresses the volume of the prism using these layers.

S: 10 cubic cm + 10 cubic cm = 20 cubic cm → 2 cubic cm × 10 cubic cm = 20 cubic cm.

T: Let's record that information in our table. (Record.) Work with your partner to find one last way that we can partition this prism into layers. Label the layers with the number of cubes on the third prism in the row, and write a number sentence to explain your thinking.

S: (Work to draw the third figure and write the number sentences.)

T: I'll record this last bit of information in our table. (Record.)

T: Now, let's draw the different layers together. Use the last prism in the row of your recording sheet.

Step 1: Draw vertical lines to show the 5 layers of 4 cubes each that remind us of bread slices. (Point to table's first line.)

Step 2: Draw a horizontal line to show the two layers of 10 cubes each that remind us of layers of cake. (Point to table's second line.)

Number of Layers	Cubes in Each Layer	Volume
5	4	20 cm^3
2	10	20 cm^3
2	10	20 cm^3

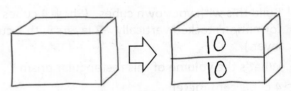

$10\,cm^3 + 10\,cm^3 = 20\,cm^3$

2×10 cubic cm = 20 cubic cm

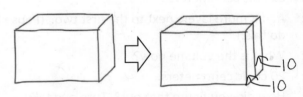

$10\,cm^3 + 10\,cm^3 = 20\,cm^3$

2×10 cubic cm = 20 cubic cm

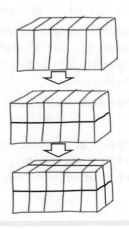

Lesson 3:   Compose and decompose right rectangular prisms using layers.
Date: 1/10/14

5.

© 2014 Common Core, Inc. All rights reserved. commoncore.org

Step 3: Draw both a horizontal and a vertical line to show the 2 front and back layers of 10 each. (Point to table's last line.)

T: What is the volume of the cube?

S: 20 cubic centimeters.

T: Build a prism with a partner that has one 3 cube by 3 cube layer. (Demonstrate building this with cubes.)

T: What is the volume?

S: 9 cubic centimeters.

T: Add another layer of cubes on top.

T: What is the volume now? How do you know?

S: It's 18 cubic centimeters, because now we have 2 groups of 9 cubic centimeters. → Two layers with 9 cubes each is 18 cubic centimeters.

T: Now add another layer. What is the volume?

S: 27 cubic centimeters.

T: What is the overall shape of your rectangular prism?

S: A cube!

T: Use the set of cubes on your recording sheet to show the three ways of layering using the same system we just did with our 2 by 2 by 5 rectangular prism.

S: (Work.)

T: (Project or draw an image of a 3 × 4 × 5 rectangular prism. Direct students to the set of vertical prisms on the prism recording sheet.) Imagine what the bottom layer of this prism would look like. Describe it to your partner and then build it.

S: There would be 3 rows with 4 cubes in each row. → There would be 12 cubes in all. It would be 3 cubes wide and 4 cubes long and 1 cube high. → This would be like a 4 by 3 rectangle but it is 1 centimeter tall. (Build.)

T: Here's the same prism, but without the unit cubes drawn. How might we represent the bottom layer on this picture? Use your recording sheet, and talk to your partner.

S: We could draw a horizontal slice toward the bottom and label it with 12. → I can see in the drawing that there are 5 layers in all, so I'll need to make the bottom about 1 fifth of the prism and put 12 on it.

T: What is the volume of the single layer?

NOTES ON MULTIPLE MEANS OF ENGAGEMENT:

Challenge students who quickly grasp the decompositions by asking them to determine a "rule" for finding the volume and test it for different rectangular prisms. They might also be asked to calculate the volume of the prisms as if they were built from 2-cm cubes. Ask them to explain what would happen to the volume if the dimensions of the cubes were doubled or tripled.

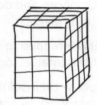

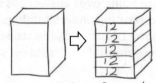

$12 \, cm^3 + 12 \, cm^3 + 12 \, cm^3 + 12 \, cm^3 + 12 \, cm^3 = 60 \, cubic \, cm$
$5 \times 12 \, cubic \, cm = 60 \, cubic \, cm$

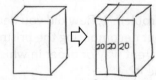

$20 \, cm^3 + 20 \, cm^3 + 20 \, cm^3 = 60 \, cubic \, cm$
$3 \times 20 \, cubic \, cm = 60 \, cubic \, cm$

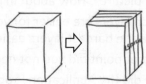

$15 \, cm^3 + 15 \, cm^3 + 15 \, cm^3 + 15 \, cm^3 = 60 \, cubic \, cm$
$4 \times 15 \, cubic \, cm = 60 \, cubic \, cm$

Lesson 3:   Compose and decompose right rectangular prisms using layers.
Date: 1/10/14

5.A.31

2014 Common Core, Inc. All rights reserved. commoncore.org

S: 12 cubic centimeters.

T: What is the volume of the prism with 5 of these layers?

S: It's 12 × 5, so 60. → I know there are 5 layers that are the same, so 12 + 12 + 12 + 12 + 12, so 60.

T: What other ways could we partition this prism into layers? Turn and talk, then draw a picture of your thinking on the recording sheet.

S: (Draw.)

Problem Set (10 minutes)

Students should do their personal best to complete the Problem Set within the allotted 10 minutes. For some classes, it may be appropriate to modify the assignment by specifying which problems they work on first. All problems do not specify a method for solving. Students solve these problems using the RDW approach used for Application Problems.

Student Debrief (10 minutes)

Lesson Objective: Compose and decompose right rectangular prisms using layers.

The Student Debrief is intended to invite reflection and active processing of the total lesson experience.

Invite students to review their solutions for the Problem Set. They should check work by comparing answers with a partner before going over answers as a class. Look for misconceptions or misunderstandings that can be addressed in the Debrief. Guide students in a conversation to debrief the Problem Set and process the lesson.

You may choose to use any combination of the questions below to lead the discussion.

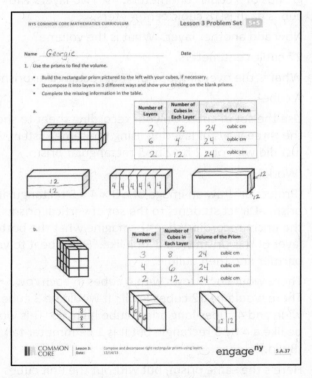

- In Problem 1, how did you decide how to go about decomposing the prisms? Is there a different way or order in which you could have done it?

- Problem 4 uses meters instead of centimeters. What, if anything, did that change in how you drew your picture? How about in how you figured out the volume?

- Which layers are easier for you to visualize? Which are the hardest? What do you think about to make the hardest layers easier to see? What was Josh having a hard time visualizing in Problem 2?

- At what point did you not need to model with the physical cubes anymore?

- How did the Application Problem connect to today's lesson? How are stacks of ice trays different from the prisms in the lesson?

© 2014 Common Core, Inc. All rights reserved. **commoncore.org**

Exit Ticket (3 minutes)

After the Student Debrief, instruct students to complete the Exit Ticket. A review of their work will help you assess the students' understanding of the concepts that were presented in the lesson today and plan more effectively for future lessons. You may read the questions aloud to the students.

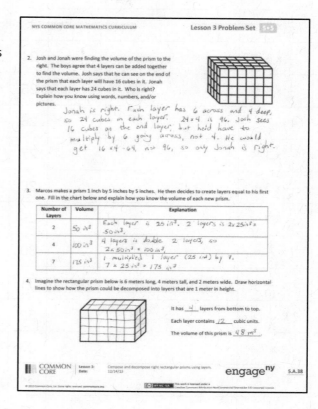

COMMON CORE

Lesson 3:   Compose and decompose right rectangular prisms using layers.
Date: 1/10/14

5.A.33

© 2014 Common Core, Inc. All rights reserved. commoncore.org

A

Correct _____

Solve.

#	Problem		#	Problem	
1	$\frac{1}{5} \times 2 =$		23	$\frac{5}{6} \times 12 =$	
2	$\frac{1}{5} \times 3 =$		24	$\frac{1}{3} \times 15 =$	
3	$\frac{1}{5} \times 4 =$		25	$\frac{2}{3} \times 15 =$	
4	$4 \times \frac{1}{5} =$		26	$15 \times \frac{2}{3} =$	
5	$\frac{1}{8} \times 3 =$		27	$\frac{1}{5} \times 15 =$	
6	$\frac{1}{8} \times 5 =$		28	$\frac{2}{5} \times 15 =$	
7	$\frac{1}{8} \times 7 =$		29	$\frac{4}{5} \times 15 =$	
8	$7 \times \frac{1}{8} =$		30	$\frac{3}{5} \times 15 =$	
9	$3 \times \frac{1}{10} =$		31	$15 \times \frac{3}{5} =$	
10	$7 \times \frac{1}{10} =$		32	$18 \times \frac{1}{6} =$	
11	$\frac{1}{10} \times 7 =$		33	$18 \times \frac{5}{6} =$	
12	$4 \div 2 =$		34	$\frac{5}{6} \times 18 =$	
13	$4 \times \frac{1}{2} =$		35	$24 \times \frac{1}{4} =$	
14	$6 \div 3 =$		36	$\frac{3}{4} \times 24 =$	
15	$\frac{1}{3} \times 6 =$		37	$32 \times \frac{1}{8} =$	
16	$10 \div 5 =$		38	$32 \times \frac{3}{8} =$	
17	$10 \times \frac{1}{5} =$		39	$\frac{5}{8} \times 32 =$	
18	$\frac{1}{3} \times 9 =$		40	$32 \times \frac{7}{8} =$	
19	$\frac{2}{3} \times 9 =$		41	$\frac{5}{9} \times 54 =$	
20	$\frac{1}{4} \times 8 =$		42	$63 \times \frac{7}{9} =$	
21	$\frac{3}{4} \times 8 =$		43	$56 \times \frac{3}{7} =$	
22	$\frac{1}{6} \times 12 =$		44	$\frac{6}{7} \times 49 =$	

COMMON CORE   **Lesson 3:**   Compose and decompose right rectangular prisms using layers.
                 Date: 1/10/14

© 2014 Common Core, Inc. All rights reserved. **commoncore.org**

B

Improvement _____   # Correct _____

Solve.

1	$\frac{1}{7} \times 2 =$		23	$\frac{3}{4} \times 8 =$	
2	$\frac{1}{7} \times 3 =$		24	$\frac{1}{5} \times 15 =$	
3	$\frac{1}{7} \times 4 =$		25	$\frac{2}{5} \times 15 =$	
4	$4 \times \frac{1}{7} =$		26	$\frac{4}{5} \times 15 =$	
5	$\frac{1}{10} \times 3 =$		27	$\frac{3}{5} \times 15 =$	
6	$\frac{1}{10} \times 7 =$		28	$15 \times \frac{3}{5} =$	
7	$\frac{1}{10} \times 9 =$		29	$\frac{1}{3} \times 15 =$	
8	$9 \times \frac{1}{10} =$		30	$\frac{2}{3} \times 15 =$	
9	$3 \times \frac{1}{8} =$		31	$15 \times \frac{2}{3} =$	
10	$5 \times \frac{1}{8} =$		32	$24 \times \frac{1}{6} =$	
11	$\frac{1}{8} \times 5 =$		33	$24 \times \frac{5}{6} =$	
12	$10 \div 5 =$		34	$\frac{5}{6} \times 24 =$	
13	$10 \times \frac{1}{5} =$		35	$20 \times \frac{1}{4} =$	
14	$9 \div 3 =$		36	$\frac{3}{4} \times 20 =$	
15	$\frac{1}{3} \times 9 =$		37	$24 \times \frac{1}{8} =$	
16	$10 \div 2 =$		38	$24 \times \frac{3}{8} =$	
17	$10 \times \frac{1}{2} =$		39	$\frac{5}{8} \times 24 =$	
18	$\frac{1}{3} \times 6 =$		40	$24 \times \frac{7}{8} =$	
19	$\frac{2}{3} \times 6 =$		41	$\frac{5}{9} \times 63 =$	
20	$\frac{1}{6} \times 12 =$		42	$54 \times \frac{7}{9} =$	
21	$\frac{5}{6} \times 12 =$		43	$49 \times \frac{3}{7} =$	
22	$\frac{1}{4} \times 8 =$		44	$\frac{6}{7} \times 56 =$	

COMMON CORE

Lesson 3:   Compose and decompose right rectangular prisms using layers.
Date: 1/10/14

5.A.35

© 2014 Common Core, Inc. All rights reserved. commoncore.org

Name _____   Date _____

Use these rectangular prisms to record the layers that you count.

 | **Lesson 3:** | Compose and decompose right rectangular prisms using layers.
| **Date:** | 1/10/14

5.A.

© 2014 Common Core, Inc. All rights reserved. **commoncore.org**

Name _____   Date _____

1. Use the prisms to find the volume.

    ▪ Build the rectangular prism pictured below to the left with your cubes, if necessary.
    ▪ Decompose it into layers in three different ways, and show your thinking on the blank prisms.
    ▪ Complete the missing information in the table.

a.

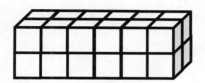

Number of Layers	Number of Cubes in Each Layer	Volume of the Prism
		cubic cm
		cubic cm
		cubic cm

 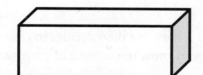 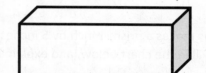

b.

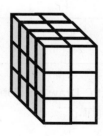

Number of Layers	Number of Cubes in Each Layer	Volume of the Prism
		cubic cm
		cubic cm
		cubic cm

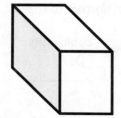 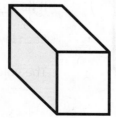 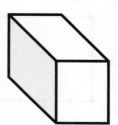

COMMON CORE™   Lesson 3:   Compose and decompose right rectangular prisms using layers.
                     Date: 1/10/14

5.A.37

© 2014 Common Core, Inc. All rights reserved. commoncore.org

2. Josh and Jonah were finding the volume of the prism to the right. The boys agree that 4 layers can be added together to find the volume. Josh says that he can see on the end of the prism that each layer will have 16 cubes in it. Jonah says that each layer has 24 cubes in it. Who is right? Explain how you know using words, numbers, and/or pictures.

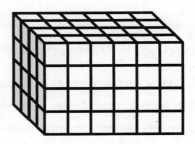

3. Marcos makes a prism 1 inch by 5 inches by 5 inches. He then decides to create layers equal to his first one. Fill in the chart below, and explain how you know the volume of each new prism.

Number of Layers	Volume	Explanation
2		
4		
7		

4. Imagine the rectangular prism below is 6 meters long, 4 meters tall, and 2 meters wide. Draw horizontal lines to show how the prism could be decomposed into layers that are 1 meter in height.

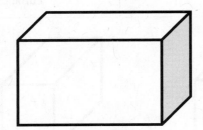

It has _____ layers from bottom to top.

Each layer contains _____ cubic units.

The volume of this prism is _____.

Lesson 3: Compose and decompose right rectangular prisms using layers.
Date: 1/10/14

5.A.3

© 2014 Common Core, Inc. All rights reserved. commoncore.org

Name _____   Date _____

1. Use unit cubes to build the figure to the right and fill in the missing information.

    Number of layers: _____

    Number of cubes in each layer: _____

    Volume: _____ cubic centimeters

    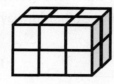

2. This prism measures 3 units by 4 units by 2 units. Draw the layers as indicated.

    Number of layers: 4

    Number of cubic units in each layer: 6

    Volume: _____ cubic centimeters

    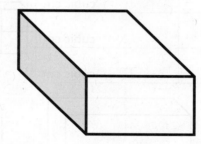

© 2014 Common Core, Inc. All rights reserved. **commoncore.org**

Name _____   Date _____

1. Use the prisms to find the volume.

- The rectangular prisms pictured below were constructed with 1-cm cubes
- Decompose each prism into layers in three different ways, and show your thinking on the blank prisms.
- Complete each table

Number of Layers	Number of Cubes in Each Layer	Volume of the Prism
		cubic cm
		cubic cm
		cubic cm

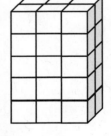

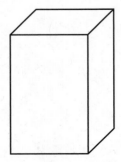 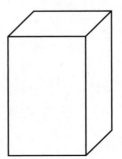 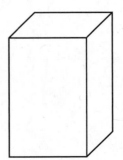

Number of Layers	Number of Cubes in Each Layer	Volume of the Prism
		cubic cm
		cubic cm
		cubic cm

© 2014 Common Core, Inc. All rights reserved. **commoncore.org**

2. Stephen and Chelsea want to increase the volume of this prism by 72 cubic centimeters. Chelsea wants to add eight layers and Stephen says they only need to add four layers. Their teacher tells them they are both correct. Explain how this is possible.

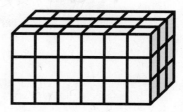

3. Juliana makes a prism 4 inches across and 4 inches wide, but only 1 inch tall. She then decides to create layers equal to her first one. Fill in the chart below and explain how you know the volume of each new prism.

Number of Layers	Volume	Explanation
3		
5		
7		

4. Imagine the rectangular prism below is 4 meters long, 3 meters tall, and 2 meters wide. Draw horizontal lines to show how the prism could be decomposed into layers that are 1 meter in height.

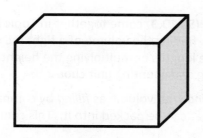

It has _____ layers from left to right.

Each layer contains _____ cubic units.

The volume of this prism is _____.

© 2014 Common Core, Inc. All rights reserved. **commoncore.org**

Mathematics Curriculum

Topic B

Volume and the Operations of Multiplication and Addition

5.MD.3, 5.MD.5

Focus Standard:	5.MD.3	Recognize volume as an attribute of solid figures and understand concepts of volume measurement.
		a. A cube with side length 1 unit, called a "unit cube," is said to have "one cubic unit" of volume, and can be used to measure volume.
		b. A solid figure which can be packed without gaps or overlaps using *n* unit cubes is said to have a volume of *n* cubic units.
	5.MD.5	Relate volume to the operations of multiplication and addition and solve real world and mathematical problems involving volume.
		a. Find the volume of a right rectangular prism with whole-number side lengths by packing it with unit cubes, and show that the volume is the same as would be found by multiplying the edge lengths, equivalently by multiplying the height by the area of the base. Represent threefold whole-number products as volume, e.g., to represent the associative property of multiplication.
		b. Apply the formulas $V = l \times w \times h$ and $V = b \times h$ for rectangular prisms to find volumes of right rectangular prisms with whole-number edge lengths in the context of solving real world and mathematical problems.
		c. Recognize volume as additive. Find volumes of solid figures composed of two non-overlapping right rectangular prisms by adding the volumes of the non-overlapping parts, applying this technique to solve real world problems.
Instructional Days:	6	
Coherence -Links from:	G3–M4	Multiplication and Area
-Links to:	G6–M5	Area, Surface Area, and Volume Problems

Concrete understanding of volume and multiplicative reasoning (**5.MD.3**) come together in Topic B as the systematic counting from Topic A leads naturally to formulas for finding the volume of a right rectangular prism (**5.MD.5**). Students come to see that multiplying the edge lengths or multiplying the height by the area of the base yields an equivalent volume to that found by packing and counting unit cubes.

Next, students solidify the connection between volume as *packing* with volume as *filling* by comparing the amount of liquid that fills a container to the number of cubes that can be packed into it. This connection is

© 2014 Common Core, Inc. All rights reserved. commoncore.org

formalized as students see that 1 cubic centimeter is equal to 1 milliliter. Complexity increases as students use their knowledge that volume is additive to partition and calculate the total volume of solid figures composed of non-overlapping rectangular prisms.

Word problems involving the volume of rectangular prisms with whole number edge lengths solidify understanding and give students opportunity to reason about scaling in the context of volume. This topic concludes with a design project that allows students to apply the concepts and formulas they have learned throughout Topics A and B to create a sculpture of a specified volume composed of varied rectangular prisms with parameters stipulated in the project description.

A Teaching Sequence Towards Mastery of Volume and the Operations of Multiplication and Addition
Objective 1: **Use multiplication to calculate volume.** **(Lesson 4)**
Objective 2: **Use multiplication to connect volume as *packing* with volume as *filling*.** **(Lesson 5)**
Objective 2: **Find the total volume of solid figures composed of two non-overlapping rectangular prisms.** **(Lesson 6)**
Objective 3: **Solve word problems involving the volume of rectangular prisms with whole number edge lengths.** **(Lesson 7)**
Objective 4: **Apply concepts and formulas of volume to design a sculpture using rectangular prisms within given parameters.** **(Lessons 8–9)**

Topic B: Volume and the Operations of Multiplication and Addition
Date: 1/10/14

© 2014 Common Core, Inc. All rights reserved. **commoncore.org**

Lesson 4

Objective: Use multiplication to calculate volume.

Suggested Lesson Structure

■ Fluency Practice   (12 minutes)
■ Application Problem   (5 minutes)
■ Concept Development   (33 minutes)
■ Student Debrief   (10 minutes)
  Total Time   **(60 minutes)**

Fluency Practice (12 minutes)

- Multiply Fractions **5.NF.4**   (4 minutes)
- Find the Area **4.MD.3**   (4 minutes)
- Find the Volume **5.MD.3**   (4 minutes)

Multiply Fractions (4 minutes)

Materials: (S) Personal white boards

Note: This fluency reviews G5–Module 4 content.

T: (Write $\frac{1}{3}$ of $\frac{4}{5}$ is _____.) Write the fraction of a set as a multiplication sentence.

S: $\frac{1}{3} \times \frac{4}{5}$.

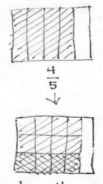

T: Draw a rectangle and shade in $\frac{4}{5}$.

S: (Draw a rectangle, partition it into 5 equal units, and shade 4 of the units.)

T: To show $\frac{1}{3}$ of $\frac{4}{5}$, how many equal parts to we need?

S: 3.

T: Show 1 third of 4 fifths.

S: (Partition the 4 fifths into thirds and shade 1 third.)

T: Make the other units the same size as the double shaded ones.

S: (Extend the horizontal thirds across the remaining units using dotted lines.)

T: What unit do we have now?

S: Fifteenths.

COMMON CORE | Lesson 4: | Use multiplication to calculate volume.
| Date: | 1/10/14

5.B.

© 2014 Common Core, Inc. All rights reserved. commoncore.org

T: How many fifteenths are double shaded?

S: Four.

T: Write the product and say the sentence.

S: (Write $\frac{1}{3} \times \frac{4}{5} = \frac{4}{15}$.) $\frac{1}{3}$ of $\frac{4}{5}$ is 4 fifteenths.

Continue this process with the following possible sequence: $\frac{2}{3} \times \frac{4}{5}$, $\frac{3}{5} \times \frac{2}{3}$, and $\frac{3}{5} \times \frac{5}{8}$.

Find the Area (4 minutes)

Materials: Personal white boards

Note: Reviewing this Grade 4 concept prepares students to calculate volume.

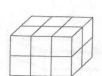
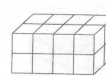
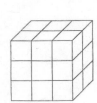

T: (Project square with side lengths 10 cm.)

T: How long are the square's sides?

S: 10 cm.

T: (Write __ cm × __ cm = __ cm².) On your boards, write the area of the square as a multiplication sentence, including the units.

S: (Write 10 cm × 10 cm = 100 cm².)

T: (Project a 3 ft by 13 ft rectangle.)

T: What is the measure of the rectangle's longest side?

S: 13 ft.

T: What is the measure of the rectangle's shortest side?

S: 3 ft.

T: (Write __ ft × __ ft = __ ft².) On your boards, write the area of the rectangle as a multiplication sentence starting with the length of the longest side.

S: (Write 13 ft × 3 ft = 39 ft².)

Continue this process with the other rectangles and squares.

Find the Volume (4 minutes)

Materials: Personal white boards

Note: This fluency reviews G5–M5–Lessons 1–2.

T: (Project the first image to the right. Number of layers = 2.) Each cube is 1 cubic centimeter.

T: (Underneath, write *Number of cubes in each layer*: __.) Fill in the blank.

S: (Write *Number of cubes in each layer*: 6.)

T: (Write *Number of cubes in each layer: 6*. Beneath it,

Lesson 4:   Use multiplication to calculate volume.
Date: 1/10/14

5.B.4

© 2014 Common Core, Inc. All rights reserved. **common**core.org

write *Volume = __ cubic centimeters + __ cubic centimeters.*) Fill in the blanks.

S: (Write *Volume = 6 cubic centimeters + 6 cubic centimeters.*)

T: (Write *Volume = 6 cubic centimeters + 6 cubic centimeters.* Beneath it, write *Volume = __ cubic centimeters.*)

S: (Write *Volume = 12 cubic centimeters.*)

Continue this process for the remaining prisms.

Application Problem (5 minutes)

Draw a 2 cm × 2 cm × 1 cm rectangular prism on the board, or project an image of one on the board.

Karen says that the volume of this prism is 5 cm^3 and that she calculated it by adding the sides together. Give the correct volume of this prism, and explain Karen's error.

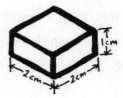

Note: To find the volume of this figure, Karen could add 2 and 2 (the number of centimeter cubes in each row), but not by adding all three dimensions.

Concept Development (33 minutes)

Materials: (T) Images of rectangular prisms to project (S) Personal white boards, rectangular prism recording
            sheet from G5–M5–Lesson 3

Part 1: Find the volume of multi-layer prisms using multiplication.

T: (Project the leftmost image below.) Record the length, width, and height of this rectangular prism on your recording sheet. Then decompose the prism into layers three different ways to find the volume like we did together yesterday.

S: (Work on the recording sheet to show the three different decompositions pictured.)

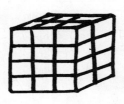

$\ell = 3\,cm$
$w = 2\,cm$
$h = 4\,cm$

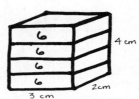

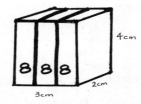

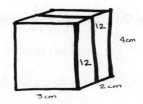

© 2014 Common Core, Inc. All rights reserved. commoncore.org

T: Let's record some information about our prism in this table. Look at this layer on the top. How many cubes are in each layer? How do you know?

S: There are 6 cubes. It is 3 cubes by 2 cubes. → I counted them. → It's like an array, 3 × 2 = 6.

T: (Record in table as 3 × 2.)

Cubes in Each Layer	Number of Layers	Volume
(3 × 2)	4	24cm^3
(2 × 4)	3	24 cm^3
(3 × 4)	2	24 cm^3

Follow a similar sequence to record the other decompositions.

T: How do we use this information to find the volume of the prism? Turn and talk.

S: With 4 layers, that's 4 copies of the same array of cubes, 4 times 6. That's 24 cubic centimeters. → I see 3 layers that each have 8 cubes in them. Eight cubes 3 times is 24 cubes. That's 24 cubic centimeters. → Three times 4 shows the cubes in the first layer on the front, but I need 2 of those, so 2 twelves make 24 cubic centimeters. → Count the layers. Four layers and each layer is a 3 cm by 2 cm by 1 cm prism, 6 fours is 24. The volume is 24 cubic centimeters.

T: (Record the number of layers and volumes in the table.)

T: (Hold up a cube.) We know that this is 1 cubic centimeter. Look at one face of this cube (point to one face), what is the area of this face?

S: 1 square centimeter.

T: (Point to the face on the top of the first prism.) If 1 square unit is the area of one cube's face, and there are 6 cubes that make up this face, what is the area of this face? Write a number sentence to show the area. Be sure to include the units.

S: 3 cm × 2 cm = 6 cm^2.

T: What do you notice about the area of this face and the number of cubes in this layer?

MP.2

S: They are the same.

T: A moment ago, we said that to find the volume, we had to account for the number of layers in the prism. How many layers are under this face?

S: 4.

T: Which dimension of the prism gives us that number?

S: The height.

T: How many centimeters is the height? Give me the unit, too.

S: 4 centimeters.

T: So, we can find the volume by multiplying the area of this face by the height. (Write (3 cm × 2 cm).) The height, 4 cm, happens to tell us the number of the layers. Show me the multiplication sentence you can use to find the volume of this prism that matches this way of seeing the layers.

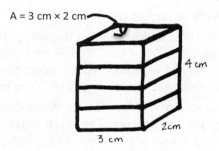

A = 3 cm × 2 cm

4 cm

3 cm   2cm

(3cm × 2cm) × 4cm = 24cm^3

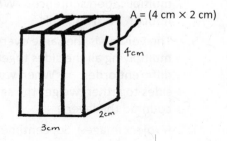

A = (4 cm × 2 cm)

4cm

3cm   2cm

(4cm × 2cm) × 3cm = 24cm^3

© 2014 Common Core, Inc. All rights reserved. commoncore.org

S: V = 3 cm × 2 cm × 4 cm = 24 cubic cm. → V = 6 cm^2 × 4 cm = 24 cm^3.

T: (Write V = 3 cm × 2 cm × 4 cm = 24 cm^3 and 6 cm^2 × 4 cm = 24 cm^3 on the board.) I notice some of you wrote 6 cm^2 × 4 cm, and others multiplied centimeters by centimeters by centimeters. What happens to the square units when you multiply them by the third factor? Why? Talk with a partner.

S: Each square unit becomes cubic. → You start out with length units, the second factor makes them square units, and the third factor makes them cubic units. → To measure area we use squares. To measure volume we use cubes. The third factor means we don't just have flat squares, but cubes.

T: Is this the same volume we found when we counted by the number of cubes in each layer?

S: Yes.

T: Let's use this method again, but I'd like to use the area of this face. (Point to the layer on the end.) Write a multiplication expression that shows how to find the area of this face.

S: 2 cm × 4 cm.

T: (Write (2 cm × 4 cm).) To find volume, we need to know how many layers are to the left of this face. What dimension of this prism tells us how many layers this time? How many centimeters is that? Turn and talk.

S: This time there are 3 layers. → The length is the one that shows how many layers this time. It's 3 centimeters. → The prism is 3 centimeters long. This shows the layers beside this face.

T: (Write (4 cm × 2 cm) × 3 cm.) Multiply to find the volume.

S: (Work to find 24 cm^3.)

T: Now, let's look at this last decomposition. Find the area of the front face. Tell which dimension shows the layers, and work with your partner to write an expression to find the volume. Turn and talk.

S: The area of this face is 3 cm times 4 cm. That's 12 square centimeters. There are 2 layers that are each 1 cm. 3 × 4 × 2 = 24. The volume is 24 cubic centimeters. → The area is 12 square centimeters, and the width is 2 cm. Twelve square centimeters times 2 centimeters is 24 cubic centimeters.

T: This is the same volume as before. Look at all three multiplication sentences. What patterns do you notice? Turn and talk.

S: The volume is the same every time. → We are multiplying all the sides together, but they are in a different order. → When we multiply the length of the sides together, we get the same volume as when we counted the layers.

T: (Project image.) So, centimeters times centimeters times centimeters gives us centimeters cubed? True? Why or why not? Turn and talk.

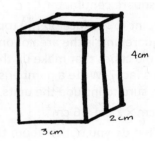

(3cm × 4cm) × 2cm = 24 cm^3

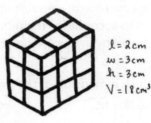

l = 2 cm
w = 3 cm
h = 3 cm
V = 18 cm^3

$\left(3\,cm \times 2\,cm\right) \times 3\,cm = 18\,cm^3$

$\left(2\,cm \times 3\,cm\right) \times 3\,cm = 18\,cm^3$

$\left(3\,cm \times 3\,cm\right) \times 2\,cm = 18\,cm^3$

	Lesson 4:	Use multiplication to calculate volume.
	Date:	1/10/14

5.B.

© 2014 Common Core, Inc. All rights reserved. commoncore.org

S: True. There are three measurements that are centimeters, and then the answer is in cubic units.
→ True. There are three factors that have centimeter units. So, the product has to be cubic units because cubes measure space in three dimensions!

T: Let's see if this pattern holds. Record the dimensions of this prism. What's different about it?

S: It's the same width and length, but now it's 1 cm shorter. → There are 6 fewer cubic centimeters in this one. → There are still some 2 × 3 layers in this one.

T: How would you find its volume? Turn and talk.

S: I can subtract 6 cubic units from the 24 cubic units in the 4-layer prism. That makes the volume 18 cubic centimeters. → I can multiply the 6 cubes in the top layer by 3 layers. That's 18 cubic centimeters. → I can multiply 2 cm times 2 cm times 3 cm, which is 18 cubic centimeters. → The end has a 6 cm^2 area and 3 layers, so 6 cm^2 × 3 cm = 18 cm^3. → The front face is different now. It is 3 cm by 3 cm. There are 2 layers behind it. 3 cm × 3 cm × 2 cm = 18 cm^3.

T: Let's record this. (Record.)

T: What can we conclude about finding volume from these examples?

S: We can multiply the sides to find the volume. → If we know the area of one face and multiply by the number of those layers, we can find volume. → Yeah, but the number of layers is just the length of the remaining side.

Part 2: Calculate the volume when the area of one side is given.

T: (Post the image of 2 cm × 2 cm square illustrated to the right.) This square shows the top face of a rectangular prism. If the prism is made of 1-cm cubes, what is the area of this face?

S: 4 square centimeters.

T: (Write A = 4 cm^2. Then post the image of prism with a height of 4 cm.) If the rectangular prism that sits below this face is built of centimeter cubes and has a height of 4 cm, how many layers of centimeter cubes are in the prism?

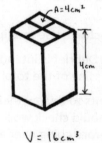

S: 4 layers.

T: How can we use the layers to find the volume? Turn and talk.

S: I can see that the length is 2 cm and the width is also 2 cm, so if the height is 4 cm, I can multiply 2 by 2 by the number of layers, which is 4, to get the volume. → Since the area of the top is 2 cm times 2 cm, which is 4 cm^2, we can just multiply the area times the height to find the volume.

$V = 16\,cm^3$

T: Show me the multiplication sentence you can use to find the volume of this prism.

S: V = 2 cm × 2 cm × 4 cm = 16 cubic cm. → V = 4 cm^2 × 4 cm = 16 cm^3.

T: (Write V = 16 cm^3 on board.)

T: (Post the image at right on board.) What's different about this prism?

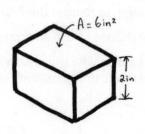

S: We can't see the individual cubes in the face with the area. → We don't know the dimensions of the top face, just the area.

COMMON CORE

| Lesson 4: | Use multiplication to calculate volume. |
| Date: | 1/10/14 |

5.B.8

© 2014 Common Core, Inc. All rights reserved. commoncore.org

T: Do we need the dimensions of that top face to find the volume? Why or why not?

S: No, we can use the area. → We don't want to know anything about how many cubes are in each layer. We just want the total volume. The area and the height are enough to find volume.

T: Work with a neighbor to find the volume of this prism.

S: (Work to show V = 6 in^2 × 2 in = 12 in^3.)

T: (Post the final image, at right, on the board.) Compare this prism to the last one. Turn and talk.

S: This one shows just the area again. → This one shows the area of the front and the width. We can still just multiply them. → This time we have the area of a different face. We have the front one and the depth of the prism, which tells how many layers behind the front face.

T: Find the volume of this prism.

S: (Work to show V = 3 m^2 × 3 m = 9 m^3.)

Problem Set (10 minutes)

Students should do their personal best to complete the Problem Set within the allotted 10 minutes. For some classes, it may be appropriate to modify the assignment by specifying which problems they work on first. All problems do not specify a method for solving. Students solve these problems using the RDW approach used for Application Problems.

Student Debrief (10 minutes)

Lesson Objective: Use multiplication to calculate volume.

The Student Debrief is intended to invite reflection and active processing of the total lesson experience.

Invite students to review their solutions for the Problem Set. They should check work by comparing answers with a partner before going over answers as a class. Look for misconceptions or misunderstandings that can be addressed in the Debrief. Guide students in a conversation to debrief the Problem Set and process the lesson.

You may choose to use any combination of the questions below to lead the discussion.

- Explain why the prisms in Problems 1(d) and 3(b) have the same volume but different dimensions. How is that possible? Identify the dimensions of a third prism that would have an equivalent volume.

Lesson 4:   Use multiplication to calculate volume.
Date: 1/10/14

5.B.9

© 2014 Common Core, Inc. All rights reserved. **commoncore.org**

- Explain how we get cubic units when we multiply to find volume.

- Connect the term *face* with the term *base.* Discuss with students that these two terms may be used interchangeably when dealing with right rectangular prisms. Why could we think of any face as the base of our prism? Discuss the fact that if we imagine rotating the prism so that the chosen face lies at the bottom (what we typically think of as the base), the remaining dimension can be thought of as the height of the prism.

- What would happen to the volume of Tyron's box if he doubled the height to 16 cm? If he halved the length? If he doubled the height while halving the length?

- Explain your thought process on Problem 5 as you found the error in Aaron's thinking.

- Compare your earlier strategies for finding volume to the method we learned today. How is the formula for finding the volume of rectangular prisms helpful?

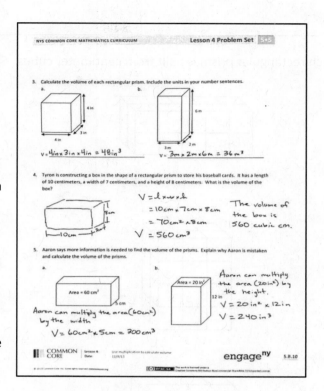

Exit Ticket (3 minutes)

After the Student Debrief, instruct students to complete the Exit Ticket. A review of their work will help you assess the students' understanding of the concepts that were presented in the lesson today and plan more effectively for future lessons. You may read the questions aloud to the students.

© 2014 Common Core, Inc. All rights reserved. **commoncore.org**

Name _____   Date _____

1. Each rectangular prism is built from centimeter cubes. State the dimensions and find the volume.

    a.

    Length: _____ cm

    Width: _____ cm

    Height: _____ cm

    Volume: _____ cm³

    b.

    Length: _____ cm

    Width: _____ cm

    Height: _____ cm

    Volume: _____ cm³

    c.

    Length: _____ cm

    Width: _____ cm

    Height: _____ cm

    Volume: _____ cm³

    d.

    Length: _____ cm

    Width: _____ cm

    Height: _____ cm

    Volume: _____ cm³

2. Write a multiplication sentence that you could use to calculate the volume for each rectangular prism in Problem 1. Include the units in your sentences.

    a. _____   b. _____

    c. _____   d. _____

Lesson 4:   Use multiplication to calculate volume.
Date: 1/10/14

5.B.1

© 2014 Common Core, Inc. All rights reserved. commoncore.org

3. Calculate the volume of each rectangular prism. Include the units in your number sentences.

a.

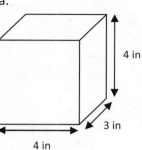

4 in

3 in

4 in

V = _____

b.

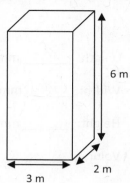

6 m

2 m

3 m

V = _____

4. Tyron is constructing a box in the shape of a rectangular prism to store his baseball cards. It has a length of 10 centimeters, a width of 7 centimeters, and a height of 8 centimeters. What is the volume of the box?

5. Aaron says more information is needed to find the volume of the prisms. Explain why Aaron is mistaken, and calculate the volume of the prisms.

a.

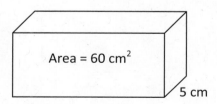

Area = 60 cm²

5 cm

b.

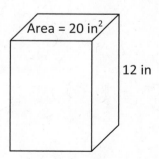

Area = 20 in²

12 in

COMMON CORE

Lesson 4:   Use multiplication to calculate volume.
Date: 1/10/14

5.B.12

© 2014 Common Core, Inc. All rights reserved. **commoncore.org**

Name _____ Date _____

Calculate the volume of each prism.

a.

Length: _____ mm

Width: _____ mm

Height: _____ mm

Volume: _____ mm^3

Write the multiplication sentence that shows how you calculated the volume. Be sure to include the units.

b. A rectangular prism has a top face with an area of 20 ft^2 and a height of 5 ft. What is the volume of this rectangular prism?

© 2014 Common Core, Inc. All rights reserved. **commoncore.org**

Name _____   Date _____

1.   Each rectangular prism is built from centimeter cubes. State the dimensions and find the volume.

a.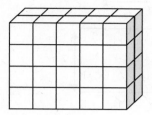

Length: _____ cm

Width: _____ cm

Height: _____ cm

Volume: _____ cm^3

b.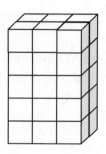

Length: _____ cm

Width: _____ cm

Height: _____ cm

Volume: _____ cm^3

c.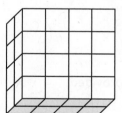

Length: _____ cm

Width: _____ cm

Height: _____ cm

Volume: _____ cm^3

d.

Length: _____ cm

Width: _____ cm

Height: _____ cm

Volume: _____ cm^3

2.   Write a multiplication sentence that you could use to calculate the volume for each rectangular prism in Problem 1. Include the units in your sentences.

a. _____   b. _____

c. _____   d. _____

© 2014 Common Core, Inc. All rights reserved. **commoncore.org**

3. Calculate the volume of each rectangular prism. Include the units in your number sentences.

a.

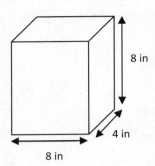

8 in

4 in

8 in

b.

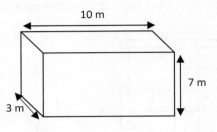

10 m

7 m

3 m

Volume:_____

Volume:_____

4. Mrs. Johnson is constructing a box in the shape of a rectangular prism to store clothes for the summer. It has a length of 28 inches, a width of 24 inches, and a height of 30 inches. What is the volume of the box?

5. Calculate the volume of each rectangular prism using the information that is provided.

a. Face area: 56 square meters, height: 4 meters.

b. Face area: 169 square inches, height: 14 inches.

COMMON CORE

Lesson 4:   Use multiplication to calculate volume.
Date: 1/10/14

5.B.1

© 2014 Common Core, Inc. All rights reserved. commoncore.org

Lesson 5

Objective: Use multiplication to connect volume as *packing* with volume as *filling*.

Suggested Lesson Structure

■ Fluency Practice   (12 minutes)
　 Concept Development   (38 minutes)
■ Student Debrief   (10 minutes)
　 Total Time   **(60 minutes)**

Fluency Practice (12 minutes)

▪ Count by Cubic Centimeters **5.MD.1**   (2 minutes)
▪ Find the Area **4.MD.3**   (4 minutes)
▪ Find the Volume **5.MD.3**   (6 minutes)

Count by Cubic Centimeters (2 minutes)

Note: This fluency will prepare students for today's lesson.

　　T:　Count by 100 cubic centimeters to 1,000 cubic centimeters. (Write as students count.)

100 cm³	200 cm³	300 cm³	400 cm³	500 cm³	600 cm³	700 cm³	800 cm³	900 cm³	1,000 cm³
100 mL³	200 mL³	300 mL³	400 mL³	500 mL³	600 mL³	700 mL³	800 mL³	900 mL³	1 liter

　　S:　100 cm^3, 200 cm^3, 300 cm^3, 400 cm^3, 500 cm^3, 600 cm^3, 700 cm^3, 800 cm^3, 900 cm^3, $1{,}000 \text{ cm}^3$.
　　T:　Count by 100 mL. (Write as students count.)
　　S:　100 mL, 200 mL, 300 mL, 400 mL, 500 mL, 600 mL, 700 mL, 800 mL, 900 mL, 1,000 mL.
　　T:　1,000 mL = 1 liter. Count by 100 mL again. This time, when you come to 1,000 mL say 1 liter. (Write as students count.)
　　S:　100 mL, 200 mL, 300 mL, 400 mL, 500 mL, 600 mL, 700 mL, 800 mL, 900 mL, 1 liter.

Find the Area (4 minutes)

Materials: (S) Personal white boards

Note: Reviewing this Grade 4 concept prepares students to calculate volume.

　　T:　(Project rectangle with side lengths of 6 cm and 4 cm.) What is the length of the rectangle's longest

---

	Lesson 5:	Use multiplication to connect volume as *packing* with volume as *filling*.	
	Date:	1/10/14	

5.B.16

© 2014 Common Core, Inc. All rights reserved. commoncore.org

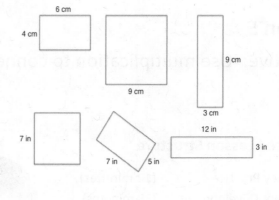

side?

S: 6 cm.

T: What is the length of the rectangle's shortest side?

S: 4 cm.

T: (Write __ cm × __ cm = __ cm^2.) On your boards, write the area of the rectangle as a multiplication sentence including the units.

S: (Write 6 cm × 4 cm = 24 cm^2.)

T: (Project a square with a given length of 9 cm.) Name the shape.

S: Square.

T: What is the length of the square's sides?

S: 9 cm.

T: (Write __ cm × __ cm = __ cm^2.) On your boards, write the area of the square as a multiplication sentence including the units.

S: (Write 9 cm × 9 cm = 81 cm^2.)

Continue this process for the other rectangles and squares.

Find the Volume (6 minutes)

Materials: (S) Personal white boards

Note: This fluency reviews G5–M5–Lesson 4.

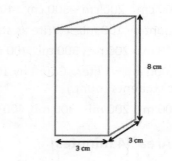

T: (Project the 4 cm by 5 cm by 2 cm rectangular prism illustrated at right.) What's the length of the rectangular prism?

S: 4 cm.

T: What's the width?

S: 5 cm.

T: What's the height?

S: 2 cm.

T: (Write __ cm × __ cm × __ cm = __ cm^3.) On your boards, calculate the volume.

S: (Write 4 cm × 5 cm × 2 cm = 40 cm^3.)

Repeat this process for the 3 cm by 3 cm by 8 cm rectangular prism.

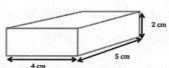

T: (Project the rectangular prism with a given area of 40 ft^2 and a given width of 7 ft given to the right.) Say the given area of the rectangular prism's front face.

S: 40 ft^2.

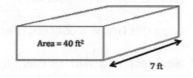

© 2014 Common Core, Inc. All rights reserved. **commoncore.org**

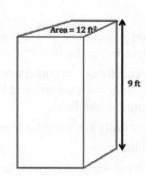

Area = 12 ft²

9 ft

T: Say the given length.

S: 7 ft.

T: (Write V = ___ft³.) On your boards, calculate the volume.

S: (Write V = 280 ft³.)

Repeat this process for the rectangular prism with a given area of 12 ft²
and a given height of 9 ft.

Concept Development (38 minutes)

Materials: (S) Per group: centimeter cubes, several small
watertight containers (preferably right rectangular
prisms) marked with a horizontal line for measuring,
small pitchers of water, beaker labeled with mL,
class data recording sheet poster, ruler or tape
measure, Problem Set

Note: Because today's lesson is a hands-on exploration, time
for the Application Problem has been given to the Concept
Development.

Before class, prepare a large poster or sheet for groups to
record their findings. Be sure to use cubes that are denser than
water for the displacement exploration.

Problem 1

Investigate 1 cm³ = 1 mL.

T: What are some ways that we can determine the
volume of the box you've been given using the
materials on your table?

S: We can pack it with cubes and count. → We can pack
the bottom layer, and then use the cubes to find how
many layers. → We could find any base, and then
count the layers. → We can measure the sides, and
then multiply the three dimensions.

T: Measure the inside dimensions of your box using the
line that's drawn as the height, and multiply to find the
volume. Then, confirm the measurement by packing
the box to the line that's drawn. Record the volume in
cubic centimeters on your Problem Set.

S: (Work.)

**NOTES ON
MULTIPLE MEANS OF
REPRESENTATION AND
MATERIALS:**

Fancy toothpicks, straight pins, and
some office supplies come in clear
rectangular boxes suitable for this
activity. The horizontal fill line for the
water can be drawn at a height that
will match the number of cubes that
can be packed into the box. If these
are not readily available, small
rectangular breath mint boxes or metal
spice boxes can be used. However,
students may have to estimate if the
corners are rounded. It is best to test
the boxes and volumes before
implementing this lesson.

An alternative approach is to gather a
collection of small gift boxes and use
salt rather than water to fill them.
While salt is not a liquid, it does
behave like one for the purposes of the
first activity.

The second activity must be done with
water and a centimeter cube that will
sink. If a dense cube is not available,
students should use a drinking straw or
coffee stirrer to submerge the cube
completely.

If resources are limited, this may be
done as a demonstration and then as a
center over the course of a few days in
small groups.

Lesson 5:	Use multiplication to connect volume as *packing* with volume as *filling*.
Date:	1/10/14

5.B.18

© 2014 Common Core, Inc. All rights reserved. commoncore.org

T: Now, I would like you to find the amount of liquid your container will hold. Any ideas how you might do this using the materials on your table? Turn and talk.

S: We could pour in some water and then measure the water with the beaker. → We could fill the container with water, and then use a measuring cup to measure the water. That would tell us the amount it will hold.

T: What units are used on the beaker?

MP.6 S: Milliliters.

T: Pour the water to the fill line. Then, measure the amount of water by carefully pouring it into the beaker. Record the liquid volume on your Problem Set. Once your group is done, have a member of your group record your data onto the class poster.

S: (Work and record.)

T: (Circulate, asking students to describe what they're doing. Encourage use of the terms *volume, capacity,* and other unit language.)

T: Now that we've recorded our findings, let's look at the volume data. What do you notice about the volume as measured by the cubes and the liquid volume?

S: They are the same. → Our box packed 36 cubes, and it held 36 mL of water. → Although our prism was a different size different than the first group's, our packing and filling was the same. → Ours was really close, just one cubic centimeter more than the milliliters.

T: What can you say about the relationship of 1 milliliter to 1 cubic centimeter?

S: They seem to be the same. → I think they are equal.

T: There's a way we can show that these two measurements are equal. Put water into your beaker to any measuring point other than the fill line. Be careful to fill it exactly to the line you choose. For example, you might fill your beaker to 15 mL.

S: (Pour.)

T: Now pour in 1 more milliliter of water and describe what happens to the water level.

S: The water went up one more line. → The water rose because we put more in.

T: Record the new amount of water on your Problem Set. What will happen to the water level if we place 1 cube in the beaker? Tell your partner.

S: It will go up again. → The water will rise because the cube pushes some of the water out of the way.

T: Let's find out how far the water will rise. Place 1 centimeter cube into the water. Describe what happens to your partner.

S: (Work and discuss.)

T: How did the water level change?

S: The water rose. → It looks like there's more water in the beaker. → The water went up 1 mL.

T: We didn't actually put more water in, and yet the cube caused a rise in the water level equal to when we put 1 mL of water in the beaker. From this investigation and from our work with the boxes, what can we say about the relationship between 1 mL of water and 1 cubic centimeter?

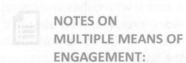

NOTES ON MULTIPLE MEANS OF ENGAGEMENT:

When dividing students into groups, be sure to choose members with different strengths. Try to assign tasks such as recorder, builder, pourer, and measurer.

Lesson 5:   Use multiplication to connect volume as *packing* with volume as *filling*.

Date: 1/10/14

5.B.1

© 2014 Common Core, Inc. All rights reserved. **commoncore.org**

S: They are equal. → I know they are equal because I measured my box and got the same number of cubes as milliliters. → I know they are equal because one cube made the water go up 1 milliliter.

T: Yes. We have seen that 1 cubic centimeter = 1 mL. (Write 1 cm³= 1 mL on the board.) This is an important relationship that will help us solve problems.

Problem 2

A rectangular tank measures 30 cm by 20 cm by 40 cm. How many milliliters of water are in the tank when it is full? How many liters is that?

T: Let's use what we've learned about volume as filling to solve this problem. We need to find the volume of the water in the tank. What do we know about the tank that can help us?

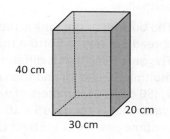

S: We know the size of the tank. → Since the water is filled to the top, the volume of the tank will be the same as the volume of the water.

T: Find the volume of the tank.

S: (Work to find 24,000 cubic centimeters.)

T: We discovered today that 1 cubic centimeter is equal to 1 mL. Since this is true, how many milliliters of water are in the tank when it is full?

S: 24,000 mL.

T: How many liters is that?

S: 24 liters.

Problem 3

a. A small fish tank is filled to the top with water. If the tank measures 15 cm by 10 cm by 10 cm, what is the volume of water in the tank? Express your answer in mL.

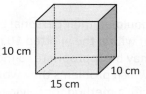

b. After a week, water evaporates out of the tank so that the water is 9 cm high. What is the volume of the water in the tank?

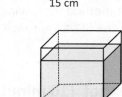

T: (Project Problem 3(a) and the accompanying image onto the board.) Using what we've talked about today, turn and talk to your partner and find the volume of water in the tank in cubic centimeters and in milliliters.

S: All we need to do is multiply the sides because the water is all the way to the top. → Since the water fills the whole tank, we can just multiply 15 × 10 × 10. That's 1,500 cubic centimeters. → It's easy to find the volume. It's 1,500 cubic centimeters. We have to say it in milliliters. That's exactly the same number, so it's 1,500 mL.

T: (Project Problem 3(b).) Let's imagine that some of the water evaporated out of the tank. Now the water is only 9 cm deep. Does this change the height of the tank? Why or why not?

S: No, because the tank doesn't change size.

Lesson 5:   Use multiplication to connect volume as *packing* with volume as *filling*.

Date: 1/10/14

5.B.20

© 2014 Common Core, Inc. All rights reserved. commoncore.org

T: Does this change the area of the bottom of the tank?

S: No, the tank is still the same size.

T: Will the volume of the water change? Why or why not?

S: The volume in the tank will be less because some of the water is gone. → The water won't be as high. → The water level will go down by 1 cm, so that's like pouring out a layer of 15 by 10 centimeters.

T: Find the volume of the water in the tank now. Turn and talk.

S: The bottom of the tank is the same, so the water is spread out on the bottom the same way as before. The only thing that is different is the height. I'll multiply 15 and 10 and then multiply by 9. That's 1,350 cubic centimeters of water. → The part of the water that is gone is 15 × 10 × 1. That's 150 cubic centimeters. I can subtract that from 1,500. That will be 1,350 cubic centimeters still in the tank.

T: What is the volume of the water in the tank now?

S: 1,350 cubic centimeters.

T: Express that in milliliters.

S: 1,350 mL.

> **NOTES ON MULTIPLE MEANS OF ENGAGEMENT:**
>
> While the relationship of 1 cm^3 = 1 mL seems a simple one numerically, the concept behind this relationship—that of volume as *filling* as well as *packing* (especially when comparing a rectangular container to a cylindrical one)—is more complex. Be sure to offer many opportunities for students to encounter this concept beyond today's lesson. Ask often if an amount of liquid will fit into rectangular containers and how it might be confirmed without pouring.

Problem Set (10 minutes)

Students should do their personal best to complete the Problem Set within the allotted 10 minutes. For some classes, it may be appropriate to modify the assignment by specifying which problems they work on first. Al problems do not specify a method for solving. Students solve these problems using the RDW approach used for Application Problems.

Student Debrief (10 minutes)

Lesson Objective: Use multiplication to connect volume as *packing* with volume as *filling*.

The Student Debrief is intended to invite reflection and active processing of the total lesson experience.

Invite students to review their solutions for the Problem Set. They should check work by comparing answers with a partner before going over answers as a class. Look for

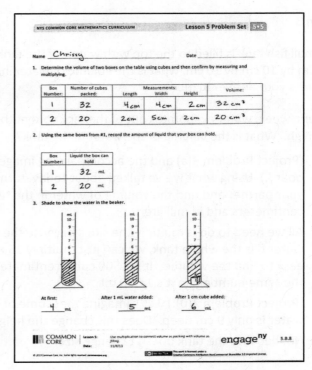

Lesson 5:   Use multiplication to connect volume as *packing* with volume as *filling*.

Date: 1/10/14

© 2014 Common Core, Inc. All rights reserved. **commoncore.org**

5.B.2

misconceptions or misunderstandings that can be addressed in the Debrief. Guide students in a conversation to debrief the Problem Set and process the lesson.

You may choose to use any combination of the questions below to lead the discussion.

- Make a real life connection for students by discussing the use of cubic centimeters and the term *cc's* in medical applications. Medicines, intravenous fluids, and injections are often ordered in cc's rather than mL. Students may not be aware that this is a cubic centimeter, equivalent to 1 milliliter.

- Problem 6 describes the height of the water using the word *depth*. Discuss the connection between these two terms. How is height like depth? When might you use the word *height* to describe a figure, and when might *depth* be more appropriate? Can the words be used interchangeably? (Have students rephrase problems from the Problem Set to test.) English language learners especially will benefit from such a discussion.

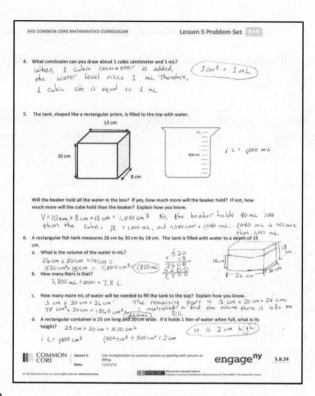

- Problem 7 asks students to extend their knowledge of cubic centimeters and milliliters to liters. Allow students to work together to think through this task if necessary and then explain their thinking to another partner group. Discuss other connections, as well. If 1 cubic centimeter is equal to 1 milliliter, to what liquid measure is 1 cubic meter equivalent? How could you find out? (Students can draw to investigate using 100 cm = 1 m.) Building a cubic container from meter sticks in the classroom will help students visualize the actual volume of 1 kiloliter. They might also imagine pouring 1,000 liter bottles of water or 500 2-liter soft drinks into that single container.

- Ask students to generate as many rectangular prisms with whole number sides as they can that would hold 1 liter of liquid. Although the dimensions will all be factors of 1,000, the shapes of the containers may be drastically different. Student might even be encouraged to draw the containers on isometric dot paper for comparison. Ask: What do the sides of all these containers have in common? (All are factors of 1,000.) Because they all have the same factors, are they all the same shape? Why or why not?

Exit Ticket (3 minutes)

After the Student Debrief, instruct students to complete the Exit Ticket. A review of their work will help you assess the students' understanding of the concepts that were presented in the lesson today and plan more effectively for future lessons. You may read the questions aloud to the students.

| COMMON CORE | Lesson 5: | Use multiplication to connect volume as *packing* with volume as *filling*. | | **5.B.22** |
| | Date: | 1/10/14 | | |

© 2014 Common Core, Inc. All rights reserved. **commoncore.org**

Name _____ Date _____

1. Determine the volume of two boxes on the table using cubes and then confirm by measuring and multiplying.

Box Number	Number of Cubes Packed	Measurements			Volume
		Length	Width	Height	

2. Using the same boxes from Problem 1, record the amount of liquid that your box can hold.

Box Number	Liquid the Box Can Hold
	mL
	mL

3. Shade to show the water in the beaker.

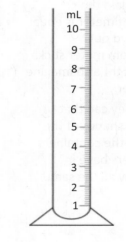 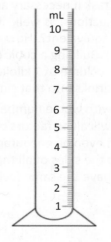

At first:	After 1 mL water added:	After 1 cm cube added:
_____mL	_____mL	_____mL

4. What conclusion can you draw about 1 cubic centimeter and 1 mL?

5. The tank, shaped like a rectangular prism, is filled to the top with water.

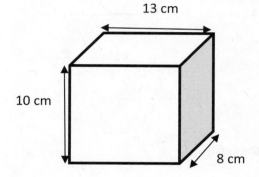
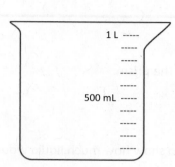

Will the beaker hold all the water in the box? If yes, how much more will the beaker hold? If not, how much more will the cube hold than the beaker? Explain how you know.

6. A rectangular fish tank measures 26 cm by 20 cm by 18 cm. The tank is filled with water to a depth of 15 cm.
    a. What is the volume of the water in mL?

    b. How many liters is that?

    c. How many more mL of water will be needed to fill the tank to the top? Explain how you know.

    d. A rectangular container is 25 cm long and 20 cm wide. If it holds 1 liter of water when full, what is its height?

© 2014 Common Core, Inc. All rights reserved. commoncore.org

Name _____   Date _____

1.

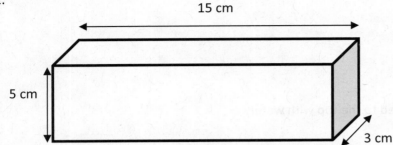 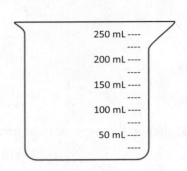

a.   Find the volume of the prism.

b.   Shade the beaker to show how much liquid would fill the box.

COMMON CORE™

Lesson 5:	Use multiplication to connect volume as *packing* with volume as *filling*.
Date:	1/10/14

5.B.2

© 2014 Common Core, Inc. All rights reserved. commoncore.org

Name _____   Date _____

1. Johnny filled a container with 30 centimeter cubes. Shade the beaker to show how much water the container will hold. Explain how you know.

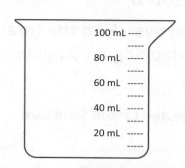

2. A beaker contains 250 mL of water. Jack wants to pour the water into a container that will hold the water. Which of the containers pictured below could he use? Explain your choices.

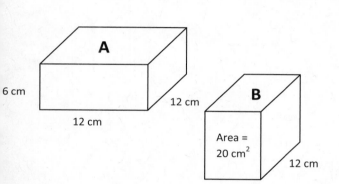

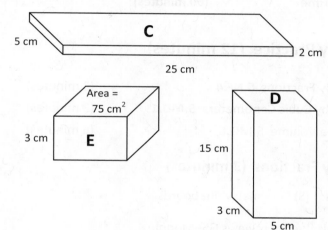

3. On the back of this paper, describe the details of the activities you did in class today. Include what you learned about cubic centimeters and milliliters. Give an example of a problem you solved with an illustration.

© 2014 Common Core, Inc. All rights reserved. commoncore.org

Lesson 6

Objective: Find the total volume of solid figures composed of two non-overlapping rectangular prisms.

Suggested Lesson Structure

■ Fluency Practice   (12 minutes)

▨ Application Problem   (8 minutes)

▢ Concept Development   (30 minutes)

■ Student Debrief   (10 minutes)

Total Time   **(60 minutes)**

Fluency Practice (12 minutes)

- Multiply Fractions **5.NF.4**   (3 minutes)
- Count by Cubic Centimeters **5.MD.1**   (3 minutes)
- Find the Volume **5.MD.C**   (6 minutes)

Multiply Fractions (3 minutes)

Materials: (S) Personal white boards

Note: This fluency reviews G5–Module 4.

T: (Write $\frac{1}{2} \times \frac{1}{2}$.) Say the number sentence.

S: $\frac{1}{2} \times \frac{1}{2} = \frac{1}{4}$.

Continue this process with $\frac{1}{2} \times \frac{1}{3}$ and $\frac{1}{2} \times \frac{1}{8}$.

T: (Write $\frac{2}{3} \times \frac{1}{5} = \_\_$.) On your boards, write the number sentence.

S: (Write $\frac{2}{3} \times \frac{1}{5} = \frac{2}{15}$.)

T: (Write $\frac{2}{3} \times \frac{1}{3} = \_\_$.) Say the number sentence.

S: $\frac{2}{3} \times \frac{1}{3} = \frac{2}{9}$.

Repeat this process with $\frac{1}{3} \times \frac{3}{3}, \frac{1}{4} \times \frac{3}{5}$, and $\frac{3}{4} \times \frac{3}{5}$.

T: (Write $\frac{2}{3} \times \frac{2}{5} = \_\_$.) Say the number sentence.

	Lesson 6:	Find the total volume of solid figures composed of two non-overlapping rectangular prisms.
	Date:	1/10/14

5.B.

© 2014 Common Core, Inc. All rights reserved. commoncore.org

S:　$\frac{2}{3} \times \frac{2}{5} = \frac{4}{15}$.

Continue this process for $\frac{3}{4} \times \frac{3}{5}$.

T:　(Write $\frac{1}{5} \times \frac{3}{4} = \underline{\quad}$.)　On your boards, write the equation.

S:　(Write $\frac{1}{5} \times \frac{3}{4} = \frac{3}{20}$.)

T:　(Write $\frac{3}{4} \times \frac{4}{3} = \underline{\quad}$.)　On your boards write the equation.

S:　(Write $\frac{3}{4} \times \frac{4}{3} = \frac{12}{12} = 1$.)

Continue this process with the following possible suggestions: $\frac{2}{3} \times \frac{3}{4}, \frac{5}{8} \times \frac{2}{3}$, and $\frac{2}{5} \times \frac{3}{8}$.

Count by Cubic Centimeters (3 minutes)

Note: This fluency will prepare students for today's lesson.

T:　Count by twos to 10. (Write as students count.)

S:　2, 4, 6, 8, 10.

T:　Count by two-hundreds to 1,000. (Write as students count.)

S:　200, 400, 600, 800, 1,000.

T:　Count by 200 cm³ to 1,000 cm³. (Write as students count.)

S:　200 cm³, 400 cm³, 600 cm³, 800 cm³, 1,000 cm³.

T:　Count by 200 cm³. This time, when you come to 1,000 cm³, say 1 liter. (Write as students count.)

S:　 200 cm³, 400 cm³, 600 cm³, 800 cm³, 1 liter.

2	4	6	8	10
200	400	600	800	1,000
200 cm³	400 cm³	600 cm³	800 cm³	1,000 cm³
200 cm³	400 cm³	600 cm³	800 cm³	1 liter

Find the Volume (6 minutes)

Materials:　(S) Personal white boards

Note: This fluency reviews G5–M5–Lesson 4.

T:　(Project 3 cm by 4 cm by 2 cm rectangular prism.) What's the length of the rectangular prism?

S:　3 cm.

T:　What's the width?

S:　4 cm.

T:　What's the height?

S:　2 cm.

T:　(Write $\underline{\quad}$ cm × $\underline{\quad}$ cm × $\underline{\quad}$ cm = $\underline{\quad}$ cm³.) On your boards, calculate the volume.

S:　(Write 3 cm × 4 cm × 2 cm = 24 cm³.)

NOTES ON MULTIPLE MEANS OF REPRESENTATION:

Have students skip-count as a group as they did in Grades K and 1 when they were counting by twos and threes. When they get to 1,000 cm³, they should say 1 liter.

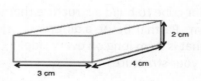

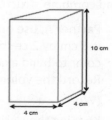

Lesson 6:　Find the total volume of solid figures composed of two non-overlapping rectangular prisms.

Date:　1/10/14

5.B.28

© 2014 Common Core, Inc. All rights reserved. commoncore.org

Repeat process for the 4 cm by 4 cm by 10 cm rectangular prism.

T: (Project rectangular prism that has a given volume of 40 in^3, length of 4 in, and width of 5 in.) What's the length of the rectangular prism?

S: 4 in.

T: What's the width of the rectangular prism?

S: 5 in.

T: What's the volume of the rectangular prism?

S: 40 in^3.

T: (Write 40 in^3 = 4 in × 5 in × __ in.) On your boards, fill in the missing side length. If you need to, write a division sentence to calculate your answer.

S: (Write 40 in^3 = 4 in × 5 in × 2 in.)

Repeat process for the rectangular prism with a given volume of 120 in^3, length of 3 in, and width of 4 in.

T: (Project the rectangular prism with a face having a given area of 30 ft^2 and a given width of 6 ft.) Say the given area of the prism's front face.

S: 30 ft^2.

T: Say the given width.

S: 6 ft.

T: (Write V = __ ft^3.) On your boards, calculate the volume.

S: (Write V = 180 ft^3.)

Repeat process for rectangular prism with a given area of 12 ft^2 and a given height of 8 ft.

Concept Development (30 minutes)

Materials: (T) Drawing of rectangular prism figures (S) Centimeter cubes, dot paper

Problem 1

Build and combine structures then find the total volume.

T: Partner A, use one color cube to build a structure that is 3 cm by 2 cm by 2 cm. Partner B, use a different color to build a cube that is 2 cm long on every side. Record the volume of your structures.

S: (Work.)

T: Keeping their original dimensions, how could you combine the two structures you've built? Turn and talk. Then find the volume of your new structure.

S: We could put the cube on top of the rectangular prism. → We could put them beside each other on the end. → We could make an L. → The volume is 20 cubic units.

T: Now, build a different structure using the two prisms and find the volume.

S: (Work.)

T: How did you find the volume of your new structures?

S: We counted all the blocks. → We knew that one was 12 cubic units and the other one was 8. We just added that together to get 20 cubic units.

T: When you built the second structure, did the volume change? Why or why not?

S: It did not change the volume. There were still 20 cubic units. → It doesn't matter how we stacked the two prisms together. The volume of each one is the same every time, and the volume of the whole thing is still 20 cubic units. → The total volume is always going to be the volume of the red one plus the volume of the green one, no matter how we stack them.

Problem 2

T: (Project or draw on the board the 3 m × 2 m × 7 m prism at right.) What is the volume of this prism?

S: 42 m^3.

T: Imagine another prism identical to this one. If we glued them together to make a bigger prism, how could we find the volume? Turn and talk. Then find the volume.

S: We already know that the volume of the first one is 42m^3. We could just add another 42 m^3 to it. That would be 84 m$^{3.}$ → We could multiply 42 by 2 since they are just alike. That's 84 m^3.

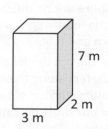

7 m

2 m

3 m

Problem 3

T: (Project or draw on the board the composite structure.) How is this drawing different from the last one?

S: There are two different size boxes this time. → The little box on top only has measurements on the length and the height.

T: There are a lot of markings on this figure. We'll need to be careful that we use the right ones when we find the volume. Find the volume of the bottom box.

S: (Work to find 120 cubic inches.)

T: What about the one on the top? I heard someone say that there isn't a width measurement on the

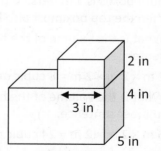

2 in

3 in

4 in

5 in

6 in

COMMON CORE™

Lesson 6: Find the total volume of solid figures composed of two non-overlapping rectangular prisms.

Date: 1/10/14

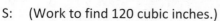

5.B.30

© 2014 Common Core, Inc. All rights reserved. **commoncore.org**

drawing. How will we find the volume? Turn and talk.

S: The boxes match up exactly in the drawing on the width. That means the width of the top box is the same as the bottom one, so it's still 5 inches wide. → You can tell the top and bottom box are the same width, so just multiply 3 × 5 × 2.

T: What is the volume of the top box?

S: 30 cubic inches.

T: How could we find the total volume?

S: Add the two together.

T: Say the number sentence with the units.

S: 120 cubic inches + 30 cubic inches = 150 cubic inches.

Problem 4

T: (Project or draw the figure given at right.) Compare this figure to the last one.

S: There are two different boxes again. → There's a little one and a big one, like last time. → This time, there's a bracket on the height of both boxes. → There's no length or width or height measurement on the top box this time.

T: If there are no measurements on the top box alone, how might we still calculate the volume? Turn and talk.

S: We can tell the length of the top box by looking at the 6 meters along the bottom. The other box has 4 meters sticking out on the top of the box. That means the box must be 2 meters long. → The length is 6 minus 4. That's 2. → The width is easy. It's the same as the bottom box, so that's 2 meters. → The height of both boxes is 4 meters. If the bottom box is 2 meters, then the top box must also be 2 meters.

T: What is the volume of the top prism? Say the number sentence.

S: 2 m × 2 m × 2 m = 8 cubic meters.

T: What is the volume of the bottom prism? Say the number sentence.

S: 6 m × 2 m × 2 m = 24 cubic meters.

T: What's the total volume of both? Say the number sentence.

S: 8 cubic meters + 24 cubic meters = 32 cubic meters.

NOTES ON
MULTIPLE MEANS OF
ENGAGEMENT:

Continuing to use the cubes to construct the prisms can help to keep kinesthetic learners on task. The calculation of the volume can still be made with the formula.

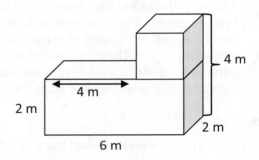

4 m

4 m

2 m

2 m

6 m

NOTES ON
MULTIPLE MEANS OF
ENGAGEMENT:

Challenge students whose spatial skills allow them to see these figures easily by having them draw a figure consisting of three different prisms on dot paper with just enough information given to calculate the volume of the figure. They should calculate the volume of their own figure and then exchange figures with a partner.

Students can write about the minimum information necessary to calculate the volume of a composite figure.

Lesson 6: Find the total volume of solid figures composed of two non-overlapping rectangular prisms.

Date: 1/10/14

5.B.3

© 2014 Common Core, Inc. All rights reserved. commoncore.org

Problem 5

Two rectangular prisms have a combined volume of 135 cubic meters. Prism A has double the volume of Prism B.

a. What is the volume of each prism?

b. If one face of Prism A has an area of 10 square meters, what is its height?

T: Let's use tape diagramming to help us with this problem. Read it with me.

T/S: (Read.)

T: What can we draw from the first sentence?

S: A tape for each prism. → Two tapes labeled Prism A's volume and Prism B's volume. → A bracket on both to show they are 135 cubic meters total. → Their total volume is 135 cubic meters.

T: What does the next sentence tell us and how can we represent it?

S: Prism A is double the volume of Prism B. → We need 2 units for Prism A. → Prism A's tape should be twice as long as Prism B's.

T: Show that in your diagram. Then use this information to solve for the volumes of both prisms.

S: (Work.)

T: What are the volumes of each prism?

S: Prism A is 90 cubic meters, and Prism B is 45 cubic meters.

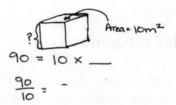

A ▭▭ } 135
B ▭

3 units = 135
1 unit = $\frac{135}{3}$ = 45

Prism A's volume is 2 × 45 cm³ = 90 cm³.
Prism B's volume is 45 cm³.

Area = 10 m²
?
90 = 10 × ___

$\frac{90}{10}$ = ___

Prism A is 9 meters high.

T: To find the height of Prism B, what do we need to think about? Turn and talk, then solve.

S: We know the area of one face. If we multiply the area by something we should get the volume of 90 m³. The area is 10 m², and 10 times 9 is 90. It is 9 meters tall. → We can divide 90 by 10 and get 9 meters tall.

Cube: 64 m³
4
4

Double:
could be 8m × 4m × 4m = 128 m³
Most floor space:
8m × 16m (or 128 m² base)
and 1 m high
Most height: 1 m × 1 m × 128 m

Application Problem (8 minutes)

A storage company advertises three different choices for all your storage needs: "The Cube," a true cube with a volume of 64 m³, "The Double" (double the volume of the cube), and "The Half" (half the volume of the cube). What could be the dimensions of the three storage units? How might they be oriented to give the most floor space? The most height?

Half:
Could be 4 m × 4 m × 2 m = 32 m³
Most floor space:
8 m × 4 m (or 32 m² base)
and 1 m high
Most height: 1 m × 1 m × 32 m

Lesson 6: Find the total volume of solid figures composed of two non-overlapping rectangular prisms.

Date: 1/10/14

5.B.32

© 2014 Common Core, Inc. All rights reserved. commoncore.org

Note: Students use the knowledge that a cube's sides are all equal to find the side as 4 meters. (Side × side × side = 64 m³, so each side must be 4 m.) While students may approach halving or doubling the other storage units using different approaches (e.g., doubling any of the dimensions singly) this problem affords an opportunity to discuss the many options of orienting the storage units to give the most practical increase or decrease in square footage or height for storage of various items. The problem also reinforces the part to whole relationships of volume.

Problem Set (10 minutes)

Students should do their personal best to complete the Problem Set within the allotted 10 minutes. For some classes, it may be appropriate to modify the assignment by specifying which problems they work on first. All problems do not specify a method for solving. Students solve these problems using the RDW approach used for Application Problems.

Student Debrief (10 minutes)

Lesson Objective: Find the total volume of solid figures composed of two non-overlapping rectangular prisms.

The Student Debrief is intended to invite reflection and active processing of the total lesson experience.

Invite students to review their solutions for the Problem Set. They should check work by comparing answers with a partner before going over answers as a class. Look for misconceptions or misunderstandings that can be addressed in the Debrief. Guide students in a conversation to debrief the Problem Set and process the lesson.

You may choose to use any combination of the questions below to lead the discussion.

- What advice would you give to a friend who was having trouble picturing the dimensions on a composite figure? What helps you to figure out missing dimensions?

- If all students use an addition strategy to find the total volume of the figures, suggest to them the alternate strategy of subtracting the missing part. For example, Problem 1(d) offers such a strategy.

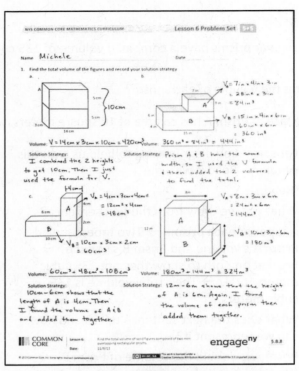

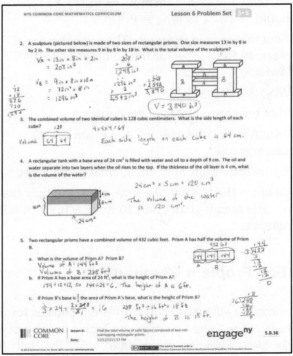

Lesson 6: Find the total volume of solid figures composed of two non-overlapping rectangular prisms.

Date: 1/10/14

5.B.

Ask students to imagine that the top prism was once identical to the bottom prism (much like the figure in Problem 1(a)). Ask: If these two prisms were identical, what would the total volume be? (360 cubic meters.) Now imagine that the end was removed from the top prism. What would the volume of that removed part be? (2 m × 3 m × 6 m = 36 cubic meters.) If we wanted to know the total volume of the figure with this part removed, how could we do that? (Subtract. 360 m^3 − 36 m^3 = 324 m^3.) Is this the same volume we found when we added the two prisms? (Yes!)

- How did the Application Problem help you solve Problem 3?

- Compare your approach to solving Problem 4 with that of the person sitting next to you. How is your thinking alike? How is it different?

- Allow students to share the tape diagrams that they used to solve Problem 5. If students need more scaffolding, use the suggested sequence in the Concept Development to guide their drawing. Ask: How is the problem like the one we did together? How is it different? (It uses the word half instead of double. This time Prism B is the larger.) What was the effect on the height of the two prisms by making the base of Prism B smaller than the one on Prism A?

- Is a shorter container always a smaller volume? Give some examples of prisms to support your answer.

Exit Ticket (3 minutes)

After the Student Debrief, instruct students to complete the Exit Ticket. A review of their work will help you assess the students' understanding of the concepts that were presented in the lesson today and plan more effectively for future lessons. You may read the questions aloud to the students.

© 2014 Common Core, Inc. All rights reserved. **commoncore.org**

Name _____   Date _____

1. Find the total volume of the figures and record your solution strategy.

a.

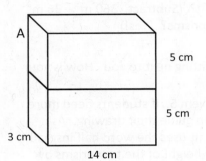

Volume: _____

Solution Strategy:

b.

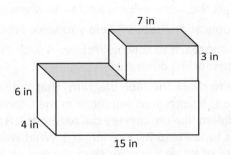

Volume: _____

Solution Strategy:

c.

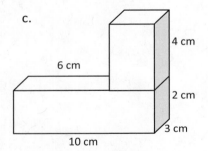

Volume: _____

Solution Strategy:

d.

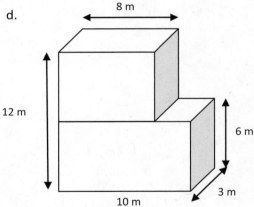

Volume: _____

Solution Strategy:

Lesson 6:   Find the total volume of solid figures composed of two non-
             overlapping rectangular prisms.
Date: 1/10/14

5.B.

© 2014 Common Core, Inc. All rights reserved. commoncore.org

2. A sculpture (pictured below) is made of two sizes of rectangular prisms. One size measures 13 in by 8 in by 2 in. The other size measures 9 in by 8 in by 18 in. What is the total volume of the sculpture?

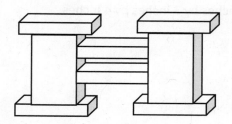

3. The combined volume of two identical cubes is 128 cubic centimeters. What is the side length of each cube?

4. A rectangular tank with a base area of 24 cm² is filled with water and oil to a depth of 9 cm. The oil and water separate into two layers when the oil rises to the top. If the thickness of the oil layer is 4 cm, what is the volume of the water?

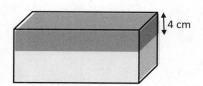

4 cm

5. Two rectangular prisms have a combined volume of 432 cubic feet. Prism A has half the volume of Prism B.

   a. What is the volume of Prism A? Prism B?

   b. If Prism A has a base area of 24 ft², what is the height of Prism A?

   c. If Prism B's base is $\frac{2}{3}$ the area of Prism A's base, what is the height of Prism B?

Lesson 6:	Find the total volume of solid figures composed of two non-overlapping rectangular prisms.	
Date:	1/10/14	5.B.36

© 2014 Common Core, Inc. All rights reserved. commoncore.org

Name _____ Date _____

1. Find the total volume of soil in the three planters. Planter A is 15 inches by 3 inches by 3 inches. Planter B is 9 inches by 3 inches by 4 inches.

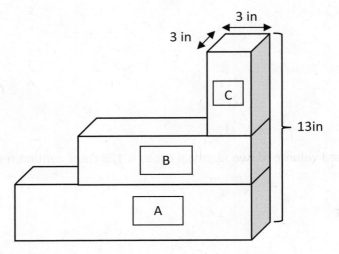

COMMON CORE

Lesson 6: Find the total volume of solid figures composed of two non-overlapping rectangular prisms.

Date: 1/10/14

5.B.

© 2014 Common Core, Inc. All rights reserved. commoncore.org

Name _____ Date _____

1. Find the total volume of the figures and record your solution strategy.

a.

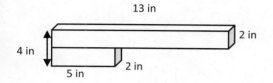

Volume: _____

Solution Strategy:

b.

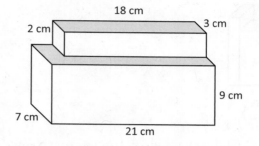

Volume: _____

Solution Strategy:

c.

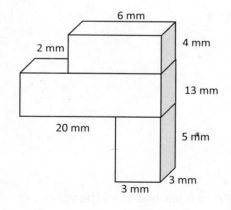

Volume: _____

Solution Strategy:

d.

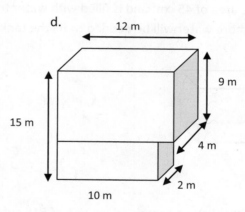

Volume: _____

Solution Strategy:

COMMON CORE | **Lesson 6:** Find the total volume of solid figures composed of two non-overlapping rectangular prisms.
Date: 1/10/14

5.B.38

© 2014 Common Core, Inc. All rights reserved. commoncore.org

2. A planting box (pictured below) is made of two sizes of rectangular prisms. One type of prism measures 3 inches by 6 inches by 14 inches. The other type measures 18 inches by 9 inches by 10 inches. What is total volume of three such boxes?

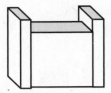

3. The combined volume of two identical cubes is 250 cubic centimeters. What is the measure of one cube's edge?

4. A fish tank has a base area of 45 cm^2 and is filled with water to a depth of 12 cm. If the height of the tank is 25 cm, how much more water will be needed to fill the tank to the brim?

5. Three rectangular prisms have a combined volume of 518 cubic feet. Prism A has one-third the volume of Prism B, and Prisms B and C have equal volume. What is the volume of each prism?

COMMON CORE | **Lesson 6:** Find the total volume of solid figures composed of two non-overlapping rectangular prisms. 5.B.

Date: 1/10/14

© 2014 Common Core, Inc. All rights reserved. commoncore.org

Lesson 7

Objective: Solve word problems involving the volume of rectangular prisms with whole number edge lengths.

Suggested Lesson Structure

■ Fluency Practice   (12 minutes)
■ Concept Development   (38 minutes)
■ Student Debrief   (10 minutes)
   Total Time   **(60 minutes)**

Fluency Practice (12 minutes)

- Sprint: Multiply Fractions **5.NF.4**   (9 minutes)
- Find the Volume **5.MD.C**   (3 minutes)

Sprint: Multiply Fractions (9 minutes)

Materials: (S) Multiply Fractions Sprint

Note: This fluency reviews G5–Module 4.

Find the Volume (3 minutes)

Materials: (S) Personal white boards

Note: This fluency reviews G5–M5–Lesson 5.

- T: On your boards, write the
      formula for finding the volume
      of a rectangular prism.
- S: (Write V = l × w × h.)
- T: (Write V = l × w × h.) Project a
      rectangular prism with a length
      of 5 cm, width of 6 cm, and
      height of 2 cm.
- T: On your boards, write a
      multiplication sentence to express
      the volume of the rectangular prism.

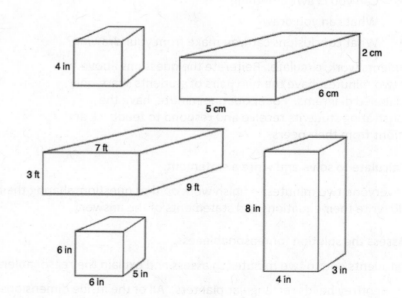

COMMON CORE™

Lesson 7:   Solve word problems involving the volume of rectangular prisms with
            whole number edge lengths.
Date: 1/10/14

5.B.40

© 2014 Common Core, Inc. All rights reserved. **commoncore.org**

S: (Beneath V = l × w × h, write V = 5 cm × 6 cm × 2 cm. Beneath it, write V = 60 cm^3.)

Continue this process with the other rectangular prisms.

T: (Project a cube with side lengths equal to 4 inches.) Name the prism.

S: Cube.

T: On your boards, write a multiplication sentence to show the volume of the cube.

S: (Write V = 4 in × 4 in × 4 in. Beneath it, write V = 64 in^3.)

Concept Development (38 minutes)

Materials: (S) Problem Set

Note: The time normally allotted for the Application Problem has been included in the Concept Development portion of today's lesson.

Suggested Delivery of Instruction for Solving Lesson 7's Word Problems

1.   Model the problem.

Have two pairs of students who can successfully model the problem work at the board while the others work independently or in pairs at their seats. Review the following questions before beginning the first problem:

- Can you draw something?
- What can you draw?
- What conclusions can you make from your drawing?

As students work, circulate. Reiterate the questions above. After two minutes, have the two pairs of students share only their labeled diagrams. For about one minute, have the demonstrating students receive and respond to feedback and questions from their peers.

2.   Calculate to solve and write a statement.

Give everyone two minutes to finish work on that question, sharing their work and thinking with a peer. All should write their equations and statements of the answer.

3.   Assess the solution for reasonableness.

Give students one to two minutes to assess and explain the reasonableness of their solution.

Note: Geoffrey builds rectangular planters. All of the inside dimensions of the planters are whole numbers.

NOTES ON
**MULTIPLE MEANS OF
ENGAGEMENT:**

The problems in today's lesson are focused on planters and gardening. The lesson could serve as a springboard for planning a school garden. Students could plan planters as Geoffrey does in the lesson given parameters of height or base area. Students might also research optimal soil depths (and thus volume) for particular plants and vegetables to incorporate into their designs.

Bringing their designs into reality is the ultimate real world problem connection. If it is possible, let them try. Writing a proposal to present the designs (along with estimated costs) to the principal or school board encompasses many skills, but even cardstock planters with paper flowers can be a rewarding experience.

Lesson 7:   Solve word problems involving the volume of rectangular prisms with
              whole number edge lengths.
Date: 1/10/14

5.B.4

© 2014 Common Core, Inc. All rights reserved. **commoncore.org**

Problem 1

Geoffrey's first planter is 8 feet long and 2 feet wide. The container is filled with soil to a height of 3 feet in the planter. What is the volume of soil in the planter? Explain your work using a diagram.

In this problem students are given three dimensions (length, width, and height) and asked to find the volume of the soil in the planter. The use of the volume formula allows students to find the number of cubic feet of soil in the planter. A non-scaled illustration of the planter is the most logical diagram to accompany this work.

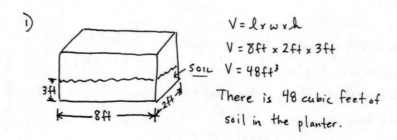

$V = l \times w \times h$

$V = 8ft \times 2ft \times 3ft$

$V = 48ft^3$

There is 48 cubic feet of soil in the planter.

Problem 2

Geoffrey wants to grow some tomatoes in four large planters. He wants each planter to have a volume of 320 cubic feet, but he wants them all to be different. Show four different ways Geoffrey can make these planters, and draw diagrams with the planters' measurements on them.

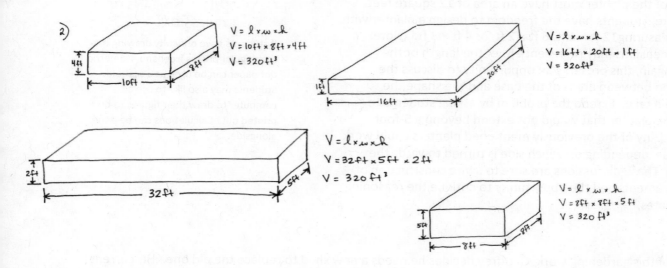

$V = l \times w \times h$
$V = 10ft \times 8ft \times 4ft$
$V = 320ft^3$

$V = l \times w \times h$
$V = 16ft \times 20ft \times 1ft$
$V = 320ft^3$

$V = l \times w \times h$
$V = 32ft \times 5ft \times 2ft$
$V = 320 ft^3$

$V = l \times w \times h$
$V = 8ft \times 8ft \times 5ft$
$V = 320 ft^3$

In Problem 2, students are asked to come up with four sets of differing dimensions that will all result in a volume of 320 cubic feet. This problem requires students to think in terms of whole to part. They will need to find factors of 32 tens to generate the dimensions. The illustrations are just four such examples. Encourage students to come up with different values for each dimension rather than just changing the name of the same dimensions (length, width, and height) repeatedly, although that method would result in the same volume. Simply changing the shape of the planter can provide opportunities for discussion of which shape might be best to use for different situations. For example, in a small yard, planting a tree which would need more depth than length might be the best option. There are a wide variety of dimensions that would be acceptable here, but be sure to have students check their multiplication using the volume formula.

COMMON CORE™

Lesson 7: Solve word problems involving the volume of rectangular prisms with whole number edge lengths.
Date: 1/10/14

5.B.42

© 2014 Common Core, Inc. All rights reserved. commoncore.org

Problem 3

Geoffrey wants to make one planter that extends from the ground to just below his back window. The window starts 3 feet off the ground. If he wants the planter to hold 36 cubic feet of soil, name one way he could build the planter so it is not taller than 3 feet. Explain how you know.

Since Geoffrey wants to build a planter with a height of 3 feet & a volume of 36 cubic feet, the base of the planter should have an area of 12 sq. ft. I drew a planter with a length of 4 ft, a width of 3 ft, & a height of 3 ft.

$36 \div 3 = 12$

$12 = 4 \times 3$

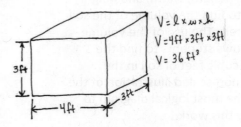

$V = l \times w \times h$
$V = 4ft \times 3ft \times 3ft$
$V = 36 ft^3$

This problem requires students to work backwards and reason that since Geoffrey needs 36 cubic feet of volume and that the height of Geoffrey's planter is 3 feet, then division shows that the base of the planter must have an area of 12 square feet. From there, students have the freedom to design a planter with a base measuring 12 ft × 1 ft, 6 ft × 2 ft, or 4 ft × 3 ft. (Note: These dimensions may represent either the length or the width.) Again, this presents an opportunity to discuss the connection between areas of the base and the shape the planter will take. Extend the problem by asking students to choose the planter that would not extend beyond a 5-foot window. (Any of the previously mentioned planters could work in this case, depending on which side is turned towards the window.) These discussions are sure to invite construction of viable arguments and the opportunity to critique the reasoning of classmates.

NOTES ON MULTIPLE MEANS OF EXPRESSION:

If students have difficulty drawing the rectangular prisms freehand, isometric dot paper can be used as a scaffold. Students may also like to use a computer to draw their figures to be printed out. Calculations can be done alongside.

Problem 4

After all of this gardening work, Geoffrey decides he needs a new shed to replace the old one. His current shed is a rectangular prism that measures 6 feet long by 5 feet wide by 8 feet high. He realizes he needs a shed with 480 cubic feet of storage.

Lesson 7: Solve word problems involving the volume of rectangular prisms with whole number edge lengths.

Date: 1/10/14

© 2014 Common Core, Inc. All rights reserved. commoncore.org

4a)   SHED : $V = 6ft \times 5ft \times 8ft$
                  $V = 240 ft^3$

SHED
DIMENSIONS : $V = 240 ft^3 \times 8$
DOUBLED
                $V = 1,920 ft^3$

Geoffrey's current shed has a volume of 240 cubic ft, which is half the volume he needs. By doubling each dimension of the shed, Geoffrey will get a shed that is 8 times the current size (because $2 \times 2 \times 2 = 8$). To double the volume he needs only to double one dimension, not all three.

a. Will he achieve his goal if he doubles each dimension? Why or why not?

This part of Problem 4 gives students a chance to explore the exponential growth potential of doubling all three dimensions simultaneously. Doubling the length, width, and height of Geoffrey's shed will result in a volume that is 8 times that of his current shed ($l \times 2$) × ($w \times 2$) × ($h \times 2$) = ($l \times w \times h$) × 8. While this size shed certainly provides the 480 cubic feet he is looking for, students can reason that doubling each dimension would lead to a shed that is far larger than Geoffrey needs. This may lead to students trying to double only two of the dimensions and then realizing that simply doubling one of the dimension of his shed gives Geoffrey double the volume. This discussion can also include an exploration of which dimension makes the most sense to double given that this is a garden shed. Would doubling the height give more usable space for gardening equipment? Does it make more sense to double either the length or the width? Challenge: Is there a way to change two dimensions and still simply double the space?

b. If he wants to keep the height the same, what could the other dimensions be so that he gets the volume he wants?

This problem builds on the students' thinking from the previous problem and asks them to identify dimensions that would yield a shed volume of 480 cubic feet while maintaining a height of 8 feet. Most students will correctly reason that you simply need to double one of the other dimensions (the length or the width) in order to create a doubled volume. However, there are additional ways to create a volume of 480 cubic feet with a height of 8 feet, including halving the length and quadrupling the width. Engage students in a discussion about why this is possible (think back to Problem 3) and have them share their alternate solutions.

4b) Since Geoffrey wants to double the volume of his shed
     & keep the height the same, he could double the length
     & keep the width the same too. Or he could double the
     width & keep the length the same.

          $l = 12ft$ $l = 6ft$
          $w = 5 ft$ OR $w = 10ft$
          $h = 8 ft$ $h = 8 ft$

Lesson 7:   Solve word problems involving the volume of rectangular prisms with
            whole number edge lengths.
Date: 1/10/14

5.B.44

© 2014 Common Core, Inc. All rights reserved. commoncore.org

c.   If he uses the dimensions in Part (b), what would be the area of the new shed's floor?

Part (c) requires students to remember their work from G5–M5–Lesson 4 and multiply the length times the width to find the area of the shed floor. Since students will be using their varied answers from Part (b) to answer this question, expect to find variety in responses here as well. However, this is another opportunity to engage students in a discussion about why the area must be 60 square feet, despite using different dimensions from Part (b).

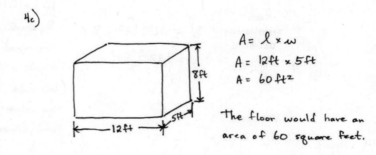

Problem Set (10 minutes)

Students should do their personal best to complete the Problem Set within the allotted 10 minutes. For some classes, it may be appropriate to modify the assignment by specifying which problems they work on first. All problems do not specify a method for solving. Students solve these problems using the RDW approach used for Application Problems.

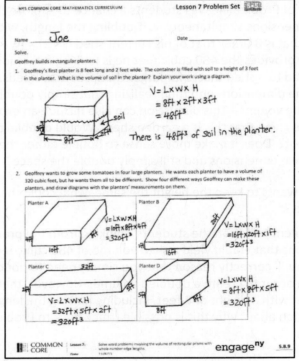

Student Debrief (10 minutes)

Lesson Objective: Solve word problems involving the volume of rectangular prisms with whole number edge lengths.

The Student Debrief is intended to invite reflection and active processing of the total lesson experience.

Invite students to review their solutions for the Problem Set. They should check work by comparing answers with a partner before going over answers as a class. Look for misconceptions or misunderstandings that can be addressed in the Debrief. Guide students in a conversation to debrief the Problem Set and process the lesson.

You may choose to use any combination of the questions below to lead the discussion.

- What effect does doubling one dimension have on the volume? Doubling two dimensions? Doubling all dimensions? Why?

- What effect would doubling one dimension while halving another have on the volume? Why?

- How many prisms can you think of that have a volume of 100 cm^3?

- If Geoffrey had been using fractional lengths for the dimensions for his planters, how would that have changed the possible answers to these questions?

Lesson 7:	Solve word problems involving the volume of rectangular prisms with whole number edge lengths.
Date:	1/10/14

5.B.4

© 2014 Common Core, Inc. All rights reserved. commoncore.org

Exit Ticket (3 minutes)

After the Student Debrief, instruct students to complete the Exit Ticket. A review of their work will help you assess the students' understanding of the concepts that were presented in the lesson today and plan more effectively for future lessons. You may read the questions aloud to the students.

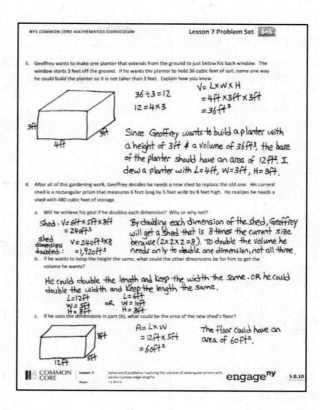

NYS COMMON CORE MATHEMATICS CURRICULUM   Lesson 7 Problem Set

3. Geoffrey wants to make one planter that extends from the ground to just below his back window. The window starts 3 feet off the ground. If he wants the planter to hold 36 cubic feet of soil, name one way he could build the planter so it is not taller than 3 feet. Explain how you know.

$36 \div 3 = 12$
$12 = 4 \times 3$

$V = L \times W \times H$
$= 4ft \times 3ft \times 3ft$
$= 36 ft^3$

Since Geoffrey wants to build a planter with a height of 3ft & a volume of 36ft³, the base of the planter should have an area of 12ft². I drew a planter with L=4ft, W=3ft, H=3ft.

4. After all of this gardening work, Geoffrey decides he needs a new shed to replace the old one. His current shed is a rectangular prism that measures 6 feet long by 5 feet wide by 8 feet high. He realizes he needs a shed with 480 cubic feet of storage.

a. Will he achieve his goal if he doubles each dimension? Why or why not?

Shed: V = 6ft × 5ft × 8ft
= 240 ft³

shed dimensions doubled: V = 240ft³ × 8
= 1,920 ft³

By doubling each dimension of the shed, Geoffrey will get a shed that is 8 times the current size because (2×2×2=8). To double the volume he needs only to double one dimension, not all three.

b. If he wants to keep the height the same, what could the other dimensions be for him to get the volume he wants?

He could double the length and keep the width the same. OR he could double the width and keep the length the same.

L=12ft   L=6ft
W=5ft   OR   W=10ft
H=8ft   H=8ft

c. If he uses the dimensions in part (b), what could be the area of the new shed's floor?

$A = L \times W$
$= 12ft \times 5ft$
$= 60 ft^2$

The floor could have an area of 60 ft².

COMMON CORE   Lesson 7:   Solve word problems involving the volume of rectangular prisms with whole number edge lengths.
Date:

engage^ny   5.B.10

COMMON CORE   **Lesson 7:**   Solve word problems involving the volume of rectangular prisms with
                 Date: whole number edge lengths.
                 1/10/14   5.B.46

© 2014 Common Core, Inc. All rights reserved. commoncore.org

A

Correct _____

Multiply, but don't simplify.

1	$\frac{1}{2} \times \frac{1}{2} =$		23	$\frac{2}{5} \times \frac{5}{3} =$	
2	$\frac{1}{2} \times \frac{1}{3} =$		24	$\frac{3}{5} \times \frac{5}{2} =$	
3	$\frac{1}{2} \times \frac{1}{4} =$		25	$\frac{1}{3} \times \frac{1}{3} =$	
4	$\frac{1}{2} \times \frac{1}{7} =$		26	$\frac{1}{3} \times \frac{2}{3} =$	
5	$\frac{1}{7} \times \frac{1}{2} =$		27	$\frac{2}{3} \times \frac{2}{3} =$	
6	$\frac{1}{3} \times \frac{1}{2} =$		28	$\frac{2}{3} \times \frac{3}{2} =$	
7	$\frac{1}{3} \times \frac{1}{3} =$		29	$\frac{2}{3} \times \frac{4}{3} =$	
8	$\frac{1}{3} \times \frac{1}{6} =$		30	$\frac{2}{3} \times \frac{5}{3} =$	
9	$\frac{1}{3} \times \frac{1}{5} =$		31	$\frac{3}{2} \times \frac{3}{5} =$	
10	$\frac{1}{5} \times \frac{1}{3} =$		32	$\frac{3}{4} \times \frac{1}{5} =$	
11	$\frac{1}{5} \times \frac{2}{3} =$		33	$\frac{3}{4} \times \frac{4}{5} =$	
12	$\frac{2}{5} \times \frac{2}{3} =$		34	$\frac{3}{4} \times \frac{5}{5} =$	
13	$\frac{1}{4} \times \frac{1}{3} =$		35	$\frac{3}{4} \times \frac{6}{5} =$	
14	$\frac{1}{4} \times \frac{2}{3} =$		36	$\frac{1}{4} \times \frac{6}{5} =$	
15	$\frac{3}{4} \times \frac{2}{3} =$		37	$\frac{1}{7} \times \frac{1}{7} =$	
16	$\frac{1}{6} \times \frac{1}{3} =$		38	$\frac{1}{8} \times \frac{3}{5} =$	
17	$\frac{5}{6} \times \frac{1}{3} =$		39	$\frac{5}{6} \times \frac{1}{4} =$	
18	$\frac{5}{6} \times \frac{2}{3} =$		40	$\frac{3}{4} \times \frac{3}{4} =$	
19	$\frac{5}{4} \times \frac{2}{3} =$		41	$\frac{2}{3} \times \frac{6}{6} =$	
20	$\frac{1}{5} \times \frac{1}{5} =$		42	$\frac{3}{4} \times \frac{6}{2} =$	
21	$\frac{2}{5} \times \frac{2}{5} =$		43	$\frac{7}{8} \times \frac{7}{9} =$	
22	$\frac{2}{5} \times \frac{3}{5} =$		44	$\frac{7}{12} \times \frac{9}{8} =$	

COMMON CORE　|　**Lesson 7:**　Solve word problems involving the volume of rectangular prisms with whole number edge lengths.

Date:　1/10/14

5.B.4

© 2014 Common Core, Inc. All rights reserved. commoncore.org

B

Multiply, but don't simplify.

Improvement _____   # Correct _____

1	$\frac{1}{2}$ x $\frac{1}{3}$ =		23	$\frac{3}{5}$ x $\frac{5}{4}$ =	
2	$\frac{1}{2}$ x $\frac{1}{4}$ =		24	$\frac{4}{5}$ x $\frac{5}{3}$ =	
3	$\frac{1}{2}$ x $\frac{1}{5}$ =		25	$\frac{1}{4}$ x $\frac{1}{4}$ =	
4	$\frac{1}{2}$ x $\frac{1}{9}$ =		26	$\frac{1}{4}$ x $\frac{3}{4}$ =	
5	$\frac{1}{9}$ x $\frac{1}{2}$ =		27	$\frac{3}{4}$ x $\frac{3}{4}$ =	
6	$\frac{1}{5}$ x $\frac{1}{2}$ =		28	$\frac{3}{4}$ x $\frac{4}{3}$ =	
7	$\frac{1}{5}$ x $\frac{1}{3}$ =		29	$\frac{3}{4}$ x $\frac{5}{4}$ =	
8	$\frac{1}{5}$ x $\frac{1}{7}$ =		30	$\frac{3}{4}$ x $\frac{6}{4}$ =	
9	$\frac{1}{5}$ x $\frac{1}{3}$ =		31	$\frac{4}{3}$ x $\frac{4}{6}$ =	
10	$\frac{1}{3}$ x $\frac{1}{5}$ =		32	$\frac{2}{3}$ x $\frac{1}{5}$ =	
11	$\frac{1}{3}$ x $\frac{2}{5}$ =		33	$\frac{2}{3}$ x $\frac{4}{5}$ =	
12	$\frac{2}{3}$ x $\frac{2}{5}$ =		34	$\frac{2}{3}$ x $\frac{5}{5}$ =	
13	$\frac{1}{3}$ x $\frac{1}{4}$ =		35	$\frac{2}{3}$ x $\frac{6}{5}$ =	
14	$\frac{1}{3}$ x $\frac{3}{4}$ =		36	$\frac{1}{3}$ x $\frac{6}{5}$ =	
15	$\frac{2}{3}$ x $\frac{3}{4}$ =		37	$\frac{1}{9}$ x $\frac{1}{9}$ =	
16	$\frac{1}{3}$ x $\frac{1}{6}$ =		38	$\frac{1}{5}$ x $\frac{3}{8}$ =	
17	$\frac{2}{3}$ x $\frac{1}{6}$ =		39	$\frac{3}{4}$ x $\frac{1}{6}$ =	
18	$\frac{2}{3}$ x $\frac{5}{6}$ =		40	$\frac{2}{3}$ x $\frac{2}{3}$ =	
19	$\frac{3}{2}$ x $\frac{3}{4}$ =		41	$\frac{3}{4}$ x $\frac{8}{8}$ =	
20	$\frac{1}{5}$ x $\frac{1}{5}$ =		42	$\frac{2}{3}$ x $\frac{6}{3}$ =	
21	$\frac{3}{5}$ x $\frac{3}{5}$ =		43	$\frac{6}{7}$ x $\frac{8}{9}$ =	
22	$\frac{3}{5}$ x $\frac{4}{5}$ =		44	$\frac{7}{12}$ x $\frac{8}{7}$ =	

Lesson 7:   Solve word problems involving the volume of rectangular prisms with whole number edge lengths.

Date: 1/10/14

5.B.48

© 2014 Common Core, Inc. All rights reserved. commoncore.org

Name _____   Date _____

Geoffrey builds rectangular planters.

1. Geoffrey's first planter is 8 feet long and 2 feet wide. The container is filled with soil to a height of 3 feet in the planter. What is the volume of soil in the planter? Explain your work using a diagram.

2. Geoffrey wants to grow some tomatoes in four large planters. He wants each planter to have a volume of 320 cubic feet, but he wants them all to be different. Show four different ways Geoffrey can make these planters, and draw diagrams with the planters' measurements on them.

Planter A	Planter B
Planter C	Planter D

Lesson 7:   Solve word problems involving the volume of rectangular prisms with
          whole number edge lengths.
Date: 1/10/14

5.B.

3. Geoffrey wants to make one planter that extends from the ground to just below his back window. The window starts 3 feet off the ground. If he wants the planter to hold 36 cubic feet of soil, name one way he could build the planter so it is not taller than 3 feet. Explain how you know.

4. After all of this gardening work, Geoffrey decides he needs a new shed to replace the old one. His current shed is a rectangular prism that measures 6 feet long by 5 feet wide by 8 feet high. He realizes he needs a shed with 480 cubic feet of storage.

   a. Will he achieve his goal if he doubles each dimension? Why or why not?

   b. If he wants to keep the height the same, what could the other dimensions be for him to get the volume he wants?

   c. If he uses the dimensions in Part (b), what could be the area of the new shed's floor?

COMMON CORE   Lesson 7:   Solve word problems involving the volume of rectangular prisms with
whole number edge lengths.
Date: 1/10/14

5.B.50

© 2014 Common Core, Inc. All rights reserved. **commoncore.org**

Name _____   Date _____

1. A storage shed is a rectangular prism and has dimensions of 6 meters by 5 meters by 12 meters. If Jean were to double these dimensions, she believes she would only double the volume. Is she correct? Explain why or why not. Include a drawing in your explanation.

 **Lesson 7:**   Solve word problems involving the volume of rectangular prisms with whole number edge lengths.

Date: 1/10/14

5.B.

Name _____   Date _____

Wren makes some rectangular display boxes.

1. Wren's first display box is 6 inches long, 9 inches wide, and 4 inches high. What is the volume of the display box? Explain your work using a diagram.

2. Wren wants to put some artwork into three large display boxes. She knows they all need a volume of 60 cubic inches, but she wants them all to be different. Show three different ways Wren can make these boxes by drawing diagrams and labeling the measurements.

Shadow Box A	Shadow Box B

Shadow Box C

Lesson 7:	Solve word problems involving the volume of rectangular prisms with whole number edge lengths.
Date:	1/10/14

5.B.52

© 2014 Common Core, Inc. All rights reserved. **commoncore.org**

3. Wren wants to build a box to organize her scrapbook supplies. She has a stencil set that is 12 inches wide that needs to lay flat in the bottom of the box. The supply box must also be no taller than 2 feet. Name one way she could build a toy box with a volume of 72 cubic inches.

4. After all of this organizing, Wren decides she also needs more storage for her soccer equipment. Her current storage box measures 1 foot long by 2 feet wide by 2 feet high. She realizes she needs to replace it with a box with 12 cubic feet of storage, so she doubles the width.

    a. Will she achieve her goal if she does this? Why or why not?

    b. If she wants to keep the height the same, what could the other dimensions be for a 12-cubic-foot storage box?

    c. If she uses the dimensions in Part (b), what is the area of the new storage box's floor?

    d. How has the area of the bottom in her new storage box changed? Explain how you know.

Lesson 7:   Solve word problems involving the volume of rectangular prisms with whole number edge lengths.

Date: 1/10/14

5.B.

© 2014 Common Core, Inc. All rights reserved. commoncore.org

Lesson 8

Objective: Apply concepts and formulas of volume to design a sculpture using rectangular prisms within given parameters.

Suggested Lesson Structure

■ Fluency Practice   (12 minutes)
  Concept Development   (38 minutes)
■ Student Debrief   (10 minutes)
  Total Time   **(60 minutes)**

Fluency Practice (12 minutes)

- Multiply Whole Numbers and Decimals **5.NBT.7**   (4 minutes)
- Mixed Numbers to Improper Fractions **4.NF.4**   (4 minutes)
- Multiply Mixed Numbers **5.NF.4**   (4 minutes)

Multiply Whole Numbers and Decimals (4 minutes)

Materials: (S) Personal white boards

Note: This fluency reviews G5–M4–Lesson 17.

T: (Write 3 × 2.) Say the number sentence.

S: 3 × 2 = 6.

T: (Write 3 × 0.2.) On your boards, write the number sentence and solve.

S: (Write 3 × 0.2 = 0.6.)

T: (Write 0.3 × 0.2.) On your boards, write the number sentence.

S: (Write 0.3 × 0.2 = 0.06.)

T: (Write 0.03 × 0.2.) On your boards, write the number sentence.

S: (Write 0.03 × 0.2 = 0.006.)

3 × 2 = 6	3 × 0.2 = 0.6	3 × 0.02 = 0.06	0.3 × 0.2 = 0.06
2 × 7 = 14	2 × 0.7 = 1.4	2 × 0.7 = 1.4	0.02 × 0.7 = 0.014
5 × 3 = 15	0.5 × 3 = 1.5	0.5 × 0.3 = 0.15	0.5 × 0.03 = 0.015

Continue the process for the following possible sequence: 2 × 7, 2 × 0.7, 0.2 × 0.7, 0.02 × 0.7, 5 × 3, 0.5 × 3, 0.5 × 0.3, and 0.5 × 0.03.

Lesson 8:   Apply concepts and formulas of volume to design a sculpture using
Date: rectangular prisms within given parameters.
            1/10/14

5.B.54

© 2014 Common Core, Inc. All rights reserved. commoncore.org

Mixed Numbers to Improper Fractions (4 minutes)

Materials: (S) Personal white boards

Note: This fluency prepares students for G5–M5–Lesson 10.

T: How many halves are in 1?

S: 2.

T: How many halves are in 2?

S: 4.

T: How many halves are in 3?

S: 6.

T: (Write $3\frac{1}{2}$ = __.) On your boards, write $3\frac{1}{2}$ as an improper fraction.

S: (Write $3\frac{1}{2} = \frac{7}{2}$.)

Continue process for the following possible sequence: $5\frac{1}{2}, 4\frac{1}{3}, 4\frac{2}{3}, 2\frac{1}{4}, 2\frac{3}{4}$, and $4\frac{5}{6}$.

NOTES ON MULTIPLE MEANS OF REPRESENTATION:

If students are having trouble with fractions, give them fraction tiles to work with. Have them build 1 whole from halves, then 2 wholes, and so on. Then have them build 3 wholes plus 1 half and have them count how many halves are in $3\frac{1}{2}$. Continue with other fractional units.

Multiply Mixed Numbers (4 minutes)

Materials: (S) Personal white boards

Note: This fluency prepares students for G5–M5–Lesson 10.

Format as illustrated to the right.

T: (Write $3\frac{1}{2} \times 2$, and below it, $(3 \times 2) + (\frac{1}{2} \times 2)$.)

T: (Point to 3×2.) Tell me the complete multiplication sentence.

S: $3 \times 2 = 6$.

T: (Point to $\frac{1}{2} \times 2$.) Tell me the complete multiplication sentence.

S: $\frac{1}{2} \times 2 = 1$.

T: Tell me the addition sentence combining two products.

S: $6 + 1 = 7$.

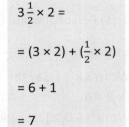

$$3\frac{1}{2} \times 2 =$$

$$= (3 \times 2) + (\frac{1}{2} \times 2)$$

$$= 6 + 1$$

$$= 7$$

Continue the process using the following possible suggestions: $4\frac{1}{3} \times 2$, $3\frac{1}{5} \times 4$, and $4\frac{2}{3} \times 3$.

Lesson 8: Apply concepts and formulas of volume to design a sculpture using rectangular prisms within given parameters.

Date: 1/10/14

5.B.

© 2014 Common Core, Inc. All rights reserved. commoncore.org

Concept Development (38 minutes)

Materials: (S) Problem Set, evaluation rubric, box patterns and lid patterns (at least three of each per group), scissors, tape, rulers

Note: The time for the Application Problem has been allocated to the Concept Development for this lesson.

Copy the flattened boxes on the thickest paper available. Each student or group will need three to five copies of each box, but they may not all be used.

Students will cut the templates to form boxes of a certain volume by adjusting the height of the sides. They should construct the boxes by taping edges together, and then turn the box open side down to create their sculpture. They may also tape lids on the open ends of their boxes to make construction easier.

Please also note the evaluation rubric included in this lesson. The rubric can be shared with students so that they understand how their work will be judged.

This activity can be done individually or in pairs.

> T: Today we will be putting our math sense and geometric skills to work as each of you design a sculpture created from a collection of rectangular prisms. Read the requirements and the rubric with a neighbor.

Distribute the Project Requirements, the Problem Set, and the evaluation rubric. Allow students time to read all three.

> T: Now that you've had an opportunity to read the requirements and the way your work will be evaluated, share your ideas about what you might like to design.
>
> S: I want to make a shape using five prisms and make it as random as possible. → I want to see if I can do a capital F, for my name. → I was going to do a scaled version of my tree house, but I'm not sure if I'll be able to scale the dimensions right.
>
> T: Here are the boxes like the ones we used in Lesson 2 that you can use to build your rectangular boxes. There are three different bases to choose from. You may adjust the volume by adjusting the height of the sides of your box. Watch me cut one of the box patterns and make a box. (Demonstrate cutting the 6 cm × 3 cm template.) If I want to build this first prism to have a volume of 36 cubic centimeters, what height will I need to measure and cut the sides?

NOTE ON
MATERIALS:

When printing the box and lid patterns, be sure the printer is set to *Actual Size*.

NOTES ON
MULTIPLE MEANS OF
ENGAGEMENT:

All students may be overwhelmed by the amount of reading and interpretation of directions required for the project. Reading the requirements as a class and having discussion after each one can be helpful. Or, place accomplished readers with those who struggle.

All students may benefit from having cubes to actually construct a model of their structure first.

NOTES ON
MULTIPLE MEANS OF
ENGAGEMENT:

Students who struggle may be encouraged to use only three prisms or be given more latitude in total volume or in the relationships between the prisms. Alternately, those whose spatial skills are well developed may be given additional restrictions to meet to fulfill the requirements, or may be asked to use more prisms to construct their design.

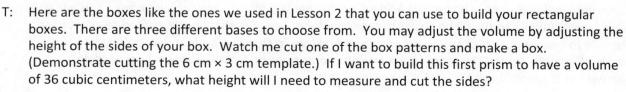

Lesson 8:   Apply concepts and formulas of volume to design a sculpture using
rectangular prisms within given parameters.
Date: 1/10/14

5.B.56

© 2014 Common Core, Inc. All rights reserved. commoncore.org

S: They would need to be 2 cm high.

T: Yes. I'll measure all my side flaps 2 cm from the base. Then I'll cut, fold, and tape them. (Demonstrate.) Talk with your neighbor about how you'll construct your first box and calculate the volume.

S: Cut the base with rectangles attached on each side that are the same height and fold them up, then calculate the volume. → Decide on the volume and find the area of the base, then cut the height to give the volume you need.

T: It might be a good idea to draw a very rough sketch of the design you're thinking of creating.

S: (Draw.)

T: Reread the third prompt with a friend. Share your ideas about how you'll meet its requirements.

S: (Share.)

T: What were your ideas?

S: I'm going to make Prism A, then try to cut one of the other prisms to make it half the volume of Prism A and call it Prism D. → I can make the biggest prism possible and then divide the volume in half and try to make another prism one-half of that volume. → I'll make a prism, then use the same base to make another prism, but cut the height in half. That will give me half of the original volume.

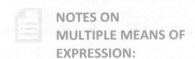

**NOTES ON
MULTIPLE MEANS OF
EXPRESSION:**

Students whose fine motor skills are less developed may enjoy producing a virtual version of this project. They might use computer-based drawing tools to draw the prisms (e.g., Google's SketchUp). These can be printed and then measured to fulfill the requirements of the project.

T: Reread the fourth prompt with a friend. Share your ideas about how you'll meet its requirements.

S: I will take Prism B and cut it up to create a prism with one-third the volume. → I can use the same big prism as before and divide the volume by 3 and find a prism with dimensions that will equal that number. → I can take one of the first three prisms and make the height one-third of the original height, and this will give me one-third of the volume.

T: The final prompt says that the total volume of your design must not exceed 1,000 cubic centimeters. Share your ideas.

S: What's the biggest prism I can do? → We can do a total of five prisms, but they can't be more than 200 cubic centimeters. One has to be half of another. Another has to be a third of another; this is going to require some thinking! → Let's just say we do one prism that's 420 cubic cm, and one that's half of that (210 cc), and then one that's a third of that (140 cc). That's 770 cubic centimeters. That means I still have 230 cubic units and two prisms to play with. I can make one 3 cm by 6 cm by 4 cm and one 5 cm x 5 cm x 4 cm for a total of 770 + 108 + 100 = 978 cubic centimeters.

T: Once you've finalized your boxes, cut a lid with tabs that will fit and tape it to your box. This will give your boxes stability so they'll be easier to tape together. I can tell that you're excited to get started. Be sure to check your math as you progress and feel free to share your ideas with a neighbor as you work. (Circulate around the room to ask clarifying questions or provide support to struggling learners as students work.)

Lesson 8:	Apply concepts and formulas of volume to design a sculpture using rectangular prisms within given parameters.
Date:	1/10/14

5.B.!

© 2014 Common Core, Inc. All rights reserved. commoncore.org

Student Debrief (10 minutes)

Lesson Objective: Apply concepts and formulas of volume to design a sculpture using rectangular prisms within given parameters.

The Student Debrief is intended to invite reflection and active processing of the total lesson experience.

Invite students to review their solutions for the Problem Set. They should check work by comparing answers with a partner before going over answers as a class. Look for misconceptions or misunderstandings that can be addressed in the Debrief. Guide students in a conversation to debrief the Problem Set and process the lesson.

You may choose to use any combination of the questions below to lead the discussion.

- What was your thought process as you designed your sculpture? Were you inspired by something you have seen or own?
- Which figure did you cut into halves or thirds when creating another shape? What was your thought process as you created a shape one-half or one-third the size? (Did you cut one dimension into halves or thirds, or did you scale the entire volume first and then select dimension to meet that volume?)
- What was your biggest challenge in designing your sculpture? Explain.

Exit Ticket (3 minutes)

After the Student Debrief, instruct students to complete the Exit Ticket. A review of their work will help you assess the students' understanding of the concepts that were presented in the lesson today and plan more effectively for future lessons. You may read the questions aloud to the students.

COMMON CORE™

Lesson 8: Apply concepts and formulas of volume to design a sculpture using rectangular prisms within given parameters.
Date: 1/10/14

© 2014 Common Core, Inc. All rights reserved. commoncore.org

Name _____ Date _____

Using the box patterns, construct a sculpture containing at least 5 but not more than 7 rectangular prisms that meets the following requirements in the table below.

1.	My sculpture has 5 to 7 rectangular prisms.	Number of prisms: _____
2.	Each prism is labeled with a letter, dimensions, and volume.	

Prism A _____ by _____ by _____ Volume _____

Prism B _____ by _____ by _____ Volume _____

Prism C _____ by _____ by _____ Volume _____

Prism D _____ by _____ by _____ Volume _____

Prism E _____ by _____ by _____ Volume _____

Prism __ _____ by _____ by _____ Volume _____

Prism __ _____ by _____ by _____ Volume _____

3.	Prism D has $\frac{1}{2}$ the volume of prism __.	Prism D Volume = _____ Prism __ Volume = _____
4.	Prism E has $\frac{1}{3}$ the volume of prism __.	Prism E Volume = _____ Prism __ Volume = _____
5.	The total volume of all the prisms is 1,000 cubic centimeters or less.	Total volume: _____ Show calculations:

Lesson 8:   Apply concepts and formulas of volume to design a sculpture using rectangular prisms within given parameters.

Date: 1/10/14

5.B.5

© 2014 Common Core, Inc. All rights reserved. **commoncore.org**

Name _____   Date _____

1. Sketch a rectangular prism that has a volume of 36 cubic cm. Label the dimensions of each side on the prism. Fill in the blanks that follow.

Height: _____ cm

Length: _____ cm

Width: _____ cm

Volume: _____ cubic cm

COMMON CORE

Lesson 8: Apply concepts and formulas of volume to design a sculpture using rectangular prisms within given parameters.
Date: 1/10/14

5.B.60

© 2014 Common Core, Inc. All rights reserved. **commoncore.org**

Name _____   Date _____

1. I have a prism with the dimensions of 6 cm by 12 cm by 15 cm. Calculate the volume of the prism, then give the dimensions of three different prisms that have $\frac{1}{3}$ of the volume.

	Length	Width	Height	Volume
Original Prism	6 cm	12 cm	15 cm	
Prism 1				
Prism 2				
Prism 3				

2. Sunni's bedroom has the dimensions of 11 ft by 10 ft by 10 ft. Her den has the same height, but double the volume. Give two sets of the possible dimensions of the den and the volume of the den.

© 2014 Common Core, Inc. All rights reserved. commoncore.org

Project Requirements

1. Each project must include 5 to 7 rectangular prisms.
2. All prisms must be labeled with a letter (beginning with A), dimensions, and volume.
3. Prism D must be $\frac{1}{2}$ the volume of another prism.
4. Prism E must be $\frac{1}{3}$ the volume of another prism.
5. The total volume of all of the prisms must be 1,000 cubic centimeters or less.

Project Requirements

1. Each project must include 5 to 7 rectangular prisms.
2. All prisms must be labeled with a letter (beginning with A), dimensions, and volume.
3. Prism D must be $\frac{1}{2}$ the volume of another prism.
4. Prism E must be $\frac{1}{3}$ the volume of another prism.
5. The total volume of all of the prisms must be 1,000 cubic centimeters or less.

Project Requirements

1. Each project must include 5 to 7 rectangular prisms.
2. All prisms must be labeled with a letter (beginning with A), dimensions, and volume.
3. Prism D must be $\frac{1}{2}$ the volume of another prism.
4. Prism E must be $\frac{1}{3}$ the volume of another prism.
5. The total volume of all of the prisms must be 1,000 cubic centimeters or less.

Lesson 8:   Apply concepts and formulas of volume to design a sculpture using
              rectangular prisms within given parameters.

Date: 1/10/14

5.B.62

© 2014 Common Core, Inc. All rights reserved. **commoncore.org**

Note: Be sure to set printer to *Actual Size* before printing.

Lesson 8:   Apply concepts and formulas of volume to design a sculpture using rectangular prisms within given parameters.

Date: 1/10/14

5.B.6

© 2014 Common Core, Inc. All rights reserved. **commoncore.org**

Lesson 8:   Apply concepts and formulas of volume to design a sculpture using
rectangular prisms within given parameters.

Date: 1/10/14

5.B.64

© 2014 Common Core, Inc. All rights reserved. **commoncore.org**

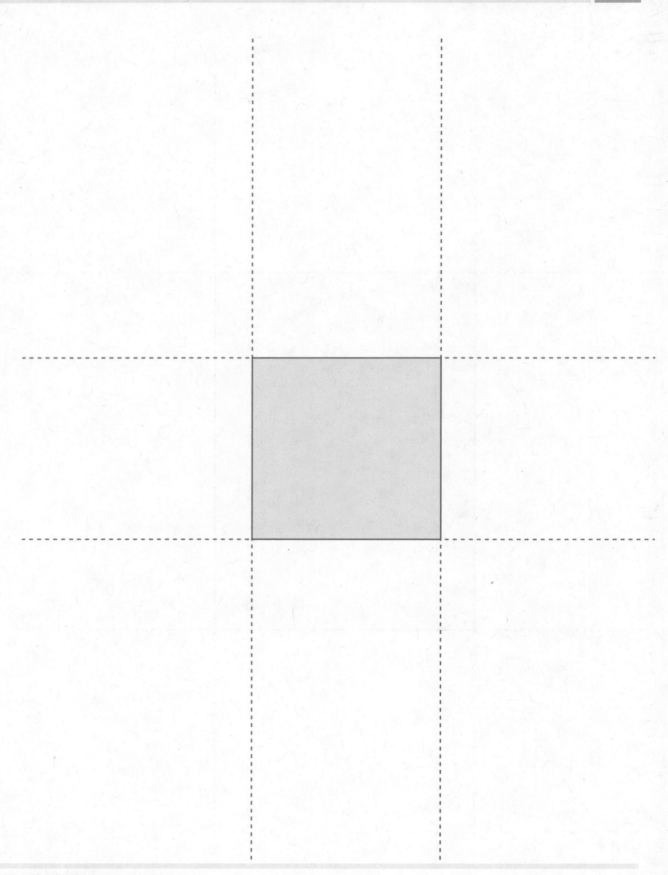

Lesson 8: Apply concepts and formulas of volume to design a sculpture using rectangular prisms within given parameters.

Date: 1/10/14

5.B.6

© 2014 Common Core, Inc. All rights reserved. **commoncore.org**

Lid patterns

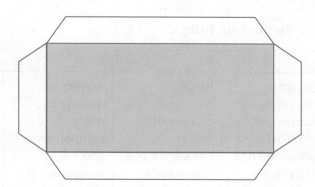

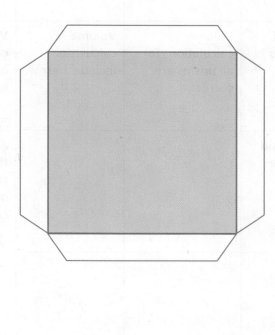

COMMON CORE

Lesson 8:   Apply concepts and formulas of volume to design a sculpture using
              rectangular prisms within given parameters.
Date: 1/10/14

5.B.66

© 2014 Common Core, Inc. All rights reserved. **common**core.org

Name _____ Date _____

Evaluation Rubric

CATEGORY	4	3	2	1	Subtotal
Completeness of Personal Project and Classmate Evaluation	All components of the project are present and correct, and a detailed evaluation of a classmate's project has been completed.	Project is missing 1 component, and a detailed evaluation of a classmate's project has been completed.	Project is missing 2 components, and an evaluation of a classmate's project has been completed.	Project is missing 3 or more components, and an evaluation of a classmate's project has been completed.	(× 4) _____/16
Accuracy of Calculations	Volume calculations for all prisms are correct.	Volume calculations include 1 error.	Volume calculations include 2–3 errors.	Volume calculations include 4 or more errors.	(× 5) _____/20
Neatness and Use of Color			All elements of the project are carefully and colorfully constructed.	All elements the project are carefully and colorfully constructed.	2) _____/4
					TOTAL: _____/40

Lesson 8:   Apply concepts and formulas of volume to design a sculpture using rectangular prisms within given parameters.

Date: 1/10/14

5.B.6

© 2014 Common Core, Inc. All rights reserved. commoncore.org

Lesson 9

Objective: Apply concepts and formulas of volume to design a sculpture using rectangular prisms within given parameters.

Suggested Lesson Structure

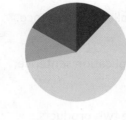

■ Fluency Practice   (7 minutes)
■ Application Problem   (7 minutes)
■ Concept Development   (36 minutes)
■ Student Debrief   (10 minutes)

Total Time   **(60 minutes)**

Fluency Practice (7 minutes)

▪ Multiply Decimals **5.NBT.7**   (3 minutes)
▪ Multiply Mixed Numbers **5.NF.4**   (4 minutes)

Multiply Decimals (3 minutes)

Materials: (S) Personal white boards

Note: This fluency reviews G5–M4–Lessons 17–18.

T: (Write 4 × 2 =_____.) Say the number sentence.
S: 4 × 2 = 8.
T: (Write 4 × 0.2 =_____.) On your boards, write number sentence.
S: (Write 4 × 0.2 = 0.8.)
T: (Write 0.4 × 0.2 =_____.) On your boards, write number sentence.
S: (Write 0.4 × 0.2 = 0.08.)

4 × 2 = 8	4 × 0.2 = 0.8	0.4 × 0.2 = 0.08	0.04 × 0.2 = 0.008
2 × 9 = 18	2 × 0.9 = 1.8	0.2 × 0.9 = 0.18	0.02 × 0.9 = 0.018
4 × 3 = 12	0.4 × 3 = 1.2	0.4 × 0.3 = 0.12	0.4 × 0.03 = 0.012

Continue the process for the following possible sequence: 2 × 9, 2 × 0.9, 0.2 × 0.9, 0.02 × 0.9, 4 × 3, 0.4 × 3, 0.4 × 0.3, and 0.4 × 0.03.

Lesson 9:   Apply concepts and formulas of volume to design a sculpture using
             rectangular prisms within given parameters.
Date: 1/10/14   5.B.68

© 2014 Common Core, Inc. All rights reserved. **commoncore.org**

Multiply Mixed Numbers (4 minutes)

Materials: (S) Personal white boards

Note: This fluency prepares students for G5–M5–Lesson 10. Format your writing as illustrated to the right.

$$4\frac{1}{3} \times 2 =$$

$$= (4 \times 2) + (\frac{1}{3} \times 2)$$

$$= 8 + \frac{2}{3}$$

$$= 8\frac{2}{3}$$

T: (Write $4\frac{1}{3} \times 2$ and below it $(4 \times 2) + (\frac{1}{3} \times 2)$.)

T: (Point to 4×2.) Tell me the complete multiplication sentence.

S: $4 \times 2 = 8$.

T: (Point to $\frac{1}{3} \times 2$.) Tell me the complete multiplication sentence.

S: $\frac{1}{3} \times 2 = \frac{2}{3}$.

T: Tell me the addition sentence combining the two products.

S: $8 + \frac{2}{3} = 8\frac{2}{3}$.

Continue process for the following possible suggestions: $7\frac{1}{5} \times 3$ and $5\frac{2}{3} \times 2$.

Application Problem (7 minutes)

The chart below shows the dimensions of various rectangular packing boxes. If possible, answer the following without calculating the volume.

a.   Which box will provide the greatest volume?

b.   Which box has a volume that is equal to the volume of the book box? How do you know?

c.   Which box is $\frac{1}{3}$ the volume of the lamp box?

Box Type	Dimensions (l × w × h)
Book Box	12 in × 12 in × 12 in
Picture Box	36 in × 12 in × 36 in
Lamp Box	12 in × 9 in × 48 in
The Flat	12 in × 6 in × 24 in

a) The picture box has the greatest volume because it has the largest dimensions of all the boxes.

b) The flat and book box have the same volume. Their lengths are the same. The flat's width is $\frac{1}{2}$ the book's, and its height is double the book's, so they have the same volume.

c) The book box is $\frac{1}{3}$ the volume of the lamp box. The lengths are the same. If you factor the width and height:

Book: 12 × 12   Lamp: 9 × 48
      3 4 3 4   3 3 4 4 3
The lamp has an extra factor of 3.

Note: This Application Problem builds on students understanding of a scaling principle. Students can use their sense of part–part–whole and scaling knowledge to answer these questions without finding the volume of the boxes.

	Lesson 9:	Apply concepts and formulas of volume to design a sculpture using rectangular prisms within given parameters.
	Date:	1/10/14

5.B.6

© 2014 Common Core, Inc. All rights reserved. **commoncore.org**

Concept Development (36 minutes)

Materials: (T) Copy of student work from G5–M5–Lesson 8, evaluation rubric (S) Rulers, 2 copies of Problem Set (1 for use during Concept Development and 1 for independent work)

Note: Before class, the projects should be labeled only with a number and no student names. The review process in today's lesson should proceed anonymously.

T: (Post image of the shape below on the board.) Here is a student's project designed according to the directions we used yesterday. I've measured the boxes and the measurements that you see on the diagram are correct. The volume of A is given. (Distribute a copy of Problem Set to each student.) Your job is to use the rubric to see if this student met all the requirements of the assignment.

T: Before we can do that, we must confirm the volumes that the student recorded. Work with a neighbor to check the work this student did to find the volumes of the prisms. (Allow students time to work and share their results.)

T: What did you find? Are the recorded volumes correct?

S: They are correct. → Prisms A and C have volumes of 36 cm^3. → Prism B has a volume of 420 cm^3. → Prism E has a volume of 140 cm^3. → Prism D's volume is 18 cm^3.

T: Now we are ready to begin our review. Look at the first item on the list. How many prisms are in this design?

S: 5.

T: Check the *Element present?* box and record the number of prisms used under *Specifics of element.*

S: (Check box and record 5 prisms.)

T: The notes box is for any positive comments we might like to give to this student on this particular element. This is also the place to tell them anything that might be missing in the design. Since this student has met this requirement, turn and talk to your partner about what positive comment you might make.

S: I like the way the prisms are sort of symmetrical. → The way the boxes are stacked from big to little looks good. → Putting the skinny box in the middle makes the design look really big even though they only used 5 boxes.

NOTES ON MULTIPLE MEANS OF ENGAGEMENT:

The high number of measurements recorded on the diagram may be overwhelming to students with visual acuity difficulties. These students may benefit from a second diagram with figures slightly separated and units listed on each dimension or a larger print version of the diagram.

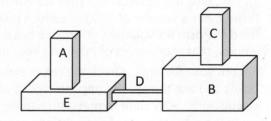

Prism A: 6 cm × 3 cm × 2 cm = 36 cm^3
Prism B: 10 cm × 7 cm × 6 cm = 420 cm^3
Prism C: 6 cm × 3 cm × 2 cm = 36 cm^3
Prism D: 6 cm × 3 cm × 1 cm = 18 cm^3
Prism E: 10 cm × 7 cm × 2 cm = 140 cm^3

Lesson 9:	Apply concepts and formulas of volume to design a sculpture using rectangular prisms within given parameters.	5.B.70
Date:	1/10/14	

© 2014 Common Core, Inc. All rights reserved. commoncore.org

T: Let's look at our next requirement. Are all the parts labeled with a letter? Record your answer.

S: Yes, they all have letters.

T: Are all prisms labeled with their dimensions and volume? Record your response.

S: Yes, all the prisms have dimensions and volume recorded.

T: Do all recorded measurements have the correct units? What are the units for the dimensions and volume?

S: Yes, all dimensions are in centimeters and volume is cubic centimeters.

T: Write that down. What's next on our list? How will we find out if this student met the requirements? Turn and talk.

S: We need to find out if the Prism D is one-half of one of the other prisms and if Prism E is one-third of another prism. → We need to calculate the volume of all of the prisms first, and then check if Prism D has one-half the volume of one of the other prisms and if Prism E has one-third the volume of one prism. → Prism D has a volume of 18 cm^3, which is one-half of Prism A's volume. → Prism E has a volume of 140 cm^3, which is one-third of Prism B's volume. → Prism E has a volume that is one-third of Prism B's volume.

MP.6 T: Record your findings. Check the requirement boxes and use the second page to record your calculations. (Circulate to make sure students are using the correct parts of the rubric to record the information.)

S: (Record.)

T: What is the total volume of this shape?

S: (Work and show that 36 + 36 + 18 + 140 + 420 = 650 cm^3.)

T: Did this student meet all the requirements of the assignment? Tell me how you know.

S: Yes, they did. The volume is 650 cm^3, which is less than 1,000 cm^3. → There are 5 prisms, and they had to have 5 to 7 prisms. → The volume of prism D is one-half the volume of Prism A's. → The volume of Prism E is one-third the volume of Prism B's.

T: Remember, if there's something that doesn't meet a requirement in the project that you review, you will record that in the notes column. You may also use the notes box to say something that you notice about their work.

NOTES ON MULTIPLE MEANS OF ENGAGEMENT:

Have students who easily grasp this concept and move quickly through the Problem Set double one or more dimensions and calculate the new volume of the figure. Another option is to ask them if the units were centimeters instead of inches, how many liters of liquid the structure would hold.

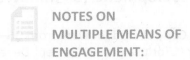

NYS COMMON CORE MATHEMATICS CURRICULUM   Lesson 9 Problem Set 5•5

Name Roberta _____   Date _____

I reviewed project number ____21____

Use the rubric below to evaluate your friend's project. Ask questions and measure the parts to determine whether he or she has all the required elements. Respond to the prompt in italics in the third column. The final column can be used to write something you find interesting about that element if you like.

Space is provided beneath the rubric for your calculations.

	Requirement	Element present? (✓)	Specifics of Element	Notes
1	Sculpture has 5 to 7 prisms.	✓	*# of prisms:* 6	
2	All prisms are labeled with a letter.	✓	*Write letters used:* A - F	
3	All prisms have correct dimensions with units written on the top.	✓	*List any prisms with incorrect dimensions or units:*	
4	All prisms have correct volume with units written on top.	✓	*List any prism with incorrect dimensions or units:*	
5	Prism D has ½ the volume of another prism.	✓	*Record on next page:*	
6	Prism E has ⅓ the volume of another prism.	✓	*Record on next page:*	
7	The total volume of all the parts together is 1,000 cubic units or less.	✓	*Total volume:* 634 cm^3	

Calculations: 210 + 180 + 72 + 90 + 70 + 12 = 634

COMMON CORE   Lesson 9:   Apply concepts and formulas of volume to design a sculpture using rectangular prisms within given parameters.
Date: 12/13/13 12:02 AM

engage^{ny} 5.B.71

Lesson 9:   Apply concepts and formulas of volume to design a sculpture using rectangular prisms within given parameters.

Date: 1/10/14

5.B.

© 2014 Common Core, Inc. All rights reserved. commoncore.org

T: I'm assigning each of you the sculpture of a fellow classmate (or pair) to review independently just as we did this one. Write the number of the project that you review on your Problem Set. Begin by confirming the measurements and volumes calculated by your classmate. (Distribute one sculpture to each student and circulate to answer questions that arise.)

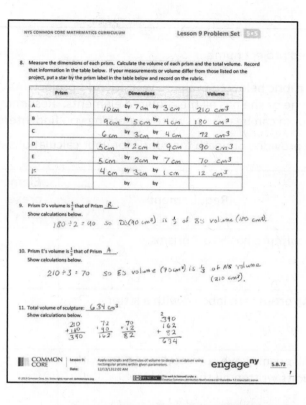

Student Debrief (10 minutes)

Lesson Objective: Apply concepts and formulas of volume to design a sculpture using rectangular prisms within given parameters.

The Student Debrief is intended to invite reflection and active processing of the total lesson experience.

Invite students to review their solutions for the Problem Set. They should check work by comparing answers with a partner before going over answers as a class. Look for misconceptions or misunderstandings that can be addressed in the Debrief. Guide students in a conversation to debrief the Problem Set and process the lesson.

You may choose to use any combination of the questions below to lead the discussion.

- How was the student work you assessed similar to and different from the design you created?

- If the work that you assessed did not meet the requirements, what feedback did you provide to help the student be successful?

- How was assessing student work different from creating your design yesterday? If you could go back and change your design, would you? In what ways?

- Students might enjoy investigating the sculptures of David Smith, particularly his *Cubi* series (as shown to the right). Many in this series of sculptures are composed exclusively of rectangular prisms.

David Smith (1906-1965), *Cubi VI*, 1963, stainless steel. Art © Estate of David Smith/Licensed by VAGA, New York, NY. Photo: Yair Talmor.

Exit Ticket (3 minutes)

After the Student Debrief, instruct students to complete the Exit Ticket. A review of their work will help you assess the students' understanding of the concepts that were presented in the lesson today and plan more effectively for future lessons. You may read the questions aloud to the students.

© 2014 Common Core, Inc. All rights reserved. **commoncore.org**

Name _____ Date _____

I reviewed project number _____.

Use the rubric below to evaluate your friend's project. Ask questions and measure the parts to determine whether he or she has all the required elements. Respond to the prompt in italics in the third column. The final column can be used to write something you find interesting about that element if you like.

Space is provided beneath the rubric for your calculations.

	Requirement	Element present? (✓)	Specifics of Element	Notes
1	Sculpture has 5 to 7 prisms.		*# of prisms:*	
2	All prisms are labeled with a letter.		*Write letters used:*	
3	All prisms have correct dimensions with units written on the top.		*List any prisms with incorrect dimensions or units:*	
4	All prisms have correct volume with units written on top.		*List any prism with incorrect dimensions or units:*	
5	Prism D has $\frac{1}{2}$ the volume of another prism.		*Record on next page:*	
6	Prism E has $\frac{1}{3}$ the volume of another prism.		*Record on next page:*	
7	The total volume of all the parts together is 1,000 cubic units or less.		*Total volume:*	

Calculations:

Lesson 9: Apply concepts and formulas of volume to design a sculpture using rectangular prisms within given parameters.

Date: 1/10/14

5.B.7

© 2014 Common Core, Inc. All rights reserved. **commoncore.org**

8. Measure the dimensions of each prism. Calculate the volume of each prism and the total volume. Record that information in the table below. If your measurements or volume differ from those listed on the project, put a star by the prism label in the table below and record on the rubric.

Prism	Dimensions		Volume
A	by	by	
B	by	by	
C	by	by	
D	by	by	
E	by	by	
	by	by	
	by	by	

9. Prism D's volume is $\frac{1}{2}$ that of Prism _____.

    Show calculations below.

10. Prism E's volume is $\frac{1}{3}$ that of Prism _____.

    Show calculations below.

11. Total volume of sculpture: _____.

    Show calculations below.

Lesson 9:   Apply concepts and formulas of volume to design a sculpture using
               rectangular prisms within given parameters.
Date: 1/10/14

5.B.74

© 2014 Common Core, Inc. All rights reserved. commoncore.org

Name _____ Date _____

1. A student designed this sculpture. Using the dimensions on the sculpture find the dimensions of each rectangular prism. Then, calculate the volume of prism.

    a.   Rectangular Prism Y

    Height: _____ inches

    Length: _____ inches

    Width: _____ inches

    Volume: _____ cubic inches

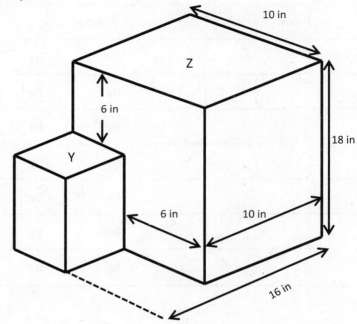

    b.   Rectangular Prism Z

    Height: _____ inches

    Length: _____ inches

    Width: _____ inches

    Volume: _____ cubic inches

    c.   Find the total volume of the sculpture. Label the answer.

COMMON CORE™

Lesson 9:   Apply concepts and formulas of volume to design a sculpture using rectangular prisms within given parameters.
Date: 1/10/14

5.B.

© 2014 Common Core, Inc. All rights reserved. **commoncore.org**

Name _____ Date _____

1. Find three rectangular prisms around your house. Describe the item you are measuring (cereal box, tissue box, etc.), then measure each dimension to the nearest whole inch and calculate the volume.

   a. Rectangular Prism A

   Item:

   Height: _____ inches

   Length: _____ inches

   Width: _____ inches

   Volume: _____ cubic inches

   b. Rectangular Prism B

   Item:

   Height: _____ inches

   Length: _____ inches

   Width: _____ inches

   Volume: _____ cubic inches

   c. Rectangular Prism C

   Item:

   Height: _____ inches

   Length: _____ inches

   Width: _____ inches

   Volume: _____ cubic inches

	Lesson 9:	Apply concepts and formulas of volume to design a sculpture using rectangular prisms within given parameters.	**5.B.76**
	Date:	1/10/14	

© 2014 Common Core, Inc. All rights reserved. commoncore.org

Name_____Date_____

Evaluation Rubric

CATEGORY	4	3	2	1	Subtotal
Completeness of Personal Project and Classmate Evaluation	All components of the project are present and correct, and a detailed evaluation of a classmate's project has been completed.	Project is missing 1 component, and a detailed evaluation of a classmate's project has been completed.	Project is missing 2 components, and an evaluation of a classmate's project has been completed.	Project is missing 3 or more components, and an evaluation of a classmate's project has been completed.	(× 4) _____/16
Accuracy of Calculations	Volume calculations for all prisms are correct.	Volume calculations include 1 error.	Volume calculations include 2–3 errors.	Volume calculations include 4 or more errors.	(× 5) _____/20
Neatness and Use of Color			All elements of the project are carefully and colorfully constructed.	All elements the project are carefully and colorfully constructed.	2) _____/4
					TOTAL: _____ /40

Lesson 9:   Apply concepts and formulas of volume to design a sculpture using rectangular prisms within given parameters.

Date: 1/10/14

5.B.

© 2014 Common Core, Inc. All rights reserved. **commoncore.org**

Mathematics Curriculum

Topic C

Area of Rectangular Figures with Fractional Side Lengths

5.NF.4b, 5.NF.6

Focus Standard:	5.NF.4b	Apply and extend previous understanding of multiplication to multiply a fraction or whole number by a fraction.
		b. Find the area of a rectangle with fractional side lengths by tiling it with unit squares of the appropriate unit fraction side lengths, and show that the area is the same as would be found by multiplying the side lengths. Multiply fractional side lengths to find areas of rectangles, and represent fraction products as rectangular areas.
	5.NF.6	Solve real world problems involving multiplication of fractions and mixed numbers, e.g., by using visual fraction models or equations to represent the problem.
Instructional Days:	6	
Coherence -Links from:	G4–M4	Angle Measure and Plane Figures
-Links to:	G6–M2	Arithmetic Operations Including Division of Fractions

In Topic C, students extend their understanding of area as they use rulers and right angle templates to construct and measure rectangles with fractional side lengths and find their areas. They apply their extensive knowledge of fraction multiplication to interpret areas of rectangles with fractional side lengths (**5.NF.4b**) and solve real world problems involving these figures (**5.NF.6**), including reasoning about scaling through contexts in which areas are compared. Visual models and equations are used to represent the problems through the Read-Draw-Write protocol.

© 2014 Common Core, Inc. All rights reserved. commoncore.org

A Teaching Sequence Towards Mastery of Area of Rectangular Figures with Fractional Side Lengths

Objective 1: Find the area of rectangles with whole-by-mixed and whole-by-fractional number side lengths by tiling, record by drawing, and relate to fraction multiplication.
(Lesson 10)

Objective 2: Find the area of rectangles with mixed-by-mixed and fraction-by-fraction side lengths by tiling, record by drawing, and relate to fraction multiplication.
(Lesson 11)

Objective 3: Measure to find the area of rectangles with fractional side lengths.
(Lesson 12)

Objective 4: Multiply mixed number factors, and relate to the distributive property and the area model.
(Lesson 13)

Objective 5: Solve real world problems involving area of figures with fractional side lengths using visual models and/or equations.
(Lessons 14–15)

Topic C: Area of Rectangular Figures with Fractional Side Lengths
Date: 1/10/14   5.C.

© 2014 Common Core, Inc. All rights reserved. commoncore.org

Lesson 10

Objective: Find the area of rectangles with whole-by-mixed and whole-by-fractional number side lengths by tiling, record by drawing, and relate to fraction multiplication.

Suggested Lesson Structure

■ Fluency Practice   (12 minutes)
■ Application Problem   (8 minutes)
■ Concept Development   (30 minutes)
■ Student Debrief   (10 minutes)
   Total Time   **(60 minutes)**

Fluency Practice (12 minutes)

▪ Multiply Decimals **5.NBT.7**   (4 minutes)
▪ Change Mixed Numbers to Fractions **4.NF.4**   (4 minutes)
▪ Multiply Mixed Numbers and Fractions **5.NF.4**   (4 minutes)

Multiply Decimals (4 minutes)

Materials: (S) Personal white boards

Note: This fluency reviews G5–M4–Lessons 17–18.

T: (Write 2 × 2 = ____.) Say the multiplication sentence.
S: 2 × 2 = 4.
T: (Write 2 × 0.2 = ____.) On your boards, write the number sentence.
S: (Write 2 × 0.2 = 0.4.)
T: (Write 0.2 × 0.2 = ____.) On your boards, write the number sentence.
S: (Write 0.2 × 0.2 = 0.04.)

2 × 2 = 4	2 × 0.2 = 0.4	0.2 × 0.2 = 0.04	0.02 × 0.2 = 0.004
2 × 6 = 12	2 × 0.6 = 1.2	0.2 × 0.6 = 0.12	0.02 × 0.6 = 0.012
5 × 7 = 35	0.5 × 7 = 3.5	0.5 × 0.7 = 0.35	0.5 × 0.07 = 0.035

Continue the process using the following possible suggestions: 3 × 4, 3 × 0.4, 0.3 × 0.4, 0.03 × 0.4, 5 × 7, 0.5 × 7, 0.5 × 0.7, and 0.5 × 0.07.

© 2014 Common Core, Inc. All rights reserved. commoncore.org

	Lesson 10:	Find the area of rectangles with whole-by-mixed and whole-by-fractional number side lengths by tiling, record by drawing and relate to fraction multiplication.	**5.C.3**
	Date:	1/10/14	

Change Mixed Numbers to Fractions (4 minutes)

Materials: (S) Personal white boards

Note: This fluency prepares students for today's lesson.

T: How many fourths are in 1?

S: 4.

T: How many fourths are in 2?

S: 8.

T: (Write $2\frac{1}{4}$ = ___.) On your boards, write $2\frac{1}{4}$ as an improper fraction.

S: (Write $2\frac{1}{4} = \frac{9}{4}$.)

Continue the process for the following possible sequence: $2\frac{3}{4}$, $2\frac{1}{2}$, $4\frac{2}{3}$, $3\frac{3}{4}$, $2\frac{5}{6}$, $3\frac{3}{8}$, $4\frac{5}{8}$, and $5\frac{7}{8}$.

Multiply Mixed Numbers and Fractions (4 minutes)

Materials: (S) Personal white boards

Note: This fluency prepares students for today's lesson.

T: (Write $3\frac{1}{2} \times 2\frac{1}{3}$ = ___. Point to $3\frac{1}{2}$.) Say $3\frac{1}{2}$ as a fraction.

S: $\frac{7}{2}$.

T: (Write = $\frac{7}{2} \times 2\frac{1}{3}$. Point to $2\frac{1}{3}$.) Say $2\frac{1}{3}$ as a fraction.

S: $\frac{7}{3}$.

T: (Write = $\frac{7}{2} \times \frac{7}{3}$. Beneath it, write = —. Beneath it, write = ___.) Multiply the fractions. Then, write the answer as a mixed number.

S: (Write $3\frac{1}{2} \times 2\frac{1}{3}$ = ___. Beneath it, write $\frac{7}{2} \times \frac{7}{3}$. Beneath it, write $\frac{49}{6}$. Beneath it, write $8\frac{1}{6}$.)

$$3\frac{1}{2} \times 2\frac{1}{3} = \underline{}$$
$$= \frac{7}{2} \times \frac{7}{3}$$
$$= \frac{49}{6}$$
$$= 8\frac{1}{6}$$

Continue the process for the following possible sequence: $3\frac{1}{3} \times 2\frac{3}{4}$ and $3\frac{4}{5} \times 4\frac{2}{3}$.

Application Problem (8 minutes)

Heidi and Andrew designed two raised flowerbeds for their garden. Heidi's flowerbed was 5 feet long by 3 feet wide, and Andrew's flowerbed was the same length, but twice as wide. Calculate how many cubic feet of soil they need to buy in order to have soil to a depth of 2 feet in both flowerbeds.

Note: This Application Problem reviews the volume work from earlier in the module.

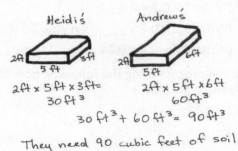

Lesson 10: Find the area of rectangles with whole-by-mixed and whole-by-fractional number side lengths by tiling, record by drawing and relate to fraction multiplication.

Date: 1/10/14

© 2014 Common Core, Inc. All rights reserved. commoncore.org

5.0

Concept Development (30 minutes)

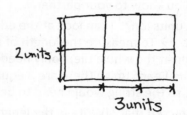

Rectangle A

Materials: (T) 3 unit × 2 unit rectangle, patty paper units for tiling, white board (S 5large mystery rectangles lettered A–E (1 of each size per group), patty paper units for tiling, Problem Set

Note: The lesson is written such that the length of one standard patty paper (5½" by 5½") is one unit. Hamburger patty paper (available from big box discount stores in boxes of 1,000) is the ideal square unit for this lesson due to its translucence and size. Measurements for the mystery rectangles are given in generic units so that any size square unit may be used to tile, as long as the tiling units can be folded. Any paper may be used if patty paper is not available. Consider color-coding Rectangles A–E for easy reference.

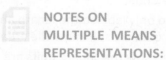

Preparation: Each group needs one copy of Rectangles A–E. The most efficient way of producing these rectangles is to use the patty paper to measure and trace the outer dimensions of one rectangle. Then use that rectangle as a template to cut the number required for the class. Rectangles should measure as follows:

Demo Rectangle A: 3 units × 2 units

Rectangle B: 3 units × $2\frac{1}{2}$ units

Rectangle C: $1\frac{1}{2}$ units × 5 units

Rectangle D: 2 units × $1\frac{3}{4}$ units

Rectangle E: $\frac{3}{4}$ unit × 5 units

NOTES ON
MULTIPLE MEANS
REPRESENTATIONS:

Folding the square units allows students to clearly see the relationship of the fractional square unit while maintaining the relationship to the whole square unit. Consequently, if students become confused about the size of the fractional square unit, the paper may be easily unfolded as a reminder.

T: We want to determine the areas of some mystery rectangles today. Find the rectangle at your table labeled A. (Allow students time to find the rectangle.)

T: If we want to find the area of this mystery rectangle, what kind of units would we use to measure it?

S: Square units.

T: (Hold up a patty paper tile.) This will be the square unit we will use to find the area of Rectangle A. Work with your partner to find the number of squares that will cover this rectangle with no space between units and no overlaps. Please start at the top left hand corner to place your first tile. (Allow students time to work.)

T: How many square units covered the rectangle?

S: 6 square units.

Lesson 10: Find the area of rectangles with whole-by-mixed and whole-by-fractional number side lengths by tiling, record by drawing and relate to fraction multiplication.

Date: 1/10/14

5.C.5

© 2014 Common Core, Inc. All rights reserved. commoncore.org

MP.2

T: Let's sketch a picture of what our tiling looks like. Draw the outside of your rectangle first. (Model as students draw.)

T: Now show the six tiles. (Allow students time to draw.)

T: Look at the longest side of your rectangle. If we wanted to measure this side with a piece of string, how many units long would the string need to be? Explain how you know to your partner.

S: It is 3 units long. I can look at the edge of the units and count. → To measure the length of the side, I'm not looking at the whole tile; I only need to count the length of each unit. There are 3 equal units on the edge, so the string would need to be 3 units long.

T: Let's record that. (Write in the length of Rectangle A in the chart.) What is the length of the shorter side?

S: 2 units.

T: Let's record that in our chart.

T: What is the area of Rectangle A?

S: 6 square units.

T: If we had only labeled the length and the width in our sketch, could we still know the area? Why or why not?

S: Yes. We know the square units are there even if we don't draw them all. → We still just multiply the sides together. We can imagine the tiles.

T: What would a sketch of this look like? Draw it with your partner. (Allow students time to draw.)

T: Now find Rectangle B. Compare its size to Rectangle A. Will its area be greater than or less than that of Rectangle A?

S: Greater.

T: We see that A and B are the same length. What about the width?

S: Rectangle B is wider than two tiles, but not as wide as three tiles.

T: Fold your tiles to decide what fraction of another tile we will need to cover the extra width. Work with your partner. (Allow students time to fold.)

T: What fraction of the tile do you need to cover this part of the rectangle? How do you know?

S: I need half a tile. I laid a whole tile over the extra part and it looked like half to me. → After I folded up the part of the tile that was hanging off the rectangle, I could see that the fold split the tile into two equal parts. That means it is halves.

NOTES ON MULTIPLE MEANS OF EXPRESSION:

Students may use the tiles to measure the outside dimensions of the rectangle before tiling. For some, marking the length and width with tick marks to show the lengths of the units may help them visualize the linear measurement more easily.

The dimensions can then be recorded on the Problem Set prior to drawing the rectangle and partial products.

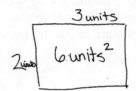

Rectangle	Length	Width	Area
A	3 units	2 units	6 units^2
B	3 units	$2\frac{1}{2}$ units	$7\frac{1}{2}$ units^2

Lesson 10: Find the area of rectangles with whole-by-mixed and whole-by-fractional number side lengths by tiling, record by drawing and relate to fraction multiplication.

Date: 1/10/14

5.C

© 2014 Common Core, Inc. All rights reserved. commoncore.org

T: Finish folding enough tiles to completely cover the width of Rectangle B.

S: (Fold to cover the rectangle completely.)

T: Let's record by sketching and filling in the blanks on the Problem Set. I will record in the chart. What is the length of Rectangle B?

S: 3 units. (Record on Problem Set.)

T: What is the width?

S: $2\frac{1}{2}$ units.

T: What is the area? How do you know?

S: The area is $7\frac{1}{2}$ units squared. I counted all of the whole square units first and then added on the halves. → I knew it was at least 6 square units, and then we had 3 more halves, so that's $7\frac{1}{2}$ square units.

→ $3 \times 2\frac{1}{2} = 6\frac{3}{2} = 7\frac{1}{2}$.

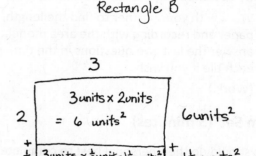

T: When we record our tiling, is it necessary to sketch each tile? Why or why not?

S: No, we can just write down how many there are. → We can show just the side lengths of 3 and $2\frac{1}{2}$. I'll know that means three squares across and two and a half squares down. → It's like the area model with whole numbers. If I know the sides, I can show the total area by just multiplying.

T: Let's sketch this rectangle again, but without the individual tiles. Draw the rectangle and label the length. (Allow students time to draw.)

T: Now, let's decompose the $2\frac{1}{2}$ units on the width as $2 + \frac{1}{2}$. (Label and draw a horizontal line across the rectangle as pictured. Allow students time to draw.)

T: Let's record the first partial product. (Point.) Three units long by 2 units wide is what area?

S: 6 square units.

T: Let's record the second partial product. (Point.) What is the length of this portion?

S: 3 units.

T: What is the width of this portion?

S: 1 half unit.

T: What is the area of this part? How do you know?

S: The area is $1\frac{1}{2}$ square units, because 3 copies of $\frac{1}{2}$ is 3 halves.

→ 3 units long by $\frac{1}{2}$ unit wide is $1\frac{1}{2}$ square units.

NOTES ON MULTIPLE MEANS OF ENGAGEMENT:

The spatial and visualization skills involved in G5–M5–Lessons 10 and 11 will be quite natural for some students, and quite challenging for others. Consequently, the time needed to accomplish the tasks will vary, but all students should be given the opportunity to tile all the rectangles. Both lessons offer two challenging questions at the end of the Problem Sets for those who finish the tiling quickly.

Lesson 10: Find the area of rectangles with whole-by-mixed and whole-by-fractional number side lengths by tiling, record by drawing and relate to fraction multiplication.

Date: 1/10/14

5.C.7

© 2014 Common Core, Inc. All rights reserved. commoncore.org

T: Does this $7\frac{1}{2}$ unit squared area make sense given our prediction? Why or why not?

S: It does make sense. It is only a little wider than the first rectangle, and $7\frac{1}{2}$ isn't that much more than 6. → You can see the first rectangle inside this one. There was a part that was 3 units by 2 units, and then a smaller part was added on that was 3 units by just half another unit. That's where the extra $1\frac{1}{2}$ square units come from. → Three times two was easy, and then I know that half of 3 is $1\frac{1}{2}$. By decomposing the mixed number, it was easy to find the total area.

T: Work with your partner to find the length, width, and area of Rectangles C, D, and E using the patty paper and recording with the area model. Record your findings on your Problem Set, and then answer the last two questions in the time remaining. You may record your tiling without drawing each tile if you wish.

S: (Work.)

Problem Set (5 minutes)

Students should do their personal best to complete the remainder of the Problem Set within the allotted five minutes if they have finished the tiling problems. All problems do not specify a method for solving. Students solve these problems using the RDW approach used for Application Problems.

Student Debrief (10 minutes)

Lesson Objective: Find the area of rectangles with whole-by-mixed and whole-by-fractional number side lengths by tiling, record by drawing, and relate to fraction multiplication.

The Student Debrief is intended to invite reflection and active processing of the total lesson experience.

Invite students to review their solutions for the Problem Set. They should check work by comparing answers with a partner before going over answers as a class. Look for misconceptions or misunderstandings that can be addressed in the Debrief. Guide students in a conversation to debrief the Problem Set and process the lesson.

You may choose to use any combination of the questions below to lead the discussion.

Record the students' answers to Task 1 to complete the class chart as answers are reviewed.

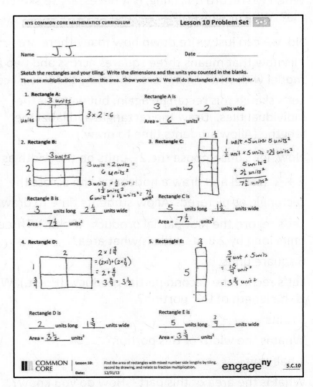

- What relationship did you notice between the areas of Rectangle C and Rectangle E? What accounts for this relationship?

- How was Rectangle E different from the other rectangles you tiled? Describe how you tiled it.

Lesson 10:   Find the area of rectangles with whole-by-mixed and whole-by-fractional number side lengths by tiling, record by drawing and relate to fraction multiplication.

Date: 1/10/14

© 2014 Common Core, Inc. All rights reserved. commoncore.org

- How did you determine the area of Rectangle E? Did you count the single units? Add repeatedly? Multiply the sides?

- Could you place these rectangles in order of greatest to least area by using relationships among the dimensions, but without actually performing the calculations? Why or why not?

- How did you determine the area of the rectangle in Problem 6?

- Analyze and compare different solution strategies for Problem 7.

Exit Ticket (3 minutes)

After the Student Debrief, instruct students to complete the Exit Ticket. A review of their work will help you assess the students' understanding of the concepts that were presented in the lesson today and plan more effectively for future lessons. You may read the questions aloud to the students.

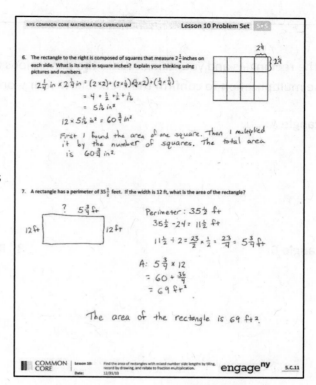

Lesson 10: Find the area of rectangles with whole-by-mixed and whole-by-fractional number side lengths by tiling, record by drawing and relate

5.C.9

Date: 1/10/14

© 2014 Common Core, Inc. All rights reserved. commoncore.org

Name _____ Date _____

Sketch the rectangles and your tiling. Write the dimensions and the units you counted in the blanks. Then use multiplication to confirm the area. Show your work. We will do Rectangles A and B together.

1. **Rectangle A:**

   Rectangle A is

   _____ units long _____ units wide

   Area = _____ units²

2. **Rectangle B:**

3. **Rectangle C:**

   Rectangle B is

   _____ units long _____ units wide

   Area = _____ units²

   Rectangle C is

   _____ units long _____ units wide

   Area = _____ units²

4. **Rectangle D:**

5. **Rectangle E:**

   Rectangle D is

   _____ units long _____ units wide

   Area = _____ units²

   Rectangle E is

   _____ units long _____ units wide

   Area = _____ units²

Lesson 10: Find the area of rectangles with whole-by-mixed and whole-by-fractional number side lengths by tiling, record by drawing and relate

Date: 1/10/14

5.C

© 2014 Common Core, Inc. All rights reserved. commoncore.org

6. The rectangle to the right is composed of squares that measure $2\frac{1}{4}$ inches on each side. What is its area in square inches? Explain your thinking using pictures and numbers.

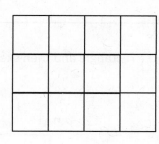

7. A rectangle has a perimeter of $35\frac{1}{2}$ feet. If the width is 12 ft, what is the area of the rectangle?

COMMON CORE

Lesson 10:   Find the area of rectangles with whole-by-mixed and whole-by-fractional number side lengths by tiling, record by drawing and relate to fraction multiplication.

Date: 1/10/14

5.C.11

© 2014 Common Core, Inc. All rights reserved. commoncore.org

Name _____ Date _____

Emma tiled a rectangle and then sketched her work. Fill in the missing information, and multiply to find the area.

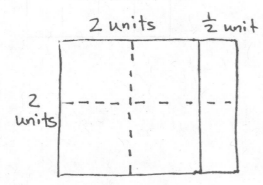

Emma's Rectangle:

_____ units long _____ units wide

Area = _____ units^2

COMMON
CORE™

Lesson 10:   Find the area of rectangles with whole-by-mixed and whole-by-
fractional number side lengths by tiling, record by drawing and relate
to fraction multiplication.

Date: 1/10/14

5.C.

© 2014 Common Core, Inc. All rights reserved. **commoncore.org**

Name _____ Date _____

1. John tiled some rectangles using square unit. Sketch the rectangles if necessary, fill in the missing information, and then confirm the area by multiplying.

   a. **Rectangle A:**

   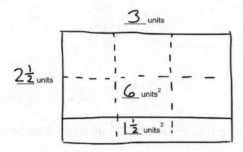

   Rectangle A is

   ___3___ units long $2\frac{1}{2}$ units wide

   Area = _____ units^2

   b. **Rectangle B:**

   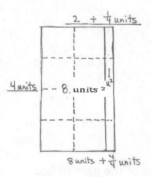

   Rectangle B is

   _____ units long   _____ units wide

   Area = _____ units^2

   c. **Rectangle C:**

   Rectangle C is

   $\frac{3}{4}$ units long   4 units wide

   Area = _____ units^2

| Lesson 10: | Find the area of rectangles with whole-by-mixed and whole-by-fractional number side lengths by tiling, record by drawing and relate to fraction multiplication. |

Date: 1/10/14

5.C.13

© 2014 Common Core, Inc. All rights reserved. commoncore.org

d. **Rectangle D:**

Rectangle D is

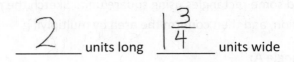

_____2_____ units long   ___$1\frac{3}{4}$___ units wide

Area = _____ units²

2. Rachel made a mosaic from different color rectangular tiles. Three tiles measured $3\frac{1}{2}$ inches × 3 inches. Six tiles measured 4 inches × $3\frac{1}{4}$ inches. What is the area of the whole mosaic in square inches?

3. A garden box has a perimeter of $27\frac{1}{2}$ feet. If the length is 9 feet, what is the area of the garden box?

Lesson 10:   Find the area of rectangles with whole-by-mixed and whole-by-
fractional number side lengths by tiling, record by drawing and relate
to fraction multiplication.

Date: 1/10/14

© 2014 Common Core, Inc. All rights reserved. **commoncore.org**

5.C.

Lesson 11

Objective: Find the area of rectangles with mixed-by-mixed and fraction-by-fraction side lengths by tiling, record by drawing, and relate to fraction multiplication.

Suggested Lesson Structure

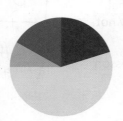

■ Fluency Practice	(12 minutes)
■ Application Problem	(5 minutes)
■ Concept Development	(33 minutes)
■ Student Debrief	(10 minutes)
Total Time	**(60 minutes)**

Fluency Practice (12 minutes)

- Sprint: Multiply Decimals **5.NBT.7**   (9 minutes)
- Multiplying Fractions **5.NF.4**   (3 minutes)

Sprint: Multiply Decimals (9 minutes)

Materials: (S) Multiply Decimals Sprint

Note: This fluency reviews G5–Module 4.

Multiplying Fractions (3 minutes)

Materials: (S) Personal white boards

Note: This fluency prepares students for G5–M5–Lesson 13.

T: (Write $\frac{1}{2} \times \frac{1}{3} =$ ___.) Say the multiplication equation.

S: $\frac{1}{2} \times \frac{1}{3} = \frac{1}{6}$.

T: (Write $\frac{1}{2} \times \frac{3}{4} =$ ___.) Say the multiplication equation.

S: $\frac{1}{2} \times \frac{3}{4} = \frac{3}{8}$.

T: (Write $\frac{2}{5} \times \frac{2}{3} =$ ___.) On your boards, write the multiplication equation.

S: (Write $\frac{2}{5} \times \frac{2}{3} = \frac{4}{15}$.)

	Lesson 11:	Find the area of rectangles with mixed-by-mixed and fraction-by-fraction side lengths by tiling, record by drawing, and relate to fraction multiplication.	**5.C.15**
	Date:	1/10/14	

© 2014 Common Core, Inc. All rights reserved. **commoncore.org**

Continue the process for the following possible sequence: $\frac{1}{2} \times \frac{1}{5}$, $\frac{1}{2} \times \frac{3}{5}$, $\frac{3}{4} \times \frac{3}{5}$, $\frac{4}{5} \times \frac{2}{3}$, and $\frac{3}{4} \times \frac{5}{6}$.

Application Problem (5 minutes)

Ms. Golden wants to cover her 6.5 foot by 4 foot bulletin board with silver paper that comes in 1-foot squares. How many squares does Mrs. Golden need to cover her bulletin board? Will there be any fractional pieces of silver paper left over? Explain why or why not. Draw a sketch to show your thinking.

Note: This Application Problem reviews G5–M5–Lesson 10's concept of tiling, now with one dimension as a decimal fraction.

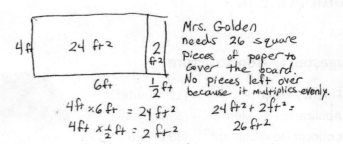

Concept Development (33 minutes)

Materials: (T) Rectangles, patty paper units for tiling, white board (S) 1 demo and 5 mystery rectangles lettered A–E (1 of each size per group), patty paper units for tiling, Problem Set

Note: Today's lesson parallels the structure of G5–M5–Lesson 10. Rectangles for each group should be prepared in advance following yesterday's instructions. The dimensions of today's rectangles are given below.

Rectangle A: $2\frac{1}{2}$ units × $4\frac{1}{2}$ units

Rectangle B: $1\frac{3}{4}$ units × $3\frac{3}{4}$ units

Rectangle C: $\frac{3}{4}$ unit × $1\frac{1}{2}$ units

Rectangle D: $\frac{3}{4}$ unit × $\frac{1}{2}$ units

Rectangle E: $\frac{2}{3}$ unit × $\frac{2}{3}$ units

The added complexities of today's lesson involve the inclusion of two mixed number or fractional side lengths. This is an application of the fraction multiplication lessons of G5–Module 4. Students will also record partial products rather than draw individual tiles.

   T: Let's start with Rectangle A. Work with your partner to place as many whole tiles on Rectangle A as you can. Remember to start at the top left corner of the rectangle.

Lesson 11:   Find the area of rectangles with mixed-by-mixed and fraction-by-fraction side lengths by tiling, record by drawing, and relate to fraction multiplication.

Date: 1/10/14

5.C.1

© 2014 Common Core, Inc. All rights reserved. commoncore.org

S: (Place whole tiles on Rectangle A.)

T: How many whole tiles fit?

S: 8.

T: Is this the area of the rectangle?

S: No.

T: Fold some of your square units to cover the rest of the rectangle's length. (Allow time for students to work.)

T: What fractional unit do you need to do this? How many?

S: I needed 2 half units. → The unit was halves. I needed 2 of them.

T: Now, fold some units to cover the rest of the rectangle's width. (Allow time for students to work.)

T: What fractional unit did you use this time, and how many?

S: I needed halves again. This time it was 4. → It was 4 half units.

T: I see that we've covered almost all of the rectangle, but there seems to be a part at the bottom that is even smaller than the halves we just placed. How can we find the fractional unit that will fit here? Turn and talk.

S: I can see that if I fold a square unit in half, it fits in one direction, but it's too long in the other direction. Maybe if I fold it again, it will fit. → If I fold it in half, it fits the length. Then if I fold that half in half again, it fits perfectly in the space. → The part is half the size of half a square unit. Half of a half is 1 fourth of a square unit.

T: Unfold the paper that you've made to fit in this part. What fraction of a whole square unit covers this part?

S: 1 fourth of a square unit.

T: Work with your partner to count the tiles to determine the area.

S: (Count tiles with partner.)

T: What is the area? How did you count it?

S: I counted the 8 squares first. I added 6 halves, or 3 more squares. Then, I added $\frac{1}{4}$ to 11. That's $11\frac{1}{4}$ square units. → I could see two rows of $4\frac{1}{2}$ units. That is 9. Then there were 4 halves and $\frac{1}{4}$ in a row.

NOTES ON MULTIPLE MEANS OF ENGAGEMENT:

Include Rectangle E as an optional challenge. Folding and tiling Rectangle E requires students to fold thirds and to reason about another area less than 1 square tile. Recording for Rectangle E should be done on separate paper, as it is not included on the Problem Set.

The last two problems on the Problem Set also offer extensions for students who finish the tiling and multiplication quickly.

NOTES ON MULTIPLE MEANS OF EXPRESSION:

For some students, it may be more effective to place a whole square unit over the last corner of the rectangle and then trace the outline or shade the corner of the rectangle on the patty paper. (Because the patty paper is translucent, the edge of the rectangle is clearly visible.) Students may then fold until only the outlined portion of the paper is visible. When the paper is unfolded, only 1 of the 4 equal parts is bordered (or shaded).

Guide students also to isolate the last corner of the rectangle and use a single piece of patty paper to model the multiplication of a fraction by a fraction to produce a double-shaded area (as in G5–Module 4). This double-shaded portion can then be laid on top of the rectangle's corner and should fit perfectly.

Lesson 11:	Find the area of rectangles with mixed-by-mixed and fraction-by-fraction side lengths by tiling, record by drawing, and relate to fraction multiplication.
Date:	1/10/14

5.C.17

© 2014 Common Core, Inc. All rights reserved. commoncore.org

That is $2\frac{1}{4} + 9 = 11\frac{1}{4}$. The area is $11\frac{1}{4}$ square units.

T: Let's record our thinking. I'll work on the board. You record on your Problem Set. Sketch the rectangle first. Decompose the length and width into ones and fractional parts.

S: (Sketch and decompose the length and width.)

T: How did you decompose the length?

S: $4 + \frac{1}{2}$.

T: (Record in the algorithm.) The width?

S: $2 + \frac{1}{2}$.

T: (Record in the algorithm.) Let's use multiplication to confirm the area we found with counting. Let's start with the ones. (Point, then record each partial product in the rectangle and in the algorithm.) 2 units × 4 units equals?

S: 8 square units.

T: (Point and record.) 2 units × $\frac{1}{2}$ unit equals?

S: 2 half square units. → 1 square unit.

T: (Point and record.) $\frac{1}{2}$ unit × 4 units equals?

S: 4 half square units → 2 square units.

T: (Point and record.) $\frac{1}{2}$ unit × $\frac{1}{2}$ unit equals?

S: $\frac{1}{4}$ square unit.

T: Find the sum.

S: (Work to find $11\frac{1}{4}$ units².)

T: Was the area the same using multiplication and the area model?

S: Yes!

T: Use your tiles to determine the area and dimensions of the other rectangles. Record your findings on your Problem Set. Then multiply to confirm the area.

NOTES ON MULTIPLE MEANS OF REPRESENTATION:

Please note that the algorithm is provided so that students are exposed to a more formal representation of the distribution. However, students should not be required to be as formal in their own calculations. Using an area model to keep track of thinking is sufficient.

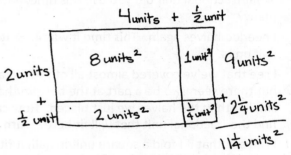

Problem Set (5 minutes)

Students should do their personal best to complete the remainder of the Problem Set within the allotted 5 minutes if they have finished the tiling problems. All problems do not specify a method for solving. Students solve these problems using the RDW approach used for Application Problems.

Lesson 11: Find the area of rectangles with mixed-by-mixed and fraction-by-fraction side lengths by tiling, record by drawing, and relate to fraction multiplication.

Date: 1/10/14

5.C.1

© 2014 Common Core, Inc. All rights reserved. commoncore.org

Student Debrief (10 minutes)

Lesson Objective: Find the area of rectangles with mixed-by-mixed and fraction-by-fraction side lengths by tiling, record by drawing, and relate to fraction multiplication.

The Student Debrief is intended to invite reflection and active processing of the total lesson experience.

Invite students to review their solutions for the Problem Set. They should check work by comparing answers with a partner before going over answers as a class. Look for misconceptions or misunderstandings that can be addressed in the Debrief. Guide students in a conversation to debrief the Problem Set and process the lesson.

You may choose to use any combination of the questions below to lead the discussion.

- Compare the rectangles we tiled today to the rectangles we tiled yesterday. What do you notice? How did that change the way we had to tile?

- Which rectangle was the easiest to tile? Which was the hardest? Why?

- Explain your strategy for tiling Rectangle D (and Rectangle E, where applicable). How was finding the area of this rectangle similar to the fraction multiplication we did in Module 4? How was it different?

- Explain your strategy for finding the areas of the rectangles in Problem 5 and how you compared them.

- How is Problem 6 in today's Problem Set like Problem 6 in yesterday's Problem Set (G5–M5–Lesson 10), and how is it different? Yesterday's problem read: A rectangle has a perimeter of $35\frac{1}{2}$ feet. If the width is 12 ft, what is the area of the rectangle?

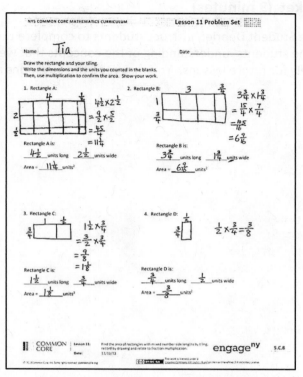

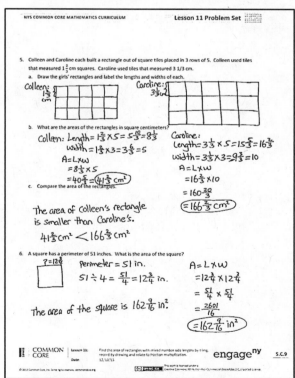

Lesson 11:   Find the area of rectangles with mixed-by-mixed and fraction-by-fraction side lengths by tiling, record by drawing, and relate to fraction multiplication.

Date: 1/10/14

5.C.19

© 2014 Common Core, Inc. All rights reserved. commoncore.org

Exit Ticket (3 minutes)

After the Student Debrief, instruct students to complete the Exit Ticket. A review of their work will help you assess the students' understanding of the concepts that were presented in the lesson today and plan more effectively for future lessons. You may read the questions aloud to the students.

Lesson 11:

Date:

Find the area of rectangles with mixed-by-mixed and fraction-by-fraction side lengths by tiling, record by drawing, and relate to fraction multiplication.

1/10/14

5.C.2

© 2014 Common Core, Inc. All rights reserved. commoncore.org

A

Multiply.   # Correct _____

1	3 x 2 =		23	0.6 x 2 =	
2	3 x 0.2 =		24	0.6 x 0.2 =	
3	3 x 0.02 =		25	0.6 x 0.02 =	
4	3 x 3 =		26	0.2 x 0.06 =	
5	3 x 0.3 =		27	5 x 7 =	
6	3 x 0.03 =		28	0.5 x 7 =	
7	2 x 4 =		29	0.5 x 0.7 =	
8	2 x 0.4 =		30	0.5 x 0.07 =	
9	2 x 0.04 =		31	0.7 x 0.05 =	
10	5 x 3 =		32	2 x 8 =	
11	5 x 0.3 =		33	9 x 0.2 =	
12	5 x 0.03 =		34	3 x 7 =	
13	7 x 2 =		35	8 x 0.03 =	
14	7 x 0.2 =		36	4 x 6 =	
15	7 x 0.02 =		37	0.6 x 7 =	
16	4 x 3 =		38	0.7 x 0.7 =	
17	4 x 0.3 =		39	0.8 x 0.06 =	
18	0.4 x 3 =		40	0.09 x 0.6 =	
19	0.4 x 0.3 =		41	6 x 0.8 =	
20	0.4 x 0.03 =		42	0.7 x 0.9 =	
21	0.3 x 0.04 =		43	0.08 x 0.8 =	
22	6 x 2 =		44	0.9 x 0.08 =	

Lesson 11: Find the area of rectangles with mixed-by-mixed and fraction-by-fraction side lengths by tiling, record by drawing, and relate to

Date: 1/10/14

5.C.21

© 2014 Common Core, Inc. All rights reserved. commoncore.org

B

Improvement _____   # Correct _____

Multiply.

1	4 x 2 =		23	0.8 x 2 =	
2	4 x 0.2 =		24	0.8 x 0.2 =	
3	4 x 0.02 =		25	0.8 x 0.02 =	
4	2 x 3 =		26	0.2 x 0.08 =	
5	2 x 0.3 =		27	5 x 9 =	
6	2 x 0.03 =		28	0.5 x 9 =	
7	3 x 3 =		29	0.5 x 0.9 =	
8	3 x 0.3 =		30	0.5 x 0.09 =	
9	3 x 0.03 =		31	0.9 x 0.05 =	
10	4 x 3 =		32	2 x 6 =	
11	4 x 0.3 =		33	7 x 0.2 =	
12	4 x 0.03 =		34	3 x 8 =	
13	9 x 2 =		35	9 x 0.03 =	
14	9 x 0.2 =		36	4 x 8 =	
15	9 x 0.02 =		37	0.7 x 6 =	
16	5 x 3 =		38	0.6 x 0.6 =	
17	5 x 0.3 =		39	0.6 x 0.08 =	
18	0.5 x 3 =		40	0.06 x 0.9 =	
19	0.5 x 0.3 =		41	8 x 0.6 =	
20	0.5 x 0.03 =		42	0.9 x 0.7 =	
21	0.3 x 0.05 =		43	0.07 x 0.7 =	
22	8 x 2 =		44	0.8 x 0.09 =	

Lesson 11:   Find the area of rectangles with mixed-by-mixed and fraction-by-
fraction side lengths by tiling, record by drawing, and relate to
fraction multiplication.

Date: 1/10/14

5.C.2

© 2014 Common Core, Inc. All rights reserved. **commoncore.org**

Name _____ Date _____

Draw the rectangle and your tiling.
Write the dimensions and the units you counted in the blanks.
Then, use multiplication to confirm the area. Show your work.

1. **Rectangle A:**

Rectangle A is

_____ units long _____ units wide

Area = _____ units²

2. **Rectangle B:**

Rectangle B is

_____ units long _____ units wide

Area = _____ units²

3. **Rectangle C:**

Rectangle C is

_____ units long _____ units wide

Area = _____ units²

4. **Rectangle D:**

Rectangle D is

_____ units long _____ units wide

Area = _____ units²

Lesson 11: Find the area of rectangles with mixed-by-mixed and fraction-by-fraction side lengths by tiling, record by drawing, and relate to fraction multiplication.

Date: 1/10/14

5.C.23

© 2014 Common Core, Inc. All rights reserved. commoncore.org

5. Colleen and Caroline each built a rectangle out of square tiles placed in 3 rows of 5. Colleen used tiles that measured $1\frac{2}{3}$ cm squares. Caroline used tiles that measured $3\frac{1}{3}$ cm.

   a. Draw the girls' rectangles, and label the lengths and widths of each.

   b. What are the areas of the rectangles in square centimeters?

   c. Compare the area of the rectangles.

6. A square has a perimeter of 51 inches. What is the area of the square?

Lesson 11:   Find the area of rectangles with mixed-by-mixed and fraction-by-fraction side lengths by tiling, record by drawing, and relate to fraction multiplication.

Date: 1/10/14

5.C.2

© 2014 Common Core, Inc. All rights reserved. commoncore.org

Name _____   Date _____

1. To find the area, Andrea tiled a rectangle and sketched her answer. Sketch the rectangle, and find the area. Show your multiplication work.

Rectangle is

$2\frac{1}{2}$ units × $2\frac{1}{2}$ units

Area = _____

COMMON CORE™   Lesson 11:   Find the area of rectangles with mixed-by-mixed and fraction-by-fraction side lengths by tiling, record by drawing, and relate to fraction multiplication.   5.C.25

Date: 1/10/14

© 2014 Common Core, Inc. All rights reserved. **commoncore.org**

Name _____   Date _____

1. Kristen tiled the following rectangles using square units. Sketch the rectangles, and find the areas. Then confirm the area by multiplying. Rectangle A has been sketched for you.

    a. **Rectangle A:**

Rectangle A is

_____ units long × _____ units wide

Area = _____ units²

    b. **Rectangle B:**

Rectangle B is

$2\frac{1}{2}$ units long × $\frac{3}{4}$ unit wide

Area = _____ units²

    c. **Rectangle C:**

Rectangle C is

$3\frac{1}{3}$ units long × $2\frac{1}{2}$ units wide

Area = _____ units²

COMMON CORE

Lesson 11:   Find the area of rectangles with mixed-by-mixed and fraction-by-fraction side lengths by tiling, record by drawing, and relate to fraction multiplication.

Date: 1/10/14

5.C.2

© 2014 Common Core, Inc. All rights reserved. commoncore.org

d. **Rectangle D:**

Rectangle D is

$3\frac{1}{2}$ units long × $2\frac{1}{4}$ units wide

Area = _____ units^2

2. A square has a perimeter of 25 inches. What is the area of the square?

COMMON CORE | Lesson 11:   Find the area of rectangles with mixed-by-mixed and fraction-by-fraction side lengths by tiling, record by drawing, and relate to   5.C.27

Date: 1/10/14

© 2014 Common Core, Inc. All rights reserved. commoncore.org

Lesson 12

Objective: Measure to find the area of rectangles with fractional side lengths.

Suggested Lesson Structure

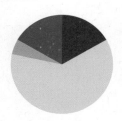

■ Fluency Practice   (10 minutes)
■ Application Problem   (3 minutes)
□ Concept Development   (37 minutes)
■ Student Debrief   (10 minutes)
  Total Time   **(60 minutes)**

Fluency Practice (10 minutes)

- Multiplying Fractions **5.NF.4**   (4 minutes)
- Find the Volume **5.MD.C**   (6 minutes)

Multiplying Fractions (4 minutes)

Materials: (S) Personal white boards

Note: This fluency prepares students for G5–M5–Lesson 13.

  T: (Write $\frac{1}{3} \times \frac{1}{4}$.) Say the multiplication number sentence.

  S: $\frac{1}{3} \times \frac{1}{4} = \frac{1}{12}$.

  T: (Write $\frac{1}{3} \times \frac{2}{5}$.) Say the multiplication number sentence.

  S: $\frac{1}{3} \times \frac{2}{5} = \frac{2}{15}$.

  T: (Write $\frac{3}{5} \times \frac{2}{3}$. Beneath it, write = ___.) On your boards, write the multiplication number sentence. Then, simplify the fraction.

  S: (Write $\frac{3}{5} \times \frac{2}{3} = \frac{6}{15}$. Beneath it, write = $\frac{2}{5}$.)

Continue the process for the following possible sequence: $\frac{1}{2} \times \frac{1}{4}, \frac{1}{2} \times \frac{3}{4}, \frac{3}{4} \times \frac{2}{3}, \frac{5}{6} \times \frac{2}{3}$, and $\frac{3}{4} \times \frac{7}{8}$.

 | Lesson 12:   Measure to find the area of rectangles with fractional side lengths.
             Date: 1/10/14   5.C.2

© 2014 Common Core, Inc. All rights reserved. **commoncore.org**

Find the Volume (6 minutes)

Materials: (S) Personal white boards

Note: This fluency reviews volume concepts and formulas.

T: (Project a prism 5 units × 2 units × 4 units. Write V = ___ units × ___ units × ___ units.) Find the volume.

S: (Write 40 units^3 = 5 units × 2 units × 4 units.)

T: How many layers of 10 cubes are in the prism?

S: 4 layers.

T: (Write 4 × 10 units^3 = _____.) Four copies of 10 cubic units is…?

S: 40 cubic units.

T: How many layers of 8 cubes are there?

S: 5 layers.

T: (Write 5 × 8 units^3 = _____.) Five copies of 8 cubic units is…?

S: 40 cubic units.

T: How many layers of 20 cubes are there?

S: 2 layers.

T: Write a multiplication sentence to find the volume of the prism, starting with the number of layers. (Point.)

S: (Write 2 units × 20 units^2 = 40 units^3.)

Repeat the process with the following prisms.

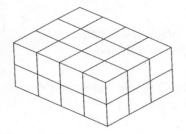

Application Problem (3 minutes)

Margo is designing a label. The dimensions of the label are $3\frac{1}{2}$ inches by $1\frac{1}{4}$ inches. What is the area of the label? Use the RDW process.

Note: Students can use the area model used in G5–Module 4 and in G5–M5–Lessons 10–11 to solve. This bridges to today's lesson, which extends the use of the area model.

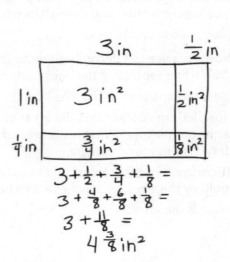

Lesson 12:   Measure to find the area of rectangles with fractional side lengths.
Date: 1/10/14

5.C.29

© 2014 Common Core, Inc. All rights reserved. commoncore.org

Concept Development (37 minutes)

Materials: (T) Ruler, projector (S) Ruler, Problem Set

Problem 1(a)

Project the first rectangle in the Problem Set.

T: We will find areas of more mystery rectangles today. What was the relationship of the areas we found using square tiles and the areas we found using multiplication?

S: We got the same answers. → Tiling or finding partial products using multiplication will always give the same area, because the rectangle we are using is the same.

T: Today we'll use a ruler to help us find area. Turn and talk to your partner about how you think a ruler might be useful in finding the area of a rectangle.

S: It's not square units, but we can measure the edges. → The ruler lets us measure the sides to find out the lengths we need to multiply.

T: Work with your partner to measure the lengths of the first rectangle of the Problem Set. Compare your measurements.

S: (Measure the first rectangle.)

T: What are the lengths of the side?

S: 2 inches and $2\frac{1}{2}$ inches.

T: Estimate the area of this rectangle. Turn and talk.

S: If this was just a 2 inch square, the area would be 4 square inches. It's a little longer than that, so it will be a little more than 4. → The longer side is between 2 and 3 inches, so the area should be somewhere between 4 square inches and 6 square inches.

T: Let's find the actual area. Decompose the longer side by marking the end of the 2 whole inches and labeling the wholes and the half inch on our rectangles. (Model on the board as shown.)

S: (Decompose and label.)

T: Now, let's use this decomposition to find the area of smaller parts of the rectangle. Using your ruler, draw a line separating the ones from the fractional units. (Model.)

S: (Separate the ones with a line.)

T: Now, let's multiply to find the areas of these sections. Let's start with the ones by ones part. Talk with your partner. What is the area of the part that is 2 inches by 2 inches? If it helps, imagine or draw tiles in your rectangle.

S: There are two going across and two rows of them, so four altogether. → I remember that I can multiply the sides, so 2 inches × 2 inches is 4 square inches.

T: What is the area?

> **NOTES ON**
> **MULTIPLE MEANS OF**
> **REPRESENTATION:**
>
> All students will benefit from drawing each square inch as a tile, connecting back to the tiling process. Others may need to use inch tile manipulatives to understand this process. (Remember that concrete materials should be foldable.)
>
> Encourage students often to return to pictorial or concrete representations as needed during any lesson to scaffold understanding.

Lesson 12:   Measure to find the area of rectangles with fractional side lengths.
Date: 1/10/14

5.C.3

© 2014 Common Core, Inc. All rights reserved. commoncore.org

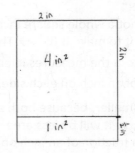

S: 4 square inches.

T: Record that.

T: Turn and talk. What is the area of the smaller part? How do you know?

S: Half of 2, so 1. → Two times $\frac{1}{2}$. Two halves make 1, so 1. → 1 square inch.

T: Yes, the area is 1 square inch. Let's write that too. (Model as shown at right.)

T: What is the total area of the rectangle? Does our answer make sense?

S: 5 square inches. → It makes sense because we said the area should be between 4 and 6 square inches and it is.

Problem 1(b)

Project the second rectangle in the Problem Set.

T: Measure the next rectangle with your ruler. (Allow students time to measure.)

T: What is the length?

S: $1\frac{3}{4}$ inches.

T: And the width?

S: $1\frac{3}{4}$ inches. → This is a square so the width is also $1\frac{3}{4}$ inches.

T: Estimate the area with your partner.

S: It's almost 2 inches by 2 inches. The area should be less than 4 square inches. → The area will be between 1 square inch and 4 square inches, but closer to 4 because the sides are almost 2 inches long.

T: Decompose the sides into ones and fractional parts and record that on your Problem Set.

Circulate and assist students. Then, project a student's work, or record on the board as shown.

T: Work with your partner to find the area of each of these four parts.

S: (Find the area of each of the four parts.)

T: What is the area of the part that is 1 inch on each side?

S: 1 square inch.

T: Then we have two parts with 1 inch on one side and $\frac{3}{4}$ inch on the other. What is the area of each of those parts? How do you know?

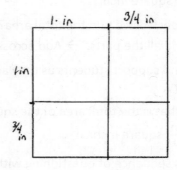

NOTES ON MULTIPLE MEANS OF ENGAGEMENT:

For students who need to review fraction multiplication, model the shaded area models from G5–Module 4 to show a fraction times a fraction, or a fraction of a fraction.

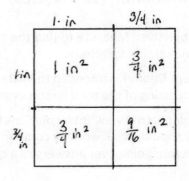

COMMON CORE™ | Lesson 12:   Measure to find the area of rectangles with fractional side lengths.
Date: 1/10/14

5.C.31

© 2014 Common Core, Inc. All rights reserved. **commoncore.org**

S: It's not a whole square inch. → A whole tile wouldn't fit in either of these places. We would have to fold it to make it fit. → Three-fourths of a square inch because 3 fourths times 1 is 3 fourths.

T: (Record the measures in each part of the area model.) Now we're left with the last little square. It is $\frac{3}{4}$ of an inch on each side. Is this area greater or less than the other parts? How do you know?

S: It's smaller, because both sides are shorter than the other parts. → It's only part of an inch on each side, so it will be less area. → The area is a fraction of a fraction. We want 3 fourths of 3 fourths. It's a fraction of an inch on each side. Three-fourths of a square inch would be like splitting a whole into four parts and taking one part off.

T: What do we need to do to find the area of this last section of our square?

S: Just like before, we need to multiply the length times the width. → We need to multiply $\frac{3}{4}$ by $\frac{3}{4}$.

T: What is the area of the small square?

S: $\frac{9}{16}$ square inch.

T: How will we find the total area?

S: Add all the parts. → Add across each row and then add the rows together.

Circulate and support students as they add the partial products. Review the need for common denominators as necessary.

T: What is the total area of the square?

S: $3\frac{1}{16}$ square inches!

Repeat this sequence of questioning with each problem as necessary. As students understand the concept, release them to work independently.

Problem Set (5 minutes)

Students should do their personal best to complete the remainder of the Problem Set within the allotted 5 minutes. All problems do not specify a method for solving. Students solve these problems using the RDW approach used for Application Problems.

Student Debrief (10 minutes)

Lesson Objective: Measure to find the area of rectangles with fractional side lengths.

The Student Debrief is intended to invite reflection and active processing of the total lesson experience.

Invite students to review their solutions for the Problem Set. They should check work by comparing answers with a partner before going over answers as a class. Look for

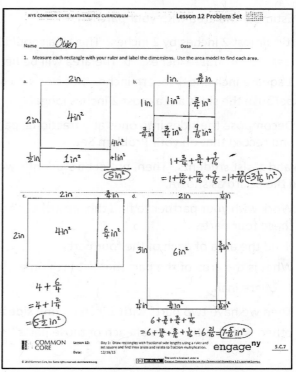

Lesson 12:   Measure to find the area of rectangles with fractional side lengths.

Date: 1/10/14

5.C.3

© 2014 Common Core, Inc. All rights reserved. commoncore.org

misconceptions or misunderstandings that can be addressed in the Debrief. Guide students in a conversation to debrief the Problem Set and process the lesson.

You may choose to use any combination of the questions below to lead the discussion.

- Look back at the area model we did together in Problem 1(b) ($1\frac{3}{4} \times 1\frac{3}{4}$). How many squares do you see in your area model? What patterns do you see whenever you have an area model of a square?

- What is the relationship between Problem 1(e) and Problem 1(f) in the Problem Set? (Both rectangles have the same area. The length of Problem 1(f) is 5 times the length of Problem 1(e). The width of Problem 1(f) is one-fifth the width of Problem 1(e).)

- Using mental math, how can you find $\frac{1}{2}$ times any fraction? (Double the denominator.)

- How is Problem 2(b) like the example we did together, $1\frac{3}{4} \times 1\frac{3}{4}$. (Both have two factors that are the same.)

Exit Ticket (3 minutes)

After the Student Debrief, instruct students to complete the Exit Ticket. A review of their work will help you assess the students' understanding of the concepts that were presented in the lesson today and plan more effectively for future lessons. You may read the questions aloud to the students.

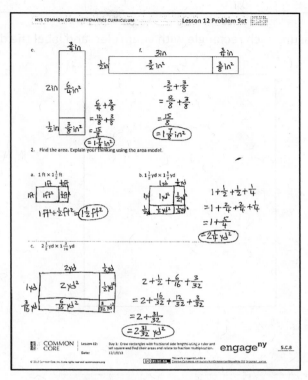

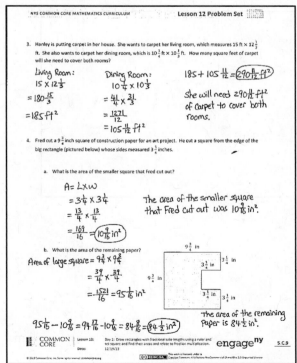

Lesson 12:   Measure to find the area of rectangles with fractional side lengths.
Date: 1/10/14

5.C.33

© 2014 Common Core, Inc. All rights reserved. commoncore.org

Name _____   Date _____

1. Measure each rectangle with your ruler, and label the dimensions. Use the area model to find each area.

a.

b.

c.

d.

Lesson 12:   Measure to find the area of rectangles with fractional side lengths.
Date: 1/10/14

5.C.3

© 2014 Common Core, Inc. All rights reserved. commoncore.org

e.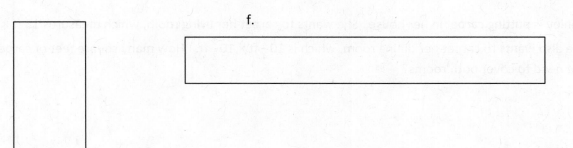

f.

2. Find the area. Explain your thinking using the area model.

a. $1 \text{ ft} \times 1\frac{1}{2} \text{ ft}$

b. $1\frac{1}{2} \text{ yd} \times 1\frac{1}{2} \text{ yd}$

c. $2\frac{1}{2} \text{ yd} \times 1\frac{3}{16} \text{ yd}$

COMMON CORE | **Lesson 12:** | Measure to find the area of rectangles with fractional side lengths.
| **Date:** | 1/10/14

5.C.35

© 2014 Common Core, Inc. All rights reserved. **commoncore.org**

3. Hanley is putting carpet in her house. She wants to carpet her living room, which measures 15 ft × $12\frac{1}{3}$ ft. She also wants to carpet her dining room, which is $10\frac{1}{4}$ ft × $10\frac{1}{3}$ ft. How many square feet of carpet will she need to cover both rooms?

4. Fred cut a $9\frac{3}{4}$ inch square of construction paper for an art project. He cut a square from the edge of the big rectangle whose sides measured $3\frac{1}{4}$ inches. (See picture below.)

   a. What is the area of the smaller square that Fred cut out?

   b. What is the area of the remaining paper?

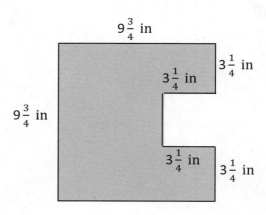

© 2014 Common Core, Inc. All rights reserved. commoncore.org

Name _____   Date _____

Measure the rectangle with your ruler, and label the dimensions. Find the area.

1.

© 2014 Common Core, Inc. All rights reserved. **commoncore.org**

Name _____ Date _____

1. Measure each rectangle with your ruler, and label the dimensions. Use the area model to find the area.

a.

b.

c.

d.

e.

Lesson 12:   Measure to find the area of rectangles with fractional side lengths.
Date: 1/10/14

5.C.3

© 2014 Common Core, Inc. All rights reserved. commoncore.org

2. Find the area. Explain your thinking using the area model.

   a. $2\frac{1}{4}$ yd $\times \frac{1}{4}$ yd

   b. $2\frac{1}{2}$ ft $\times 1\frac{1}{4}$ ft

3. Kelly buys a tarp to cover the area under her tent. The tent is 4 feet wide and has an area of 31 square feet. The tarp she bought is $5\frac{1}{3}$ feet by $5\frac{3}{4}$ feet. Can the tarp cover the area under Kelly's tent? Draw a model to show your thinking.

4. Shannon and Leslie want to carpet a $16\frac{1}{2}$ ft by $16\frac{1}{2}$ ft square room. They can't put carpet under an entertainment system that juts out. (See the drawing below.)

   a. In square feet, what is the area of the space with no carpet?

   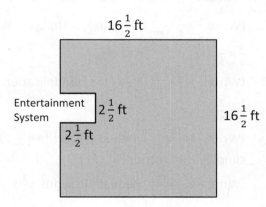

   $16\frac{1}{2}$ ft

   Entertainment System

   $2\frac{1}{2}$ ft

   $2\frac{1}{2}$ ft

   $16\frac{1}{2}$ ft

   b. How many square feet of carpet will Shannon and Leslie need to buy?

COMMON CORE | Lesson 12: Measure to find the area of rectangles with fractional side lengths.
Date: 1/10/14

5.C.39

© 2014 Common Core, Inc. All rights reserved. commoncore.org

Lesson 13

Objective: Multiply mixed number factors, and relate to the distributive property and area model.

Suggested Lesson Structure

■ Fluency Practice	(10 minutes)
■ Application Problem	(7 minutes)
■ Concept Development	(33 minutes)
■ Student Debrief	(10 minutes)
Total Time	**(60 minutes)**

Fluency Practice (10 minutes)

- Multiplying Fractions **5.NF.4**   (4 minutes)
- Find the Volume **5.MD.C**   (6 minutes)

Multiplying Fractions (4 minutes)

Materials: (S) Personal white boards

Note: This fluency prepares students for today's lesson.

T: (Write $\frac{1}{3} \times \frac{1}{5} = \_\_$.) Say the multiplication equation.

S: $\frac{1}{3} \times \frac{1}{5} = \frac{1}{15}$.

T: (Write $\frac{2}{3} \times \frac{2}{5} = \_\_$.) Say the multiplication equation.

S: $\frac{2}{3} \times \frac{2}{5} = \frac{4}{15}$.

T: (Write $\frac{3}{4} \times \frac{2}{3} = \_\_$. Beneath it, write = __.) On your boards, write the multiplication equation. Then, simplify the fraction.

S: (Write $\frac{3}{4} \times \frac{2}{3} = \frac{6}{12}$. Beneath it, write $= \frac{1}{2}$.)

Continue the process for the following possible sequence: $\frac{1}{2} \times \frac{3}{4}, \frac{2}{3} \times \frac{3}{5}, \frac{3}{4} \times \frac{4}{5}, \frac{5}{6} \times \frac{3}{4}$, and $\frac{3}{5} \times \frac{5}{6}$.

COMMON CORE | Lesson 13: Multiply mixed number factors, and relate to the distributive property and area model.
Date: 1/10/14

5.C.4

© 2014 Common Core, Inc. All rights reserved. commoncore.org

Find the Volume (6 minutes)

Materials: (S) Personal white boards

Note: This fluency reviews volume concepts and formulas.

T: (Project a prism 4 units × 2 units × 3 units. Write V = __ units × ___ units × ___ units.) Find the volume.

S: (Write 24 units³ = 4 units × 2 units × 3 units.)

T: How many layers of 6 cubes are in the prism?

S: 4 layers.

T: (Write 4 × 6 units³.) Four copies of 6 cubic units is…?

S: 24 cubic units.

T: How many layers of 8 cubes are there?

S: 3 layers.

T: (Write 3 × 8 units³.) Three copies of 8 cubic units is…?

S: 24 cubic units.

T: How many layers of 12 cubes are there?

S: 2 layers.

T: Write a multiplication equation to find the volume of the prism, starting with the number of layers.

S: (Write 2 × 12 units³ = 24 units³.)

Repeat the process for the prisms pictured.

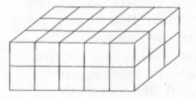

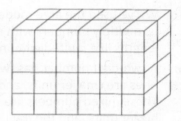

Application Problem (7 minutes)

The Colliers want to put new flooring in a $6\frac{1}{2}$ foot by $7\frac{1}{3}$ foot bathroom. The tiles they want come in 12-inch squares. What is the area of the bathroom floor? If the tile costs $3.25 per square foot, how much will they spend on the flooring?

Note: This type of tiling applies the work from G5–M5–Lessons 10–13 and bridges to today's lesson on the distributive property.

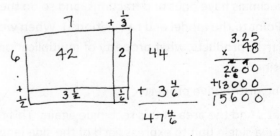

The area of the bathroom is $47\frac{2}{3}$ ft². They will pay $156 to tile the floor.

| Lesson 13: | Multiply mixed number factors, and relate to the distributive property and area model. |
| Date: | 1/10/14 |

5.C.41

© 2014 Common Core, Inc. All rights reserved. commoncore.org

Concept Development (33 minutes)

Materials: (S) Personal white boards

In this lesson, students reason about the most efficient strategy to use to multiply mixed numbers: distributing with the area model or multiplying improper fractions and canceling to simplify.

Problem 1

Find the area of a rectangle $1\frac{1}{3}$ inches × $3\frac{3}{4}$ inches and discuss strategies for solving.

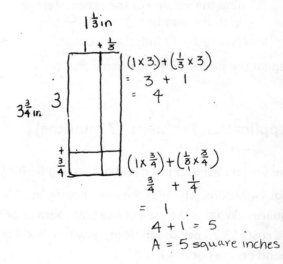

T: (Project Rectangle 1.) How is this rectangle different from the rectangles we've been working with?

S: We know the dimensions of this one. → The side lengths are given to us, so we don't need to tile or measure.

T: Find the area of this rectangle. Use an area model to show your thinking.

S: (Find the area using a model.)

T: What is the area of this rectangle?

S: 5 inches squared.

T: We've used the area model many times in Grade 5 to help us multiply numbers with mixed units. How are these side lengths like multi-digit numbers? Turn and talk.

MP.4 S: A two-digit number has two different size units in it. The ones are smaller units, and the tens are the bigger units. These mixed numbers are like that. The ones are the bigger units, and the fractions are the smaller units. → Mixed numbers are another way to write decimals. Decimals have ones and fractions, and so do these.

T: (Point to the model and calculations.) When we add partial products, what property of multiplication are we using?

S: The distributive property.

T: Let's find the area of this rectangle again. This time let's use a single unit to express each of the side lengths. What is $1\frac{1}{3}$ expressed only in thirds?

S: 4 thirds.

T: (Record on the rectangle.) Express $3\frac{3}{4}$ using only fourths.

S: 15 fourths.

T: (Record on the rectangle.) Multiply these fractions to find the area.

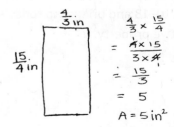

Lesson 13:   Multiply mixed number factors, and relate to the distributive property
and area model.

Date: 1/10/14

5.C.4

© 2014 Common Core, Inc. All rights reserved. commoncore.org

S: (Multiple to find the area.)

T: What is the area?

S: 5 in².

T: Which strategy did you find to be more efficient? Why?

S: This way was a lot faster for me! → These fractions were easy to simplify before I multiplied, so there were fewer calculations to do to find the area.

T: Do you think it will always be true that multiplying the fractions will be the most efficient? Why or why not?

S: This seems easier, because it's multiplying whole numbers. → I like the distributive property better because the numbers stay smaller doing one part at a time. → I'm not sure, some larger mixed numbers might be a lot more challenging.

T: Lots of different viewpoints here. Let's try another example to test these strategies again.

NOTES ON
MULTIPLE MEANS OF
ENGAGEMENT:

All students may need a quick refresher on changing mixed numbers to improper fractions or vice versa. Student should be reminded that a mixed number is an addition sentence, so when converting to an improper fraction, the whole number can be expressed in the unit of the fractional part and then both like fractions added.

Problem 2

Determine when the distributive property or the multiplication of fractions is more efficient to solve for area.

T: (Draw a rectangle with side lengths $16\frac{1}{2}$ in and $4\frac{1}{4}$ in.) Which strategy do you think might be more efficient to find the area of this rectangle? Turn and talk.

S: The fractions are pretty easy, so I think the distributive property will be quicker. → The numerators will be big. I think distribution will be easier. → I like to simplify fractions, so I think improper fractions will work easier.

T: Work with a partner to find the area of this rectangle. Partner A, use the distributive property with an area model. Partner B, express the sides using fractions greater than 1. (Allow students time to work.)

T: What is the area? Which strategy was more efficient?

S: The improper fractions were messy. When I converted to improper fractions, the numerators I got were 33 and 17, and there weren't any common factors to help me simplify. The area is $\frac{561}{8}$ in², which is right, but it's weird. I had to use long division to figure out that the area was $70\frac{1}{8}$ square inches. → The distributive property was much easier on this one. The partial products were all easy to do in my head. I just added the sums of the rows and got $70\frac{1}{8}$ square inches.

T: Does the method that you choose matter? Why or why not? Turn and talk.

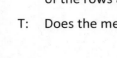

Lesson 13: Multiply mixed number factors, and relate to the distributive property and area model.

Date: 1/10/14

5.C.43

© 2014 Common Core, Inc. All rights reserved. commoncore.org

S: Either way, we got the right answer. → Depending on the numbers, sometimes distributing is easier, and sometimes just multiplying the improper fractions is easier.

Repeat the process to find the area of a square with side length $3\frac{2}{3}$ m.

T: When should you use each strategy? Talk to your partner.

S: If the numbers are small, fraction multiplication might be better, especially if some factors can be simplified. → For large mixed numbers, I think the area model is easier, especially if some of the partial products are whole numbers or have common denominators. → You can always start with one strategy and change to the other if it gets too hard.

Problem 3

An 8 inch by 10 inch picture is resting on a mat. Three-fourths inch of the mat shows around the entire edge of the picture. Find the area of the mat not covered by the picture.

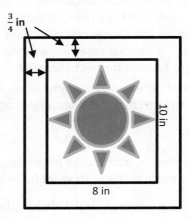

T: Compare this problem to others we've worked. Turn and talk.

S: There are two rectangles to think about here. → We have to think about how to get just the part that is the mat and not the area of the whole thing. → It is a little bit of a mystery rectangle because they are asking about the mat, but they only gave us the measurements of the picture.

T: Work with your partner and use RDW to solve. (Allow students time to work.)

T: What did you think about to solve this problem?

S: I started by imagining the mat without the picture on top. I added the extra part of the mat ($1\frac{1}{2}$ inches) to the picture to find the length and width of the mat. Then, I multiplied and found the area of the mat. I subtracted the picture's area from the mat and got the answer. → I started to use improper fractions, but the numbers were really large, so I used the area model. → I used the area model for the mat's area, because I saw the measurements were going to have fractions. Then, I just multiplied 8 × 10 to find the area of the picture. → After I figured out the area of the mat, I drew a tape diagram to show the part I knew and the part I needed to find.

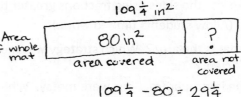

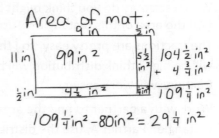

Problem Set (10 minutes)

Students should do their personal best to complete the Problem Set some classes, it may be appropriate to modify the assignment by first. All problems do not specify a method for solving. Students solve these problems using the RDW approach used for Application Problems.

Lesson 13:   Multiply mixed number factors, and relate to the distributive property
              and area model.
Date: 1/10/14

5.C.4

© 2014 Common Core, Inc. All rights reserved. commoncore.org

Student Debrief (10 minutes)

Lesson Objective: Multiply mixed number factors, and relate to the distributive property and area model.

The Student Debrief is intended to invite reflection and active processing of the total lesson experience.

Invite students to review their solutions for the Problem Set. They should check work by comparing answers with a partner before going over answers as a class. Look for misconceptions or misunderstandings that can be addressed in the Debrief. Guide students in a conversation to debrief the Problem Set and process the lesson.

You may choose to use any combination of the questions below to lead the discussion.

- What are the strategies that we have used to find the area of a rectangle? Which one do you find the easiest? The most difficult? How do you decide which strategy you will use for a given problem? What kinds of things do you think about when deciding?
- In the Problem Set, when did you use the distributive property and when did you multiply improper fractions? Why did you make those choices?
- How did you solve Problem 3?
- What are some situations in real life where finding the area of something would be needed or useful?

Exit Ticket (3 minutes)

After the Student Debrief, instruct students to complete the Exit Ticket. A review of their work will help you assess the students' understanding of the concepts that were presented in the lesson today and plan more effectively for future lessons. You may read the questions aloud to the students.

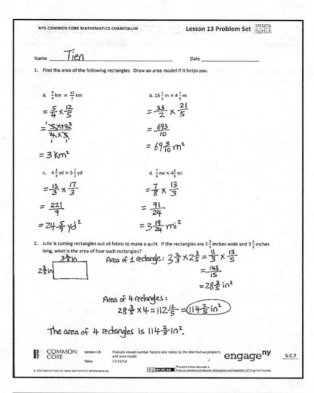

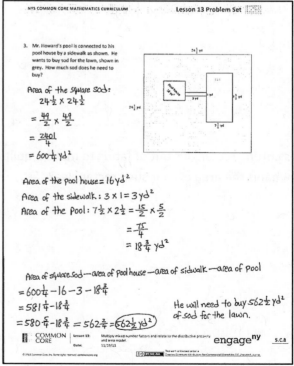

Lesson 13:	Multiply mixed number factors, and relate to the distributive property and area model.
Date:	1/10/14

5.C.45

© 2014 Common Core, Inc. All rights reserved. commoncore.org

Name _____ Date _____

1. Find the area of the following rectangles. Draw an area model if it helps you.

   a. $\frac{5}{4}$ km × $\frac{12}{5}$ km

   b. $16\frac{1}{2}$ m × $4\frac{1}{5}$ m

   c. $4\frac{1}{3}$ yd × $5\frac{2}{3}$ yd

   d. $\frac{7}{8}$ mi × $4\frac{1}{3}$ mi

2. Julie is cutting rectangles out of fabric to make a quilt. If the rectangles are $2\frac{3}{5}$ inches wide and $3\frac{2}{3}$ inches long, what is the area of four such rectangles?

Lesson 13:	Multiply mixed number factors, and relate to the distributive property and area model.
Date:	1/10/14

5.C.4

© 2014 Common Core, Inc. All rights reserved. commoncore.org

3. Mr. Howard's pool is connected to his pool house by a sidewalk as shown. He wants to buy sod for the lawn, shown in grey. How much sod does he need to buy?

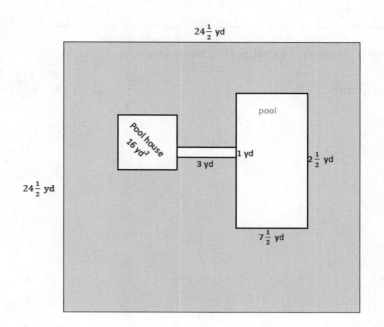

COMMON CORE

Lesson 13:   Multiply mixed number factors, and relate to the distributive property and area model.

Date: 1/10/14

5.C.47

© 2014 Common Core, Inc. All rights reserved. **commoncore.org**

Name _____   Date _____

Find the area. Draw an area model if it helps you.

1. $\frac{7}{2}$ mm × $\frac{14}{5}$ mm

2. $5\frac{7}{8}$ km × $\frac{18}{4}$ km

Lesson 13:	Multiply mixed number factors, and relate to the distributive property and area model.
Date:	1/10/14

5.C.4

© 2014 Common Core, Inc. All rights reserved. **commoncore.org**

Name _____   Date _____

1. Find the area of the following rectangles. Draw an area model if it helps you.

   a. $\frac{8}{3}$ cm $\times \frac{24}{4}$ cm

   b. $2. \frac{32}{5}$ ft $\times 3\frac{3}{8}$ ft

   c. $5\frac{4}{6}$ in $\times 4\frac{3}{5}$ in

   d. $4. \frac{5}{7}$ m $\times 6\frac{3}{5}$ m

2. Chris is making a table top from some leftover tiles. He has 9 tiles that measure $3\frac{1}{8}$ inches long and $2\frac{3}{4}$ inches wide. What is the area he can cover with these tiles?

COMMON CORE™   Lesson 13:   Multiply mixed number factors, and relate to the distributive property
                      and area model.
          Date: 1/10/14

5.C.49

© 2014 Common Core, Inc. All rights reserved. commoncore.org

3. A hotel is recarpeting a section of the lobby. Carpet covers the part of the floor as shown below in grey. How many square feet of carpeting will be needed?

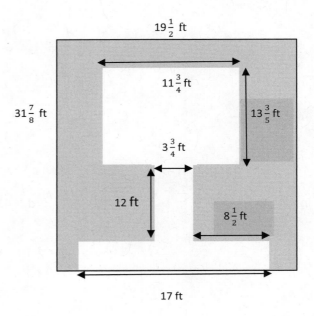

COMMON CORE | **Lesson 13:** | Multiply mixed number factors, and relate to the distributive property and area model.
| **Date:** | 1/10/14

5.C.5

© 2014 Common Core, Inc. All rights reserved. **commoncore.org**

Lesson 14

Objective: Solve real world problems involving area of figures with fractional side lengths using visual models and/or equations.

Suggested Lesson Structure

■ Fluency Practice   (12 minutes)
  Concept Development   (38 minutes)
■ Student Debrief   (10 minutes)
  Total Time   **(60 minutes)**

Fluency Practice (12 minutes)

▪ Multiply Fractions **5.NF.4**   (4 minutes)
▪ Find the Volume **5.MD.5c**   (5 minutes)
▪ Physiometry **4.G.1**   (3 minutes)

Multiply Fractions (4 minutes)

Materials: (S) Personal white boards

Note: This fluency reviews G5–M4–Lessons 13–16.

T: (Write $\frac{1}{2} \times \frac{1}{4}$.) Say the multiplication number sentence.

S: $\frac{1}{2} \times \frac{1}{4} = \frac{1}{8}$.

Continue the process with $\frac{1}{2} \times \frac{1}{5}$ and $\frac{1}{2} \times \frac{1}{9}$.

T: (Write $\frac{1}{2} \times \frac{1}{8}$.) Write the number sentence.

S: (Write $\frac{1}{2} \times \frac{1}{8} = \frac{1}{16}$.)

T: (Write $\frac{1}{2} \times \frac{5}{8}$.) Say the multiplication sentence.

S: $\frac{1}{2} \times \frac{5}{8} = \frac{5}{16}$.

Repeat the process with $\frac{1}{4} \times \frac{5}{5}$, $\frac{1}{3} \times \frac{9}{8}$, and $\frac{3}{4} \times \frac{1}{7}$.

T: (Write $\frac{3}{4} \times \frac{3}{5}$.) Write the multiplication sentence.

S: (Write $\frac{3}{4} \times \frac{3}{5} = \frac{9}{20}$.)

Lesson 14:	Solve real world problems involving area of figures with fractional side lengths using visual models and/or equations.	5.C.51
Date:	1/10/14	

© 2014 Common Core, Inc. All rights reserved. **commoncore.org**

Continue the process with $\frac{2}{3} \times \frac{3}{8}$.

T: (Write $\frac{1}{4} \times \frac{5}{12}$.) On your boards, write the number sentence.

S: (Write $\frac{1}{4} \times \frac{5}{8} = \frac{5}{32}$.)

T: (Write $\frac{2}{3} \times \frac{3}{2}$.) On your boards, write the number sentence.

S: (Write $\frac{2}{3} \times \frac{3}{2} = \frac{6}{6} = 1$.)

Find the Volume (5 minutes)

Materials: (S) Personal white boards

Note: This fluency reviews volume concepts and formulas.

T: (Project a prism 3 units × 2 units × 7 units. Write V = ___ units × ___ units × ___ units.) Find the volume.

S: (Write 42 units³ = 4 units × 2 units × 3 units.)

T: How many layers of 6 cubes are in the prism?

S: 7 layers.

T: Write a multiplication sentence to find the volume starting with the number of layers.

S: (Write 7 × 6 units³ = 42 units³.)

T: How many layers of 21 cubes are there?

S: 2 layers.

T: Write a multiplication sentence to find the volume starting with the number of layers.

S: (Write 2 × 21 units³ = 42 units³.)

T: How many layers of 14 cubes are there?

S: 3 layers.

T: Write a multiplication sentence to find the volume starting with the number of layers.

S: (Write 3 × 14 units³ = 42 units³.)

Repeat process for the other prisms.

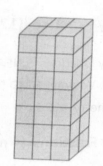
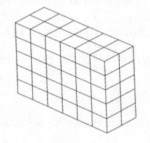
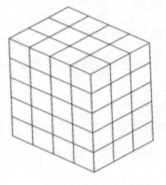

Physiometry (3 minutes)

Materials: (S) Personal white boards

Note: Kinesthetic memory is strong memory. This fluency prepares students for G5–M5–Lesson 16.

T: Stand up.

Lesson 14:   Solve real world problems involving area of figures with fractional side

Date: 1/10/14

5.C.

© 2014 Common Core, Inc. All rights reserved. commoncore.org

S: (Stand up.)

T: (Point at side wall.) Point to the wall that runs parallel to the one I'm pointing to.

S: (Point to the opposite wall.)

T: (Point to back wall.)

S: (Point to front wall.)

T: (Point to side wall.)

S: (Point to the opposite side wall.)

T: (Point at front wall.)

S: (Point at back wall.)

T: (Stretch one arm up, directly at the ceiling. Stretch the other arm directly towards a wall, parallel to the floor.) What type of angle do you think I'm modeling with my arms?

S: Right angle.

T: Model a right angle with your arms.

S: (Stretch one arm up, directly at the ceiling. Stretch another arm directly towards a wall, parallel to the floor.)

T: (Stretch the arm pointing towards a wall directly up towards the ceiling. Move the arm pointing towards the ceiling so that it points directly towards the opposite wall.) Model another right angle.

S: (Stretch the arm pointing towards a wall directly up towards the ceiling. Move the arm pointing towards the ceiling so that it points directly towards the opposite wall.)

Concept Development (38 minutes)

Materials: (S) Problem Set

Note: The Problem Set has been incorporated into the Concept Development. The problems in today's lesson can be time intensive. It may be that only two or three problems can be solved in the time allowed. Students will approach representing these problems from many perspectives. Allow students the flexibility to use the approach that makes the most sense to them.

Suggested Delivery of Instruction for Solving Lesson 14's Word Problems

1. Model the problem.

Have two pairs of student who can successfully model the problem work at the board while the others work independently or in pairs at their seats. Review the following questions before beginning the first problem:

- Can you draw something? This may or may not be a tape diagram today. An area model may be more appropriate.
- What can you draw?
- What conclusions can you make from your drawing?

As students work, circulate. Reiterate the questions above. After two minutes, have the two pairs of students share only their labeled diagrams. For about one minute, have the demonstrating students receive and

---

Lesson 14: Solve real world problems involving area of figures with fractional side
lengths using visual models and/or equations.

Date: 1/10/14

© 2014 Common Core, Inc. All rights reserved. commoncore.org

respond to feedback and questions from their peers.

2. Calculate to solve and write a statement.

Give everyone two minutes to finish work on that question, sharing their work and thinking with a peer. All should write their equations and statements of the answer.

3. Assess the solution for reasonableness.

Give students one to two minutes to assess and explain the reasonableness of their solution.

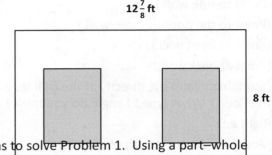

Problem 1

George decided to paint a wall with two windows. Both windows are $3\frac{1}{2}$ ft by $4\frac{1}{2}$ ft rectangles. Find the area the paint needs to cover. Students must keep track of three different areas to solve Problem 1. Using a part–whole tape diagram to represent these areas may be helpful to some students, while others may find using the area model to be more helpful. Students have choices in strategy for computing the areas as well. All may choose to use the distributive property. Others may choose to multiply improper fractions. Once students have solved, ask them to justify their choice of strategy. Were they able to tell which strategy to use from the beginning? Did they change direction once they began? If so, why? Flexibility in thinking about these types of problems should be a focus.

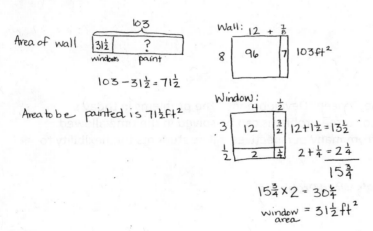

Problem 2

Joe uses square tiles, some of which he cuts in half, to make the figure below. If each square tile has a side length of $2\frac{1}{2}$ inches, what is total area of the figure?

The presence of the triangles in the design may prove challenging for some students. Students who understand area as a procedure of multiplying sides, but do not understand the meaning of area may need scaffolding to help them reason about mentally reassembling the 6 halves to find 3 whole tiles.

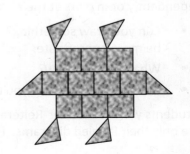

Lesson 14:   Solve real world problems involving area of figures with fractional side
              lengths using visual models and/or equations.

Date: 1/10/14

© 2014 Common Core, Inc. All rights reserved. commoncore.org

5.C.

10 whole tiles + 6 half tiles = 13 tiles

Area of a tile: $2\frac{1}{2} \times 2\frac{1}{2}$ in

$13 \times 6\frac{1}{4}$ in² = $81\frac{1}{4}$ in²

$6\frac{1}{4}$ in²

$$\begin{array}{r} 13 \\ \times\ 6 \\ \hline 78 \end{array}$$

$\frac{13}{4} = 3\frac{1}{4}$

The total area is $81\frac{1}{4}$ square inches.

$\frac{5}{2} \times \frac{5}{2} = \frac{25}{4} = 6\frac{1}{4}$

All tiles: $6\frac{1}{4} \times 13 = (6 \times 13) + (\frac{1}{4} \times 13)$

$= 78 + \frac{13}{4}$

$= 78 + 3\frac{3}{4}$

$= 81\frac{1}{4}$

NOTES ON MULTIPLE MEANS OF EXPRESSION:

If students are struggling with this problem, give them 13 square units and allow them to make designs with the tiles and find the areas. They will quickly see that the layout of the tiles does not change the area the tiles cover. They can then recreate the design in Problem 2 physically re-assembling the half tiles as necessary to reason about the wholes.

Problem 3

All-In-One Carpets is installing carpeting in three rooms. How many square feet of carpet are needed to carpet all three?

While this problem is a fairly straightforward, additive area problem, an added complexity occurs at finding the dimensions of Room C. The complexity of this problem also lies in the need to keep three different areas organized before finding the total area. Again, once students have had opportunity to work through the protocol, discuss the pros and cons of various approaches, including the reasoning for their choice of strategy.

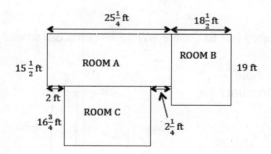

NOTES ON MULTIPLE MEANS OF ENGAGEMENT:

Problem 3 might be extended by inviting students to research actual carpet prices from local ads or the internet and calculate what such a project might cost in real life. Comparison between the costs of using different types of flooring (hardwood versus carpet, for example) may also be made.

© 2014 Common Core, Inc. All rights reserved. commoncore.org

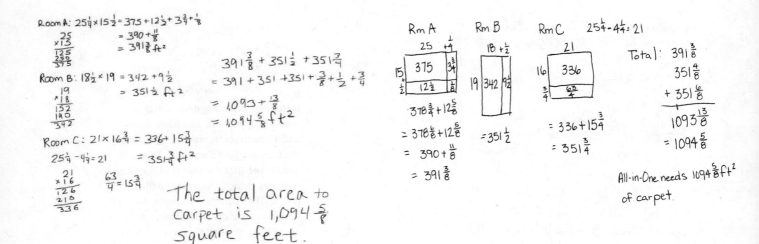

Room A: $25\frac{1}{4} \times 15\frac{1}{2} = 375 + 12\frac{1}{2} + 3\frac{3}{4} + \frac{1}{8}$
$ = 390 + \frac{11}{8}$
$ = 391\frac{3}{8}$ ft²

$\begin{array}{r} 25 \\ \times 15 \\ \hline 125 \\ 250 \\ \hline 375 \end{array}$

Room B: $18\frac{1}{2} \times 19 = 342 + 9\frac{1}{2}$
$ = 351\frac{1}{2}$ ft²

$\begin{array}{r} 19 \\ \times 18 \\ \hline 152 \\ 190 \\ \hline 342 \end{array}$

Room C: $21 \times 16\frac{3}{4} = 336 + 15\frac{3}{4}$
$25\frac{1}{4} - 4\frac{1}{4} = 21 \quad = 351\frac{3}{4}$ ft²

$\begin{array}{r} 21 \\ \times 16 \\ \hline 126 \\ 210 \\ \hline 336 \end{array}$ $\frac{63}{4} = 15\frac{3}{4}$

$391\frac{3}{8} + 351\frac{1}{2} + 351\frac{3}{4}$
$= 391 + 351 + 351 + \frac{3}{8} + \frac{1}{2} + \frac{3}{4}$
$= 1{,}093 + \frac{13}{8}$
$= 1{,}094\frac{5}{8}$ ft²

The total area to carpet is 1,094 $\frac{5}{8}$ square feet.

Rm A   Rm B   Rm C $25\frac{1}{4} - 4\frac{1}{4} = 21$

Total: $391\frac{3}{8}$
$351\frac{4}{8}$
$+ 351\frac{6}{8}$
$\overline{1093\frac{13}{8}}$
$= 1094\frac{5}{8}$

All-in-One needs $1094\frac{5}{8}$ft² of carpet.

Problem 4

Mr. Johnson needs to buy sod for his front lawn.

a. If the lawn measures $36\frac{2}{3}$ ft by $45\frac{1}{6}$ ft, how many square feet of sod will he need?

b. If sod is only sold in whole square feet, how much will Mr. Johnson have to pay?

Sod Prices

Area	Price per square foot
First 1,000 sq ft	$0.27
Next 500 sq ft	$0.22
Additional square feet	$0.19

The dimensions of the yard are larger than any others in the Problem Set to encourage use of the distributive property to find the total area. Because the total area ($1{,}656\frac{1}{9}$ ft²) is numerically closer to 1,656, students may be tempted to round down. Reasoning about the $\frac{1}{9}$ ft² area can provide an opportunity to discuss the pros and cons of sodding that last fraction of a square foot. In the final component of the protocol, ask the following or similar questions:

- Is it worth the extra money for such a small amount of area left to cover? While 19 cents is a small cost, what if the sod had been more expensive?

- What if the costs had been structured so that that last whole square foot of sod had lowered the price of the entire amount?

- What could Mr. Johnson do with the other 8 ninths?

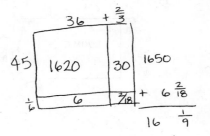

a. $36\frac{2}{3} \times 45\frac{1}{6}$

$\begin{array}{r} 45 \\ \times 36 \\ \hline 270 \\ 1350 \\ \hline 1{,}620 \end{array}$

$36 \times \frac{1}{6} = 6$
$45 \times \frac{2}{3} = 30$
$\frac{2}{3} \times \frac{1}{6} = \frac{1}{9}$
$1{,}620 + 30 + 6 + \frac{1}{9} = 1{,}656\frac{1}{9}$

He needs $1{,}656\frac{1}{9}$ ft² of sod.

b. 1,657 whole s.f.:
$1000 \times \$0.27 = \$270.00$
$500 \times \$0.22 = \$110.00$
$157 \times \$0.19 = \$ \ 29.83$
$\overline{\$409.83}$

$\boxed{\$409.83}$

He will have to pay $409.83.

Mr Johnson needs to buy 1657 sq.ft of sod and it will cost $409.83.

© 2014 Common Core, Inc. All rights reserved. commoncore.org

Problem 5

Jennifer's class decides to make a quilt. Each of the 24 students will make a quilt square that is 8 inches on each side. When they sew the quilt together, every edge of each quilt square will lose $\frac{3}{4}$ inch.

    a.   Draw one way the squares could be arranged to make a rectangular quilt. Then find the perimeter of your arrangement.

    b.   Find the area of the quilt.

There are many ways to lay out the quilt squares. Allow students to draw their layout and then compare the perimeters. Ask the following questions:

- Does the difference in perimeter affect the area? Why or why not?

- Are there advantages to one arrangement of the blocks over another? (For example, lowering cost for an edging by minimizing the perimeter or fitting the dimensions of the quilt to a specific wall or bed size.)

Problem 5 harkens back to Problem 2, but with an added layer of complexity. Students might be asked to compare and contrast the two problems. In this problem, students must account for the seam allowances on all four sides of the quilt squares before finding the area. Students find that each quilt block becomes $6\frac{1}{2}$ inches square after sewing and may simply multiply this area by 24.

NOTES ON
MULTIPLE MEANS OF
ENGAGEMENT:

This problem may be extended for students who finish early. Ask them to find the arrangement that gives the largest perimeter, then the smallest. The problem can also be changed to having seams only between squares so there are three different square areas to calculate. Another extension could be offered by asking students to find the area of the seams. (Find the unfinished area of the 24 squares and subtract the finished area.)

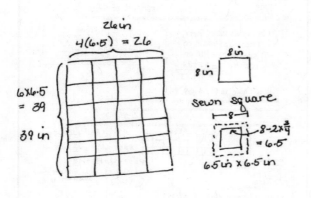

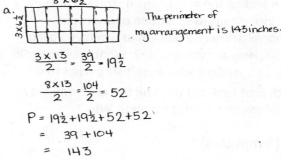

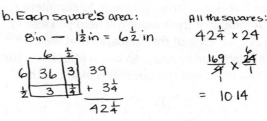

© 2014 Common Core, Inc. All rights reserved. commoncore.org

Student Debrief (10 minutes)

Lesson Objective: Solve real world problems involving area of figures with fractional side lengths using visual models and/or equations.

The Student Debrief is intended to invite reflection and active processing of the total lesson experience.

Invite students to review their solutions for the Problem Set. They should check work by comparing answers with a partner before going over answers as a class. Look for misconceptions or misunderstandings that can be addressed in the Debrief. Guide students in a conversation to debrief the Problem Set and process the lesson.

You may choose to use any combination of the questions below to lead the discussion.

- Do these problems remind you of any others that we've seen in this module? In what ways are they like other problems? In what ways are they different?

- What did you learn from looking at your classmates' drawings? Did that support your understanding of the problems in a deeper way? When you checked for reasonableness, what process did they use?

- When finding the areas, which strategy did you use more often—distribution or improper fractions? Is there a pattern to when you used which? How did you decide? What advice would you give a student who wasn't sure what to do?

- Which problems did you find the most difficult? Which one was easiest for you? Why?

Exit Ticket (3 minutes)

After the Student Debrief, instruct students to complete the Exit Ticket. A review of their work will help you assess the students' understanding of the concepts that were presented in the lesson today and plan more effectively for future lessons. You may read the questions aloud to the students.

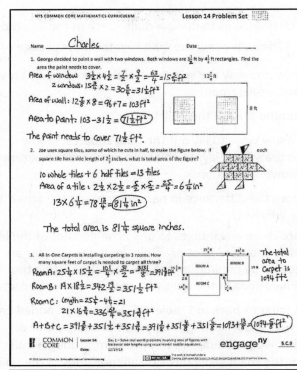

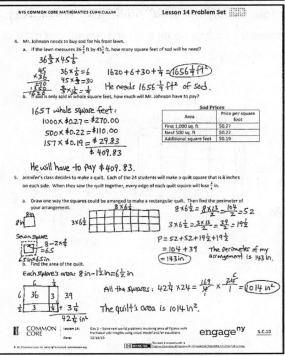

Lesson 14:
Date: 1/10/14

Solve real world problems involving area of figures with fractional side lengths using visual models and/or equations.

5.C.

© 2014 Common Core, Inc. All rights reserved. **commoncore.org**

Name _____ Date _____

1. George decided to paint a wall with two windows. Both windows are $3\frac{1}{2}$ ft by $4\frac{1}{2}$ ft rectangles. Find the area the paint needs to cover.

$12\frac{7}{8}$ ft

8 ft

2. Joe uses square tiles, some of which he cuts in half, to make the figure below. If each square tile has a side length of $2\frac{1}{2}$ inches, what is total area of the figure?

3. All-In-One Carpets is installing carpeting in three rooms. How many square feet of carpet are needed to carpet all three?

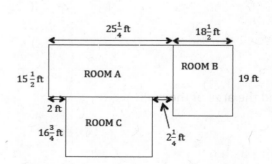

$25\frac{1}{4}$ ft $18\frac{1}{2}$ ft

ROOM B

$15\frac{1}{2}$ ft   ROOM A

19 ft

2 ft

ROOM C

$16\frac{3}{4}$ ft $2\frac{1}{4}$ ft

© 2014 Common Core, Inc. All rights reserved. commoncore.org

4. Mr. Johnson needs to buy sod for his front lawn.

   a. If the lawn measures $36\frac{2}{3}$ ft by $45\frac{1}{6}$ ft, how many square feet of sod will he need?

   b. If sod is only sold in whole square feet, how much will Mr. Johnson have to pay?

   Sod Prices

Area	Price per square foot
First 1,000 sq ft	$0.27
Next 500 sq ft	$0.22
Additional square feet	$0.19

5. Jennifer's class decides to make a quilt. Each of the 24 students will make a quilt square that is 8 inches on each side. When they sew the quilt together, every edge of each quilt square will lose $\frac{3}{4}$ inch.

   a. Draw one way the squares could be arranged to make a rectangular quilt. Then find the perimeter of your arrangement.

   b. Find the area of the quilt.

Lesson 14:   Solve real world problems involving area of figures with fractional side lengths using visual models and/or equations.

Date: 1/10/14

5.C.

© 2014 Common Core, Inc. All rights reserved. **commoncore.org**

Name _____   Date _____

1. Mr. Klimek made his wife a rectangular vegetable garden. The width is $5\frac{3}{4}$ ft and the length is $9\frac{4}{5}$ ft. What is the area of the garden?

Lesson 14:   Solve real world problems involving area of figures with fractional side
                 lengths using visual models and/or equations.
Date: 1/10/14

5.C.61

© 2014 Common Core, Inc. All rights reserved. commoncore.org

Name _____   Date _____

1. Mr. Albano wants to paint menus on the wall of his café in chalkboard paint. The grey area below shows where the rectangular menus will be. Each menu will measure 6 feet wide and $7\frac{1}{2}$ ft long.

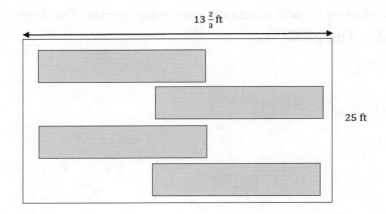

$13\frac{2}{3}$ ft

25 ft

a. How many square feet of menu space will Mr. Albano have?

b. What is the area of wall space that is not covered by chalkboard paint?

2. Mr. Albano wants to put tiles in the shape of a dinosaur at the front entrance. He will need to cut some tiles in half to make the figure. If each square tile is $4\frac{1}{4}$ inches on each side, what will the total area of the figure be?

3. A-Plus Glass is making windows for a new house that is being built. The box shows the list of sizes they must make.

> **15 windows** $4\frac{3}{4}$ ft long and $3\frac{3}{5}$ ft wide
>
> **7 windows** $2\frac{4}{5}$ ft wide and $6\frac{1}{2}$ ft long

a. How many square feet of glass will they need?

b. Each sheet of glass they use to make the windows is 9 feet long and $6\frac{1}{2}$ feet wide. How many sheets will they need in order to make the windows?

4. Mr. Johnson needs to buy seed for his backyard lawn.

a. If the lawn measures $40\frac{4}{5}$ ft by $50\frac{7}{8}$ ft, how many square feet of seed will he need?

b. One bag of seed will cover 500 square feet if he sets his seed spreader to its lowest setting and 300 square feet if he sets the spreader to its highest setting. How many bags of seed will he need if he uses the highest setting? The lowest setting?

| Lesson 14: | Solve real world problems involving area of figures with fractional side lengths using visual models and/or equations. |
| Date: | 1/10/14 |

5.C.63

© 2014 Common Core, Inc. All rights reserved. commoncore.org

Lesson 15

Objective: Solve real world problems involving area of figures with fractional side lengths using visual models and/or equations.

Suggested Lesson Structure

- ■ Fluency Practice   (10 minutes)
- ☐ Concept Development   (40 minutes)
- ■ Student Debrief   (10 minutes)
  - **Total Time**   **(60 minutes)**

Fluency Practice (10 minutes)

- Divide Whole Numbers by Unit Fractions and Unit Fractions by Whole Numbers **5.NF.7**   (6 minutes)
- Quadrilaterals **3.G.1**   (4 minutes)

Divide Whole Numbers by Unit Fractions and Unit Fractions by Whole Numbers (6 minutes)

Materials: (S) Personal white boards

Note: This fluency reviews G5–Module 4.

- T: (Write $1 \div \frac{1}{2}$.) Say the division sentence.
- S: $1 \div \frac{1}{2}$.
- T: How many halves are in 1?
- S: 2.
- T: (Write $1 \div \frac{1}{2} = 2$. Beneath it, write $2 \div \frac{1}{2}$.) How many halves are in 2?
- S: 4.
- T: (Write $2 \div \frac{1}{2} = 4$. Beneath it, write $3 \div \frac{1}{2}$.) How many halves are in 3?
- S: 6.
- T: (Write $3 \div \frac{1}{2} = 6$. Beneath it, write $7 \div \frac{1}{2}$.) Write the division sentence.
- S: (Write $7 \div \frac{1}{2} = 14$.)

Continue for the following possible suggestions: $1 \div \frac{1}{4}$, $2 \div \frac{1}{4}$, $9 \div \frac{1}{4}$, and $3 \div \frac{1}{5}$.

- T: (Write $\frac{1}{2} \div 2$.) Say the complete division sentence.

Lesson 15: Solve real world problems involving area of figures with fractional side
lengths using visual models and/or equations.

Date: 1/10/14

5.C.6

© 2014 Common Core, Inc. All rights reserved. **commoncore.org**

S: $\frac{1}{2} \div 2 = \frac{1}{4}$.

T: (Write $\frac{1}{2} \div 2 = \frac{1}{4}$. Beneath it, write $\frac{1}{2} \div 3$.) Say the complete division sentence.

S: $\frac{1}{2} \div 3 = \frac{1}{6}$.

T: (Write $\frac{1}{2} \div 3 = \frac{1}{6}$. Beneath it, write $\frac{1}{2} \div 4$.) Say the complete division sentence.

S: $\frac{1}{2} \div 4 = \frac{1}{8}$.

T: (Write $\frac{1}{2} \div 9 =$ _____.) Complete the number sentence.

S: (Write $\frac{1}{2} \div 9 = \frac{1}{18}$.)

Continue with the following possible sequence: $\frac{1}{5} \div 2$, $\frac{1}{5} \div 3$, $\frac{1}{5} \div 5$, and $\frac{1}{8} \div 4$.

Quadrilaterals (4 minutes)

Materials: (T) Shapes sheet

Note: This fluency reviews Grade 3 geometry concepts in anticipation of G5–Module 6 content. The sheet can be duplicated if preferred.

T: (Project the quadrilaterals template and the list of attributes.) Take one minute to discuss the attributes of the shapes you see. You can use the list to support you.

S: All have right angles. → All have straight sides. → They all have four sides. → B and G and maybe H and K have all equal sides. I'm not really sure.

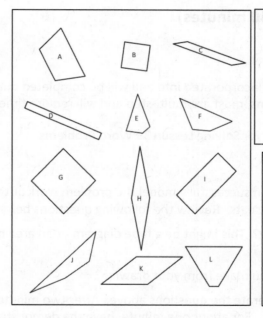

Attributes to Consider

Number of Sides

Length of Sides

Angle Measures

Shapes

Quadrilateral

Rhombus

Square

Rectangle

T: If we wanted to verify whether the sides are equal, what would we do?

S: Measure with a ruler.

T: What about the angles? How could you verify that they're right angles?

S: I could compare it to something that I know is a right angle. → I could use a set square. → I could use a protractor to measure.

T: Now, look at the shape names. Determine which shapes might fall into each category. (Post the shape names.)

Lesson 15:	Solve real world problems involving area of figures with fractional side lengths using visual models and/or equations.
Date:	1/10/14

5.C.65

© 2014 Common Core, Inc. All rights reserved. commoncore.org

S: B and G might be squares. → All of them are quadrilaterals. → H and K might be rhombuses. It's hard to know if their sides are equal. → D and I are rectangles. Oh yeah, and B and G are, too. → L and A look like trapezoids.

T: Which are quadrilaterals?

S: All of them.

T: Which shapes appear to be rectangles?

S: B, D, G, and I.

T: Which appear to have opposite sides of equal length but are not rectangles?

S: C, H, and K. → A and L have one pair of opposite sides that look the same.

T: Squares are rhombuses with right angles. Do you see any other shapes that might have four equal sides without right angles?

S: H and K.

Concept Development (40 minutes)

Materials: (S) Problem Set

Note: The Problem Set has been incorporated into and will be completed during the Concept Development. While there are only four problems, most are multi-step and will require time to solve.

Suggested Delivery of Instruction for Solving Lesson 39 Word Problems

1. Model the problem.

Have two pairs of student who can successfully model the problem work at the board while the others work independently or in pairs at their seats. Review the following questions before beginning the first problem:

- Can you draw something? This might be a tape diagram or an area model.
- What can you draw?
- What conclusions can you make from your drawing?

As students work, circulate. Reiterate the questions above. After two minutes, have the two pairs of students share only their labeled diagrams. For about one minute, have the demonstrating students receive and respond to feedback and questions from their peers.

2. Calculate to solve and write a statement.

Give everyone two minutes to finish work on that question, sharing their work and thinking with a peer. All should write their equations and statements of the answer.

3. Assess the solution for reasonableness.

Give students one to two minutes to assess and explain the reasonableness of their solution.

© 2014 Common Core, Inc. All rights reserved. commoncore.org

Problem 1

The length of a flowerbed is 4 times as long as its width. If the width is $\frac{3}{8}$ meter, what is the area?

While this problem is quite simple to calculate, two complexities must be navigated. First, the length is not given. Second, the resulting area is less than a whole meter. Once students have arrived at a solution, ask if their result makes sense and why. If students need support, discuss what this might look like if it were tiled. The length of the bed necessitates that 2 whole tiles be used. (How is it that the area is less than 1?) Students might draw or represent the problem with concrete materials to explain their thinking. The folding for these units may prove challenging but worthwhile, as these types of problems are often done procedurally by students rather than with a deep understanding of what their answer represents. As in G5–M5–Lesson 14, continue to have students explain their choice of strategy in terms of efficiency. When students are sharing their approaches with the class, encourage those who had difficulty to ask how the presenters got started with their drawing and calculations. Also encourage students to explain any false starts they experienced when solving and how and why their thinking changed.

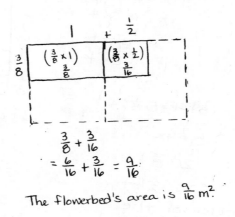

Problem 2

Mrs. Johnson grows herbs in square plots. Her basil plot measures $\frac{5}{8}$ yd on each side.

a. Find the total area of the basil plot.
b. Mrs. Johnson puts a fence around the basil. If the fence is 2 ft from the edge of the garden on each side, what is the perimeter of the fence?
c. What is the total area that the fence encloses?

As in Problem 1, the fraction multiplication involved in completing Part (a) is not rigorous. However, this problem offers an opportunity to explore the relationships of square yards to square feet and the importance of understanding the actual size of such units. The expression of the area as $\frac{25}{64}$ yd^2 may be conceptually challenging for students. They might be encouraged to relate this to a benchmark of 1 half or 1 third square yard (which is 3 square feet). Students might be asked to show what a tiling of this garden plot would look like.

Lesson 15:	Solve real world problems involving area of figures with fractional side lengths using visual models and/or equations.
Date:	1/10/14

5.C.67

© 2014 Common Core, Inc. All rights reserved. commoncore.org

It may even be helpful to use yardsticks to show the actual size of the herb plot. The area expressed as a bit more than 5 square feet may be surprising to students. Help students make connections to the shading models of G5–Module 4 and how the representation of the area model for the basil plot compares and contrasts to the representation of fraction multiplication. Part (b) offers a bit of complexity in that the dimensions of the garden are given in yards, yet the distance from the garden to the fence is given in feet. Part (c) requires that students use the fence measurements to find the total area enclosed by the fence. Multiple methods may be used to accomplish this.

NOTES ON MULTIPLE MEANS OF ENGAGEMENT:

Problem 2 may be extended by having student convert the fence perimeter back into yards and the fenced area back into square yards. The understanding that $1 \text{ yd}^2 = 9 \text{ ft}^2$ makes this an interesting challenge.

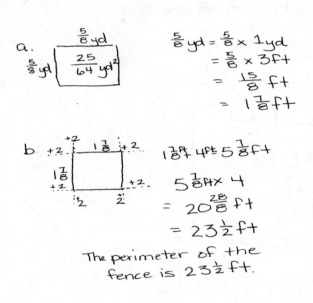

Problem 3

Janet bought 5 yards of fabric $2\frac{1}{4}$ feet wide to make curtains. She used $\frac{1}{3}$ of the fabric to make a long set of curtains and the rest to make 4 short sets.

- a. Find the area of the fabric she used for the long set of curtains.
- b. Find the area of the fabric she used for each of the short sets.

As in Problem 2, there are different units within a multi-step problem. After students have solved, allow them to share whether they converted both measurements to feet or yards and the advantages and disadvantages of both. A discussion of the relationship of the square yards to the square feet may also be fruitful. Discuss the various strategies students may have used to find the fabric left for the shorter curtains.

Lesson 15: Solve real world problems involving area of figures with fractional side lengths using visual models and/or equations.

Date: 1/10/14

5.C.6

© 2014 Common Core, Inc. All rights reserved. commoncore.org

Total area of fabric
15ft

2ft   30ft²
+
¼ft   3¾ ft²

= 33¾ft²

a. $33\frac{3}{4} \times \frac{1}{3}$

$= (33 \times \frac{1}{3}) + (\frac{3}{4} \times \frac{1}{3})$

$= 11 + \frac{1}{4}$

$= 11\frac{1}{4} . ft²$

The area of the long curtain
is $11\frac{1}{4} ft²$

b. $33\frac{3}{4} - 11\frac{1}{4} = 22\frac{1}{2}$

$22\frac{1}{2} \times \frac{1}{4}$

$= (22 \times \frac{1}{4}) + (\frac{1}{2} \times \frac{1}{4})$

$= 5\frac{1}{2} + \frac{1}{8}$

$= 5\frac{5}{8}$

The area of each set
of short curtains is $5\frac{5}{8}ft²$.

Problem 4

All wire is used to make 3 rectangles: A, B, and C. Rectangle B's dimensions are $\frac{3}{5}$ cm larger than Rectangle A's dimensions, and Rectangle C's dimensions are $\frac{3}{5}$ cm larger than Rectangle B's dimensions. Rectangle A is 2 cm by $3\frac{1}{5}$ cm.

   a. What is the total area of all three rectangles?
   b. If a 40-cm coil of wire was used to form the rectangles, how much wire is left?

The complexity of this problem stems from students making sense of the way each rectangle increases in dimension. As always, encourage students to start by drawing each of the three rectangles. As the denominators are easily expressed as hundredths, some students may use decimals to calculate these areas. Should this occur, help make the connection for other students to that learning from G5–Module 4.

NOTES ON
MULTIPLE MEANS OF
ENGAGEMENT:

Encourage students to look for patterns in the growth of the perimeters. A challenge could be offered to tell the perimeter of the fifth or tenth rectangle in the series.

For Part (b), students must shift their thinking to perimeter and use the outer dimensions of the rectangles to find the total amount of wire used. Again, students may use decimals for the calculations. Be sure to have students compare their decimal and fraction solutions with one another for equivalence and explain why they chose each type of fraction.

$3\frac{1}{5}$ [2] $\square$ $3\frac{4}{5}$ [$2\frac{3}{5}$] $\square$ $4\frac{2}{5}$ [$3\frac{1}{5}$] $\square$

                    2
3   6
$\frac{1}{5}$ $\frac{2}{5}$
$= 6\frac{2}{5}$ cm²

         2      $\frac{3}{5}$
3   6 $\frac{4}{5}$ $7\frac{4}{5}$ cm²
$\frac{4}{5}$ $1\frac{3}{5}$ $\frac{12}{25}$ $+ 2\frac{2}{25}$cm²
                      $9\frac{22}{25}$ cm²

          3   5
4   12 $\frac{4}{5}$ $12\frac{4}{5}$ cm²
$\frac{2}{5}$ $1\frac{1}{5}$ $\frac{2}{25}$ $+ 1\frac{7}{25}$ cm²
                        $14\frac{2}{25}$ cm²

COMMON CORE   Lesson 15:   Solve real world problems involving area of figures with fractional side
                                    lengths using visual models and/or equations.   5.C.69
               Date: 1/10/14

© 2014 Common Core, Inc. All rights reserved. commoncore.org

a Total area:

$6\frac{2}{5} + 9\frac{22}{25} + 14\frac{2}{25}$

$= 6\frac{10}{25} + 9\frac{22}{25} + 14\frac{2}{25}$

$= 29\frac{34}{25}$

$= 30\frac{9}{25}$ cm²

$= 30.36$ cm²

The total area is $30\frac{9}{25}$ cm².

a $2 \times 3.2 = 6.4$

$2.6 \times 3.8 = 9.88$ •

$3.2 \times 4.4 = 14.08$

$\overline{30.36}$

The total area is 30.36 cm².

b. Perimeter:

#1 $(2\times2)+(2\times3.2)$
$= 4 + 6.4$
$= 10.4$

#2 $(2\times2.6)+(2\times3.8)$
$= 5.2 + 7.6$
$= 12.8$

#3 $(2\times3.2)+(2\times4.4)$
$= 6.4 + 8.8$
$= 15.2$

Perimeter:

#1 $2 \times 5\frac{1}{5} = 10\frac{2}{5}$

#2 $2 \times 6\frac{2}{5} = 12\frac{4}{5}$

#3 $2 \times 7\frac{3}{5} = 15\frac{1}{5}$

$40 - 38\frac{2}{5}$
$= 1\frac{3}{5}$

Total Perimeter $38\frac{2}{5}$

There was $1\frac{3}{5}$ cm of wire left.

Total perimeter:

$10.4\text{cm} + 12.8\text{cm} + 15.2\text{cm} = 38.4\text{cm}$

$40\text{cm} - 38.4\text{cm} = 1.6\text{cm}$

There was 1.6 cm of wire left

Student Debrief (10 minutes)

Lesson Objective: Solve real world problems involving area of figures with fractional side lengths using visual models and/or equations.

The Student Debrief is intended to invite reflection and active processing of the total lesson experience.

Invite students to review their solutions for the Problem Set. They should check work by comparing answers with a partner before going over answers as a class. Look for misconceptions or misunderstandings that can be addressed in the Debrief. Guide students in a conversation to debrief the Problem Set and process the lesson.

You may choose to use any combination of the questions below to lead the discussion.

- Compare the problems for which the distributive property seems most efficient and the problems for which multiplying improper fractions (or using decimals to multiply) seems so. What influences your choice of strategy?

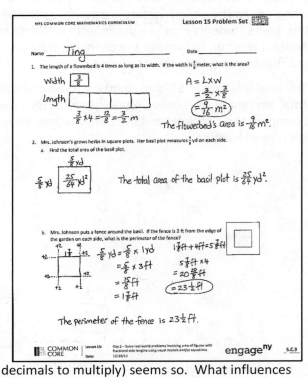

Lesson 15: | Solve real world problems involving area of figures with fractional side lengths using visual models and/or equations.

Date: | 1/10/14

5.C.7

© 2014 Common Core, Inc. All rights reserved. commoncore.org

- Sort problems from yesterday's and today's lessons (G5–M5–Lessons 14 and 15) from simple to complex. What do the problems have in common? Have students compare their sort to a partner's.

Exit Ticket (3 minutes)

After the Student Debrief, instruct students to complete the Exit Ticket. A review of their work will help you assess the students' understanding of the concepts that were presented in the lesson today and plan more effectively for future lessons. You may read the questions aloud to the students.

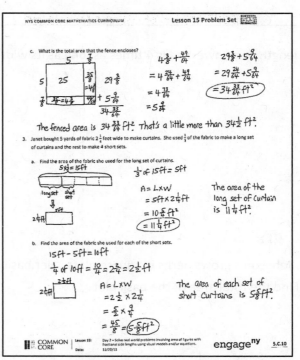

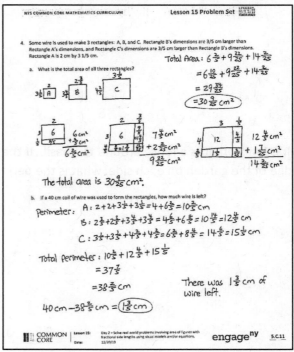

COMMON CORE

Lesson 15:   Solve real world problems involving area of figures with fractional side
              lengths using visual models and/or equations.
Date: 1/10/14

5.C.71

© 2014 Common Core, Inc. All rights reserved. commoncore.org

Name _____   Date _____

1. The length of a flowerbed is 4 times as long as its width. If the width is $\frac{3}{8}$ meter, what is the area?

2. Mrs. Johnson's grows herbs in square plots. Her basil plot measures $\frac{5}{8}$ yd on each side.

    a. Find the total area of the basil plot.

    b. Mrs. Johnson puts a fence around the basil. If the fence is 2 ft from the
        edge of the garden on each side, what is the perimeter of the fence?

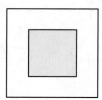

COMMON
CORE™

| Lesson 15:   Solve real world problems involving area of figures with fractional side
             lengths using visual models and/or equations.
| Date: 1/10/14

5.C.7

© 2014 Common Core, Inc. All rights reserved. commoncore.org

c. What is the total area that the fence encloses?

3. Janet bought 5 yards of fabric $2\frac{1}{4}$ feet wide to make curtains. She used $\frac{1}{3}$ of the fabric to make a long set of curtains and the rest to make 4 short sets.

a. Find the area of the fabric she used for the long set of curtains.

b. Find the area of the fabric she used for each of the short sets.

© 2014 Common Core, Inc. All rights reserved. commoncore.org

4. All wire is used to make 3 rectangles: A, B, and C. Rectangle B's dimensions are $\frac{3}{5}$ cm larger than Rectangle A's dimensions, and Rectangle C's dimensions are $\frac{3}{5}$ cm larger than Rectangle B's dimensions. Rectangle A is 2 cm by $3\frac{1}{5}$ cm.

    a.   What is the total area of all three rectangles?

    b.   If a 40-cm çoil of wire was used to form the rectangles, how much wire is left?

Lesson 15:   Solve real world problems involving area of figures with fractional side
             lengths using visual models and/or equations.
Date: 1/10/14

5.C.7

© 2014 Common Core, Inc. All rights reserved. **commoncore.org**

Name _____   Date _____

Wheat grass is grown in planters that are $3\frac{1}{2}$ inch by $1\frac{3}{4}$ inch. If there is a 6 × 6 array of these planters with no space between them, what is the area of the array?

COMMON CORE | **Lesson 15:** Solve real world problems involving area of figures with fractional side lengths using visual models and/or equations.
Date: 1/10/14

5.C.75

© 2014 Common Core, Inc. All rights reserved. **commoncore.org**

Name _____ Date _____

1. The width of a picnic table is 3 times its length. If the length is $\frac{5}{6}$ yd long, what is the area in square feet?

2. A painting company will paint this wall. The homeowner gives them the following dimensions:

   Window A is $6\frac{1}{4}$ ft × $5\frac{3}{4}$ ft

   Window B is $3\frac{1}{8}$ ft × 4 ft

   Window C is $9\frac{1}{2}$ ft square

   Door D is 8 ft × 4 ft

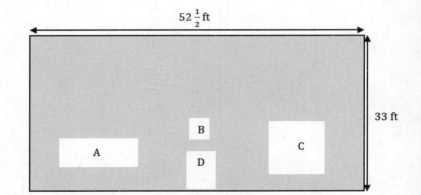

What is the area of the painted part of the wall?

COMMON CORE™

Lesson 15: Solve real world problems involving area of figures with fractional side lengths using visual models and/or equations.

Date: 1/10/14

5.C.7

© 2014 Common Core, Inc. All rights reserved. **commoncore.org**

3. A decorative wooden piece is made up of four rectangles as shown to the right. The smallest rectangle measures $4\frac{1}{2}$ inches by $7\frac{3}{4}$ inches. If $2\frac{1}{4}$ inches is added to each dimension as the rectangles get larger, what is the total area of the entire piece?

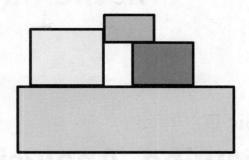

COMMON CORE

Lesson 15: Solve real world problems involving area of figures with fractional side lengths using visual models and/or equations.
Date: 1/10/14

5.C.77

© 2014 Common Core, Inc. All rights reserved. **commoncore.org**

Topic D

Drawing, Analysis, and Classification of Two-Dimensional Shapes

5.G.3, 5.G.4

Focus Standard:	5.G.3	Understand that attributes belonging to a category of two-dimensional figures also belong to all subcategories of that category. *For example, all rectangles have four right angles and squares are rectangles, so all squares have four right angles.*
	5.G.4	Classify two-dimensional figures in a hierarchy based on properties.
Instructional Days:	6	
Coherence -Links from:	G3–M7	Geometry and Measurement Word Problems
	G4–M4	Angle Measure and Plane Figures
-Links to:	G6–M4	Expressions and Equations

In Topic D, students draw two-dimensional shapes in order to analyze their attributes, and then use those attributes to classify them. Familiar figures, such as parallelograms, rhombuses, squares, and trapezoids, have all been defined in earlier grades, and by Grade 4, students have gained an understanding of shapes beyond the intuitive level. Grade 5 extends this understanding through an in-depth analysis of the properties and defining attributes of quadrilaterals.

Grade 4's work with the protractor is applied in this topic in order to construct various quadrilaterals. Using measurement tools illuminates the attributes used to define and recognize each quadrilateral (**5.G.3**). Students see, for example, that the same process that they used to construct a parallelogram will also produce a rectangle when all angles are constructed to measure 90°. Students then analyze defining attributes and create a hierarchical classification of quadrilaterals (**5.G.4**).

Topic D:	Drawing, Analysis, and Classification of Two-Dimensional Shapes
Date:	1/10/14

5.D.1

© 2014 Common Core, Inc. All rights reserved. commoncore.org

A Teaching Sequence Towards Mastery of Drawing, Analysis, and Classification of Two-Dimensional Shapes
Objective 1: Draw trapezoids to clarify their attributes, and define trapezoids based on those attributes. (Lesson 16)
Objective 2: Draw parallelograms to clarify their attributes, and define parallelograms based on those attributes. (Lesson 17)
Objective 3: Draw rectangles and rhombuses to clarify their attributes, and define rectangles and rhombuses based on those attributes. (Lesson 18)
Objective 4: Draw kites and squares to clarify their attributes, and define kites and squares based on those attributes. (Lesson 19)
Objective 5: Classify two-dimensional figures in a hierarchy based on properties. (Lesson 20)
Objective 6: Draw and identify varied two-dimensional figures from given attributes. (Lesson 21)

© 2014 Common Core, Inc. All rights reserved. commoncore.org

Lesson 16

Objective: Draw trapezoids to clarify their attributes, and define trapezoids based on those attributes.

Suggested Lesson Structure

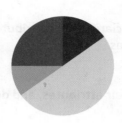

■ Fluency Practice   (9 minutes)
■ Application Problem   (6 minutes)
■ Concept Development   (30 minutes)
■ Student Debrief   (15 minutes)
  Total Time   **(60 minutes)**

Fluency Practice (9 minutes)

- Divide Whole Numbers by Unit Fractions and Unit Fractions by Whole Numbers **5.NF.7**   (5 minutes)
- Quadrilaterals **3.G.1**   (4 minutes)

Divide Whole Numbers by Unit Fractions and Unit Fractions by Whole Numbers (5 minutes)

Materials: (S) Personal white boards

Note: This fluency reviews G5–Module 4.

   T: (Write $1 \div \frac{1}{2}$.) Say the division expression.

   S: $1 \div \frac{1}{2}$.

   T: How many halves are in 1 one?

   S: 2.

   T: (Write $1 \div \frac{1}{2} = 2$. Beneath it, write $2 \div \frac{1}{2} =$_____.) How many halves are in 2 ones?

   S: 4.

   T: (Write $2 \div \frac{1}{2} = 4$. Beneath it, write $3 \div \frac{1}{2} =$_____.) How many halves are in 3 ones?

   S: 6.

   T: (Write $3 \div \frac{1}{2} = 6$. Beneath it, write $7 \div \frac{1}{2}$.) Write the division sentence.

   S: (Write $7 \div \frac{1}{2} = 14$.)

Continue with the following possible suggestions: $1 \div \frac{1}{4}$, $2 \div \frac{1}{4}$, $9 \div \frac{1}{4}$, and $3 \div \frac{1}{5}$.

Lesson 16:	Draw trapezoids to clarify their attributes, and define trapezoids based on those attributes.
Date:	1/10/14

5.D.3

© 2014 Common Core, Inc. All rights reserved. commoncore.org

T: (Write $\frac{1}{2} \div 2 =$ _____.) Say the division sentence with the answer.

S: $\frac{1}{2} \div 2 = \frac{1}{4}$.

T: (Write $\frac{1}{2} \div 2 = \frac{1}{4}$. Beneath it, write $\frac{1}{2} \div 3 =$ _____.) Say the division sentence with the answer.

S: $\frac{1}{2} \div 3 = \frac{1}{6}$.

T: (Write $\frac{1}{2} \div 3 = \frac{1}{6}$. Beneath it, write $\frac{1}{2} \div 4 =$ _____.) Say the division sentence with the answer.

S: $\frac{1}{2} \div 4 = \frac{1}{8}$.

T: (Write $\frac{1}{2} \div 9 =$ _____.) Complete the number sentence.

S: (Write $\frac{1}{2} \div 9 = \frac{1}{18}$.)

Continue with the following possible sequence: $\frac{1}{5} \div 2$, $\frac{1}{5} \div 3$, $\frac{1}{5} \div 5$, and $\frac{1}{8} \div 4$.

Quadrilaterals (4 minutes)

Materials: (T) Shape sheet from G5–M5–Lesson 15 (S) Personal white boards

Note: This fluency reviews Grade 3 geometry concepts in anticipation of G5–Module 5 content.

T: (Project the shape sheet that includes the following: square, rhombus that is not a square, rectangle that is not a square, and several quadrilaterals that are not squares, rhombuses, or rectangles.) How many sides are in each polygon?

S: 4.

T: On your boards, write down the name for any four-sided polygon.

S: (Write *quadrilateral*.)

T: (Point to the square.) This quadrilateral has four equal sides and four right angles. On your board, write what type of quadrilateral it is.

S: (Write *square*.)

T: Rhombuses are parallelograms with four equal sides. (Point to the rectangle.) Is this polygon a rhombus?

S: Yes.

T: Is it a rectangle?

S: Yes.

T: Is a square also a rhombus?

S: Yes!

T: (Point to the rhombus that is not a square.) This polygon has four equal sides. Is it a square?

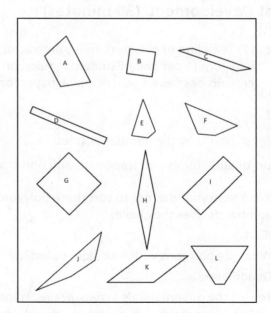

COMMON CORE

Lesson 16:   Draw trapezoids to clarify their attributes, and define trapezoids based on those attributes.

Date: 1/10/14

5.D.4

© 2014 Common Core, Inc. All rights reserved. **commoncore.org**

S: No.

T: Is a rhombus always a square?

S: No!

T: (Point to the rectangle that is not a square.) This polygon has four equal angles, but the sides are not equal. Write the name of this quadrilateral.

S: (Write *rectangle*. → *Parallelogram*. → *Trapezoid*.)

T: Draw a quadrilateral that is not a square, rhombus, or rectangle.

S: (Draw.)

Application Problem (6 minutes)

Kathy spent 3 fifths of her money on a necklace and 2 thirds of the remainder on a bracelet. If the bracelet cost $17, how much money did she have at first?

Note: Today's Application Problem should be a quick review of a fraction of a set as well as decimal multiplication from G5–Modules 2 and 4.

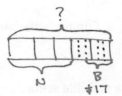

1 unit = 17 ÷ 4 = 4.25
15 units = 15 × 4.25 = 60 + 3.75
= 63.75

She had $63.75 at first.

Concept Development (30 minutes)

Materials: (T) Template of polygons, ruler, protractor, set square (or right angle template) (S) Collection of polygons (1 per pair of students), ruler, protractor, set square (or right angle template), scissors, crayons or colored pencils, blank paper for drawing

Problem 1

a. Sort polygons by the number of sides.

b. Sort quadrilaterals into trapezoids and non-trapezoids.

T: Work with your partner to sort these polygons by the number of sides they have.

S: (Sort.)

T: What are polygons with four sides called?

S: Quadrilaterals.

T: To sort the quadrilaterals in two groups, trapezoids and non-trapezoids, what attribute do you look for to separate the shapes?

S: We look for sides that are parallel. → Trapezoids have at least one set of parallel sides, so quadrilaterals with parallel sides go in the trapezoid pile.

T: Separate the trapezoids in your collection of quadrilaterals from the non-trapezoids.

NOTES ON MULTIPLE MEANS OF ENGAGEMENT:

Problem 1 in the Concept Development provides an opportunity for a quick formative assessment. If students have difficulty sorting and articulating attributes, consider a review of concepts from Grade 4–Module 4.

 **Lesson 16:** Draw trapezoids to clarify their attributes, and define trapezoids based on those attributes.
Date: 1/10/14

5.D.5

© 2014 Common Core, Inc. All rights reserved. **commoncore.org**

S: (Sort.)

T: Talk to your partner. How are the shapes you put in your trapezoid group alike? How are they different?

S: They all have four straight sides, but they don't all look the same. → They are all quadrilaterals, but they have different side lengths and angle measures. → All of the trapezoids are rhombuses, rectangles, or squares. → They all have at least one pair of sides that are parallel.

Problem 2

a. Draw a trapezoid according to the definition of a trapezoid.

b. Measure and label its angles to explore their relationships.

T: Look at our sort. I am going to ask you to draw a trapezoid in a minute. What attributes do you need to include? Turn and talk.

S: We'd have to draw four straight sides. → Two of the sides would need to be parallel to each other. → We could draw any of the shapes in our trapezoid pile. → If we have one set of parallel sides, we can draw a trapezoid.

T: Use your ruler and set square (or right angle template) to draw a pair of parallel lines on your blank paper positioned at any angle on the sheet.

MP.6 S: (Draw.)

T: Finish your trapezoid by drawing a third and fourth segment that cross the parallel pair of lines. Make sure they do not cross each other.

S: (Draw.)

T: Compare your trapezoids with your partner's. What's alike? What's different?

S: My horizontal parallel sides are closer together than my partner's. → My trapezoid is a rectangle, but my partner's isn't. → My trapezoid is taller than my partner's. → I have right angles in mine, but my partner does not.

NOTES ON DRAWING FIGURES:

If students need specific scaffolding for drawing figures, please see Grade 4– Module 4.

To draw parallel lines with a set square:

1. Draw a line.

2. Line up one side of the set square on the line.

3. Line up a ruler with the perpendicular side of the set square.

4. Slide the set square along the ruler until the desired place for a second line is reached.

5. Draw along the side of the set square to mark the second, parallel line.

6. Remove the set square and extend the second line with the ruler if necessary.

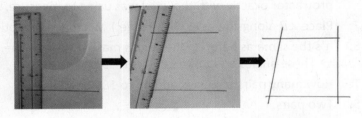

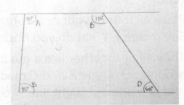

Lesson 16:   Draw trapezoids to clarify their attributes, and define trapezoids based on those attributes.

Date: 1/10/14

5.D.6

© 2014 Common Core, Inc. All rights reserved. commoncore.org

T: Label the angles of one of your trapezoids as A, B, C, and D. Now, measure the four interior angles of your trapezoid with your protractor and write the measurements inside each angle.

S: (Measure.)

T: Cut out your trapezoid.

S: (Cut.)

T: Cut your trapezoid into two parts by cutting between the parallel sides with a wavy cut. (As shown to the right.)

S: (Cut.)

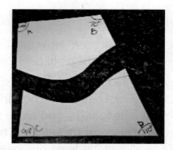

T: Place $\angle A$ alongside $\angle C$. (See image.) What do you notice in your trapezoid and in your partner's?

S: The angles line up. → The two angles make a straight line. → If I add the angles together, it is 180 degrees. → It is a straight line, but my angles only add up to something close to 180 degrees. → My partner's trapezoid did the same thing.

T: I heard you say that the angles make a straight line. What is the measure of a straight angle?

S: 180 degrees.

T: I also heard a few of you say that your angles didn't add up to exactly 180 degrees. How do you explain that?

S: It sure looked like a straight line, so maybe we read our protractor a little bit wrong. → I might not have lined up the protractor exactly with the line I was using to measure.

T: Place $\angle B$ alongside $\angle D$. (See image.) What do you notice?

S: It's the same as before. The angles make a straight line. → These angles add up to 180 degrees also.

T: How many pairs of angles add up to 180 degrees?

S: Two pairs.

T: Cut each part of your trapezoid into two pieces using a wavy cut.

S: (Cut.)

T: Place all four of your angles together at a point. (Demonstrate. See image.) What do you notice about the angles?

S: They all fit together like a puzzle. → The angles go all the way around. → Angle A and C made a straight line, and Angle B and D made a straight line. I could put the straight lines together. The two straight angles make 360 degrees.

T: How does this compare to your partner's trapezoid? Turn and talk.

S: It's the same in their trapezoid. → The angles in my partner's trapezoid weren't the same size as mine, but they still all fit together all the way around.

	Lesson 16:	Draw trapezoids to clarify their attributes, and define trapezoids based on those attributes.	5.D.7
	Date:	1/10/14	

© 2014 Common Core, Inc. All rights reserved. **commoncore.org**

T: (Distribute the Problem Set to students.) Let's practice drawing more trapezoids and thinking about their attributes by completing the Problem Set.

S: (Complete the Problem Set.)

Please note the extended time designated for the Debrief of today's lesson.

Problem Set (10 minutes)

Students should do their personal best to complete the Problem Set within the allotted 10 minutes. For some classes, it may be appropriate to modify the assignment by specifying which problems they work on first. All problems do not specify a method for solving. Students solve these problems using the RDW approach used for Application Problems. Note: Today's Problem Set should be kept for use in G5–M5–Lesson 17's Debrief as well.

Student Debrief (15 minutes)

Lesson Objective: Draw trapezoids to clarify their attributes, and define trapezoids based on those attributes.

The Student Debrief is intended to invite reflection and active processing of the total lesson experience.

Invite students to review their solutions for the Problem Set. They should check work by comparing answers with a partner before going over answers as a class. Look for misconceptions or misunderstandings that can be addressed in the Debrief. Guide students in a conversation to debrief the Problem Set and process the lesson.

You may choose to use any combination of the questions below to lead the discussion.

- Allow students to share the myriad trapezoids that are produced in Problem 1 of the Problem Set. Consolidate the lists of attributes students generated for trapezoids in Problem 4. (Where do these pairs seem to occur consistently? Is this true for all quadrilaterals? Just trapezoids?)

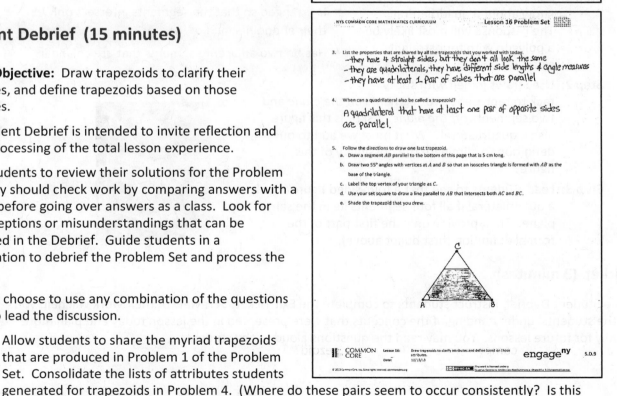

Lesson 16:   Draw trapezoids to clarify their attributes, and define trapezoids based on those attributes.
Date: 1/10/14

5.D.8

© 2014 Common Core, Inc. All rights reserved. commoncore.org

- Use the trapezoids that students produce in Problem 1 to articulate the formal definition of trapezoids. Post these definitions in the classroom for reference as the topic proceeds.

> **A trapezoid:**
> - Is a quadrilateral in which at least one pair of opposite sides is parallel.

- Begin the construction of the hierarchy diagram. (See the template following lesson.) Students might draw or glue examples of trapezoids and quadrilaterals and/or list attributes within the diagram. Encourage them to explain their placement of the figures in the hierarchy. Respond to the following statements with *true* or *false*. Explain your reasoning.

    - All trapezoids are quadrilaterals.
    - All quadrilaterals are trapezoids.

- The trapezoid you drew in Problem 5 is called an isosceles trapezoid. Think back to what you know about isosceles triangles; why is this a good name for this quadrilateral? How is it like some of the other trapezoids that you drew today? How is it different?

- Over the course of several days, students will be exploring the formal definition of a quadrilateral (see the boxed text on the right) through the examination of counter-examples.

> **Formal Definition of a Quadrilateral:**
> **(Only the first bullet is introduced today.)**
>
> - Consists of four different points A, B, C, D in the plane and four segments, $\overline{AB}, \overline{BC}, \overline{CD}, \overline{DA}$,
> - Is arranged so that the segments intersect only at their endpoints, and .
> - Has no two adjacent segments that are collinear.

  Step 1: Ask students to tell what they know about a quadrilateral. The response will most likely be a polygon with four straight sides.

  Step 2: Use straws joined with sticky tack to represent two segments *on the plane* and two segments *off the plane*. Ask: "Is this figure also a quadrilateral? What must we add to our definition to eliminate the possibility of this figure?"

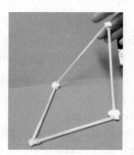

  Step 3: Lead students to see that a four-sided figure is only a quadrilateral if all four segments lie in the same plane. Then provide only the first part of the formal definition (first bullet above).

Exit Ticket (3 minutes)

After the Student Debrief, instruct students to complete the Exit Ticket. A review of their work will help you assess the students' understanding of the concepts that were presented in the lesson today and plan more effectively for future lessons. You may read the questions aloud to the students.

Lesson 16:	Draw trapezoids to clarify their attributes, and define trapezoids based on those attributes.
Date:	1/10/14

5.D.9

© 2014 Common Core, Inc. All rights reserved. commoncore.org

Name _____   Date _____

1. Draw a pair of parallel lines in each box. Then use the parallel lines to draw a trapezoid with the following:

No right angles.	Only 1 obtuse angle.
2 obtuse angles.	At least 1 right angle.

2. Use the trapezoids you drew to complete the tasks below.

   a. Measure the angles of the trapezoid with your protractor, and record the measurements on the figures.

   b. Use a marker or crayon to circle pairs of angles inside each trapezoid with a sum equal to 180°. Use a different color for each pair.

Lesson 16:   Draw trapezoids to clarify their attributes, and define trapezoids based on those attributes.

Date: 1/10/14

5.D.10

© 2014 Common Core, Inc. All rights reserved. commoncore.org

3. List the properties that are shared by all the trapezoids that you worked with today.

4. When can a quadrilateral also be called a trapezoid?

5. Follow the directions to draw one last trapezoid.
    a. Draw a segment $\overline{AB}$ parallel to the bottom of this page that is 5 cm long.
    b. Draw two 55° angles with vertices at A and B so that an isosceles triangle is formed with $\overline{AB}$ as the base of the triangle.
    c. Label the top vertex of your triangle as C.
    d. Use your set square to draw a line parallel to $\overline{AB}$ that intersects both $\overline{AC}$ and $\overline{BC}$.
    e. Shade the trapezoid that you drew.

COMMON CORE™ | **Lesson 16:**   Draw trapezoids to clarify their attributes, and define trapezoids based
on those attributes.

| **Date:**   1/10/14

5.D.1

© 2014 Common Core, Inc. All rights reserved. **commoncore.org**

Name _____ Date _____

1. Use a ruler and a set square to draw a trapezoid.

2. What attribute must be present for a quadrilateral to also be a trapezoid?

Lesson 16: Draw trapezoids to clarify their attributes, and define trapezoids based on those attributes.

Date: 1/10/14

5.D.12

© 2014 Common Core, Inc. All rights reserved. commoncore.org

Name _____ Date _____

1. Use a straightedge and the grid paper to draw:
   a. A trapezoid with exactly 2 right angles.   b. A trapezoid with no right angles.

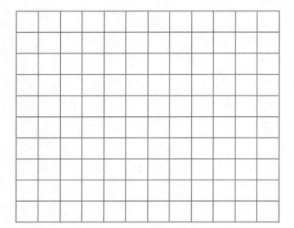   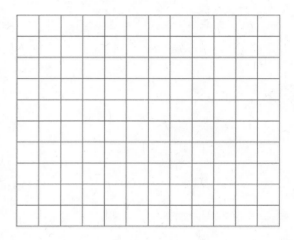

2. Kaplan incorrectly sorted some quadrilaterals into trapezoids and non-trapezoids as pictured below.
   a. Circle the shapes that are in the wrong group and tell why they are missorted.

Trapezoids	Non-Trapezoids

   b. Explain what tools would be necessary to use to verify the placement of all the trapezoids.

 | **Lesson 16:** Draw trapezoids to clarify their attributes, and define trapezoids based on those attributes.
Date: 1/10/14

5.D.1

© 2014 Common Core, Inc. All rights reserved. **commoncore.org**

3.   Use a straightedge to draw an isosceles trapezoid on the grid paper.

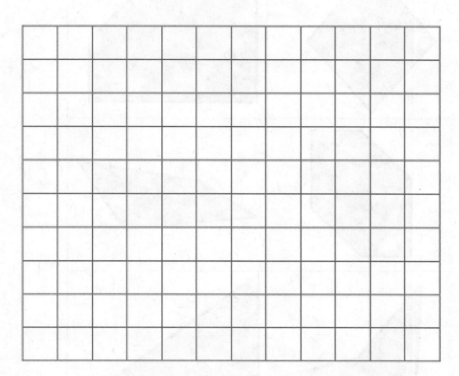

a.   Why is this shape called an isosceles trapezoid?

COMMON CORE | Lesson 16: | Draw trapezoids to clarify their attributes, and define trapezoids based on those attributes.

Date: 1/10/14

5.D.14

© 2014 Common Core, Inc. All rights reserved. commoncore.org

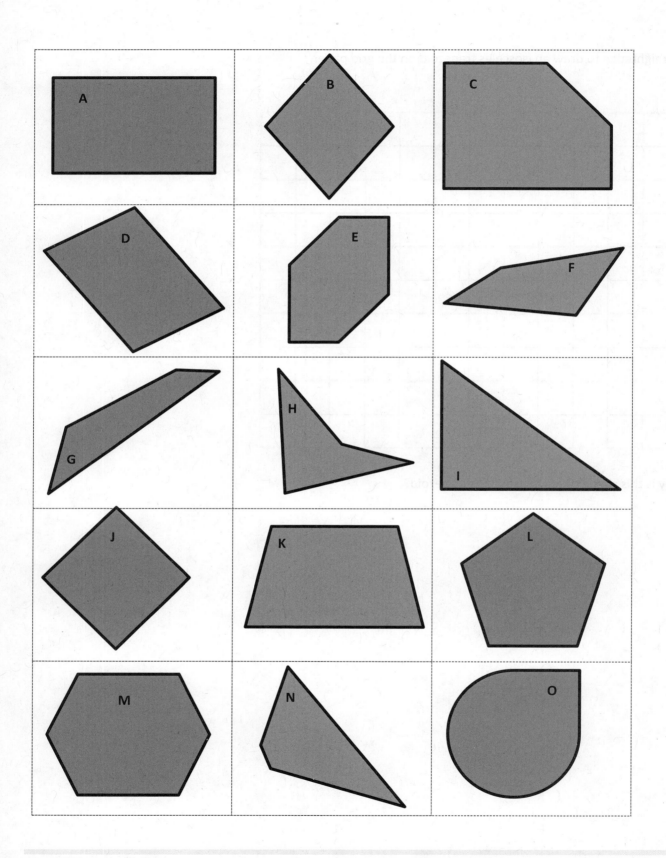

COMMON CORE

| **Lesson 16:** | Draw trapezoids to clarify their attributes, and define trapezoids based on those attributes. |
| **Date:** | 1/10/14 |

5.D.1

© 2014 Common Core, Inc. All rights reserved. commoncore.org

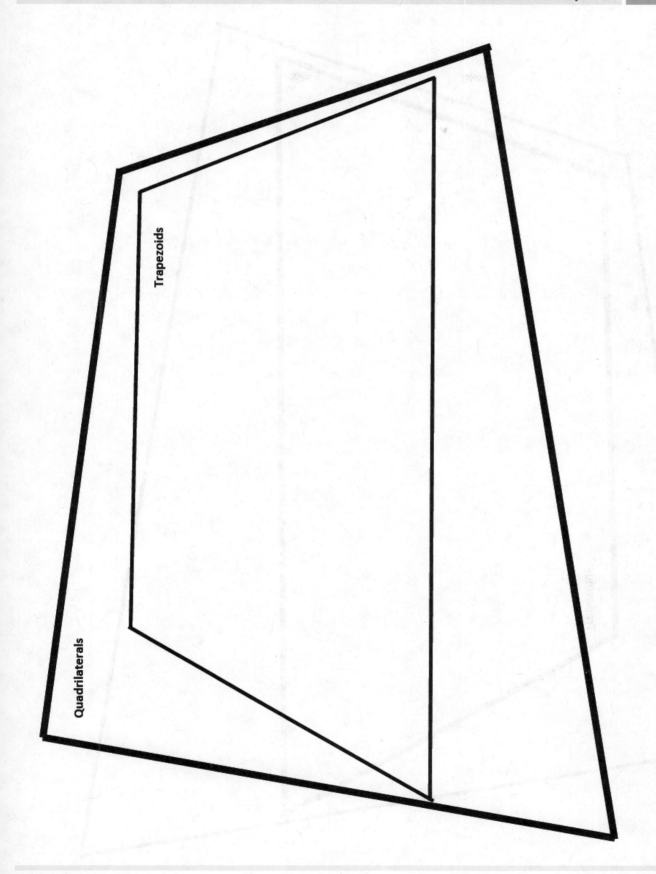

Trapezoids

Quadrilaterals

Lesson 16: Draw trapezoids to clarify their attributes, and define trapezoids based on those attributes.
Date: 1/10/14

5.D.16

© 2014 Common Core, Inc. All rights reserved. **commoncore.org**

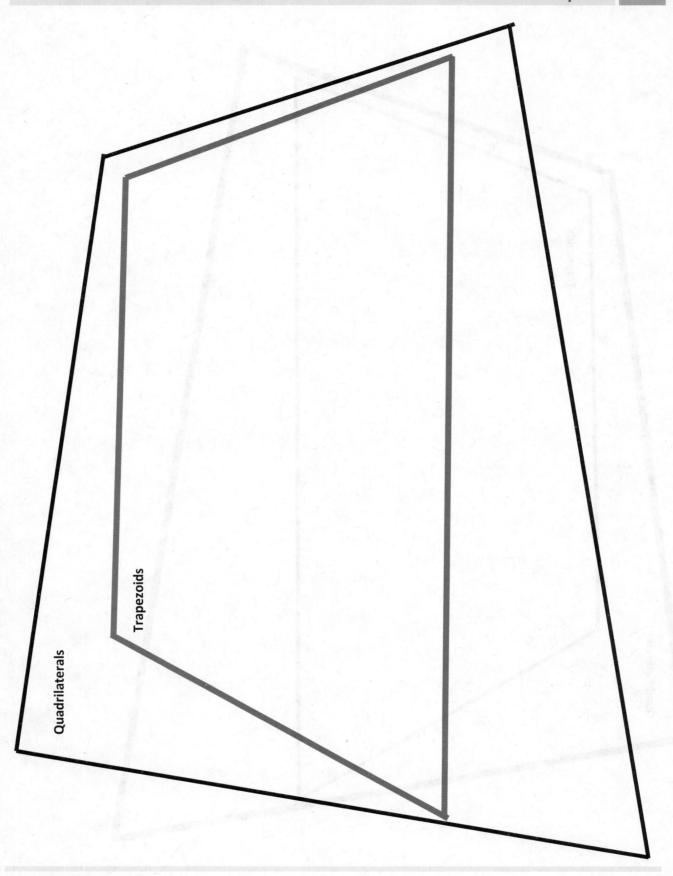

Quadrilaterals

Trapezoids

© 2014 Common Core, Inc. All rights reserved. **commoncore.org**

Lesson 17

Objective: Draw parallelograms to clarify their attributes, and define parallelograms based on those attributes.

Suggested Lesson Structure

■ Fluency Practice   (10 minutes)
■ Application Problem   (4 minutes)
■ Concept Development   (31 minutes)
■ Student Debrief   (15 minutes)
   Total Time   **(60 minutes)**

Fluency Practice (10 minutes)

- Multiply by Multiples of 10 and 100 **5.NBT.2**   (4 minutes)
- Divide Whole Numbers by Unit Fractions and Fractions by Whole Numbers **5.NF.7**   (6 minutes)

Multiply by Multiples of 10 and 100 (4 minutes)

Note: This fluency reviews G5–Modules 1 and 2.

   T: (Write $31 \times 10 =$ _____.) Say the multiplication sentence.
   S: $31 \times 10 = 310$.
   T: (Write $31 \times 10 = 310$. Below it, write $310 \times 2 =$ _____.) Say the multiplication sentence.
   S: $310 \times 2 = 620$.
   T: (Write $310 \times 2 = 620$. Below it, write $31 \times 20 = 31 \times$ _____ $\times$ _____ $=$ _____.) Say 31×20 as a three-factor multiplication sentence with 10 as one factor.
   S: $31 \times 10 \times 2 = 620$.

Follow the same process for 21×40.

   T: (Write $32 \times 30 = 32 \times$ _____ $\times$ _____ $=$ _____.) Write 32×30 as a three-factor multiplication sentence and solve.
   S: (Write $32 \times 30 = 32 \times 10 \times 3 = 960$.)

Repeat the process for 241×20.

   T: (Write $21 \times 100 =$ _____.) Say the multiplication sentence.
   S: $21 \times 100 = 2,100$.
   T: (Write $21 \times 100 = 2,100$. Below it, write $2,100 \times 3 =$_____.) Say the multiplication sentence.
   S: $2,100 \times 3 = 6,300$.

Lesson 17:	Draw parallelograms to clarify their attributes, and define parallelograms based on those attributes.	**5.D.18**
Date:	1/10/14	

© 2014 Common Core, Inc. All rights reserved. commoncore.org

T: (Write 2,100 × 3 = 6,300. Below it, write 21 × 300 = _____.) Say 21 × 300 as a three-factor multiplication sentence with 100 as one factor.

S: 21 × 3 × 100 = 6,300.

T: (Write 21 × 300 = 6,300.)

Direct students to solve using the same method for 42 × 400 and 34 × 300.

Divide Whole Numbers by Unit Fractions and Fractions by Whole Numbers (6 minutes)

Materials: (S) Personal white boards

Note: This fluency reviews G5–M4–Lessons 25–27 and prepares students for today's lesson.

T: (Write $2 \div \frac{1}{3}$.) Say the division sentence.

S: $2 \div \frac{1}{3} = 6$.

T: (Write $2 \div \frac{1}{3} = 6$. Beneath it, write $3 \div \frac{1}{5}$.) Say the division sentence.

S: $3 \div \frac{1}{5} = 15$.

T: (Write $3 \div \frac{1}{5} = 15$. Beneath it, write $6 \div \frac{1}{2}$.) On your boards, complete the division sentence.

S: (Write $6 \div \frac{1}{2} = 12$.)

Continue this process for $3 \div \frac{1}{4}$, $9 \div \frac{1}{3}$, $1 \div \frac{1}{10}$, $2 \div \frac{1}{10}$, $8 \div \frac{1}{10}$, and $10 \div \frac{1}{10}$.

T: (Write $\frac{1}{2} \div 2$.) Say the division sentence.

S: $\frac{1}{2} \div 2 = \frac{1}{4}$.

T: (Write $\frac{1}{2} \div 2 = \frac{1}{4}$. Beneath it, write $\frac{1}{3} \div 5$.) Say the division sentence.

S: $\frac{1}{3} \div 5 = \frac{1}{15}$.

T: (Write $\frac{1}{3} \div 5 = \frac{1}{15}$. Beneath it, write $\frac{1}{6} \div 5$.) On your boards, write the division sentence.

S: (Write $\frac{1}{6} \div 5 = \frac{1}{30}$.)

T: (Write $\frac{1}{4} \div 4$.) Say the division sentence.

S: $\frac{1}{4} \div 4 = \frac{1}{16}$.

Continue this process for the following possible sequence: $9 \div \frac{1}{4}$, $\frac{1}{4} \div 9$, $5 \div \frac{1}{8}$, $\frac{1}{8} \div 5$, $\frac{1}{7} \div 8$, and $8 \div \frac{1}{9}$.

© 2014 Common Core, Inc. All rights reserved. **commoncore.org**

Application Problem (4 minutes)

Ava drew the quadrilateral to the right and called it a trapezoid. Adam said Ava is wrong. Explain to your partner how a set square can be used to determine who is correct. Support your answer using the properties of trapezoids.

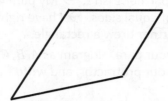

They can use a set square and ruler to see if 2 of the lines are parallel. If so, then it is a trapezoid.

Concept Development (31 minutes)

Materials: (T) Ruler, protractor, set square (or right angle template) (S) Ruler, protractor, set square (or right angle template), scissors, crayons or colored pencils, blank paper for drawing

NOTES ON MULTIPLE MEANS OF ENGAGEMENT:

If students need specific scaffolding for drawing figures, please see Grade 4–Module 4.

Problem

a. Draw a parallelogram and articulate the definition.

b. Measure and label its angles to explore their relationships.

c. Fold and measure to explore diagonals of parallelograms.

T: What name could we give to all of the shapes we drew yesterday?

S: Quadrilateral. → Trapezoid.

T: Use your ruler and set square to draw a pair of parallel lines on your blank paper positioned at any angle on the sheet.

S: (Draw.)

T: Because we are about to draw a quadrilateral beginning with one pair of parallel sides, what name can we give every figure we will draw today?

S: Trapezoid.

T: If I want to draw a trapezoid that can also be called a parallelogram, what will I need to draw next?

S: Parallelograms have two sets of parallel sides, so you have to draw another pair of parallel lines. → Draw another pair of parallel lines that cross the first ones.

T: Use your tools to draw a second pair of parallel lines that intersect your first pair.

S: (Draw.)

T: Measure the sides of your parallelogram and compare your parallelogram with your partner's. What's alike? What's different?

S: The opposite sides in my parallelogram are the same lengths and my

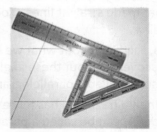

© 2014 Common Core, Inc. All rights reserved. commoncore.org

Lesson 17: Draw parallelograms to clarify their attributes, and define parallelograms based on those attributes.
Date: 1/10/14

5.D.20

MP.7

partner's are too. → My parallel sides are closer together than my partner's. → My parallelogram is a rectangle, but my partner's isn't. → My parallelogram has four equal sides, and my partner's has two different pairs of equal sides. → I have right angles in mine, but my partner does not. → I drew a square, and my partner drew a rectangle.

T: Label the angles of your parallelogram as $A, B, C,$ and D. Then, measure the angles of your parallelogram with your protractor, and write the measurements inside each angle.

S: (Measure.)

T: Cut out your parallelogram.

S: (Cut.)

T: Make a copy of your parallelogram on another blank sheet by tracing it and labeling the vertices with the same letters.

S: (Trace and label.)

T: Cut your first parallelogram into four parts by cutting between each set of parallel sides with a wavy cut.

S: (Cut.)

T: Put Angle A on top of Angle D, and Angle B on top of Angle C. What do you notice about your parallelogram's angles and about your partner's? Turn and talk.

S: Angles A and D are the same size, and so are Angles B and C. → Our parallelograms don't look anything alike, but the angles opposite each other in each of our parallelograms are equal.

T: Place your angles alongside each other, and find as many combinations that form straight lines as you can.

S: (Work.)

T: Compare your findings with your partner's. What do you notice? How many pairs did you find?

S: We both found four pairs that make straight lines. → Yesterday, some of us only had two pairs of angles that made straight lines. Today, all of us have four pairs.

T: So, thinking about what we drew and what we've discovered about these angles, when can a trapezoid also be called a parallelogram? Turn and talk.

S: When a trapezoid has more than one pair of parallel sides, it can be called a parallelogram. → Trapezoids have at least two pairs of angles that add up to 180 degrees. When they have more than that, they can also be called a parallelogram.

T: Place all four of your angles together at a point. What do you notice about the angles in your parallelogram and in your partner's?

S: (Work and share.)

NOTES ON
MULTIPLE MEANS OF
ENGAGEMENT:

The discussion of parallelograms as special trapezoids is based on the inclusive definition of a trapezoid as a quadrilateral with *at least* one set of parallel sides. That is, trapezoids may have more than one set of parallel sides.

Also note that the dialogue as written here assumes recall of Grade 4 geometric concepts. Additional, scaffolded questions may be necessary for students to verbalize the conditions necessary to classify a trapezoid as a parallelogram.

Lesson 17:   Draw parallelograms to clarify their attributes, and define
               parallelograms based on those attributes.
Date: 1/10/14

5.D.2

© 2014 Common Core, Inc. All rights reserved. commoncore.org

T: Use your ruler to draw the diagonals on the copy you made of your parallelogram.

S: (Draw.)

T: Measure each diagonal and record the measurements on your paper. Are these segments equal to each other?

S: I drew a long skinny parallelogram, and my diagonals aren't the same length. But, my partner drew a square, and his are the same length. → All people have equal diagonals, and some people don't.

T: I hear you saying that the diagonals of a parallelogram may or may not be equal to each other. Label the point where your diagonals intersect as point M.

S: (Draw and label.)

T: Measure from each corner of your parallelogram to point M. Record all of the measurements on the figure. Compare your measurements to those of your partner.

S: (Measure and compare.)

T: What do you notice about the diagonals of your parallelogram now?

S: The length from opposite corners to point M on the same diagonal is equal. → The diagonals cut each other into two equal parts. → One diagonal crosses the other at its midpoint. → M is the midpoint of both diagonals. → Even though our parallelograms look really different, our diagonals still cross at their midpoints.

T: The diagonals of a parallelogram **bisect** each other. Say, "bisect."

S: Bisect.

T: Let's break down this word into parts. Think about the first part *bi-*. How many wheels are on a bicycle?

S: Two.

T: What does the word *section* mean?

S: Parts of something.

T: *Sect* also means to cut. Turn and talk to your partner about why *bisect* is a good name for what you see in all the parallelograms' diagonals.

S: *Bi-* means two. These segments are cut in two equal parts. → *Bi-* means two, and sect means cut, so *bisect* means to cut in two parts.

T: (Distribute the Problem Set to students.) Let's practice drawing more parallelograms and thinking about their attributes by completing the Problem Set.

S: (Complete the Problem Set.)

Please note the extended time designated for the Debrief of today's lesson.

Problem Set (10 minutes)

Students should do their personal best to complete the Problem Set within the allotted 10 minutes. For some classes, it may be appropriate to modify the assignment by specifying which problems they work on first. All problems do not specify a method for solving. Students solve these problems using the

NOTES ON
MULTIPLE MEANS OF
ENGAGEMENT:

For early finishers of the Problem Set, offer this challenge:

In parallelogram $ABCD$, $\angle A$ is $\frac{1}{3}$ the measure of $\angle B$. Find the measures of all the angles of the figure.

Lesson 17:   Draw parallelograms to clarify their attributes, and define parallelograms based on those attributes.

Date: 1/10/14

5.D.22

© 2014 Common Core, Inc. All rights reserved. commoncore.org

RDW approach used for Application Problems.

Note: Today's Problem Set from G5–M5–Lessons 16 and 17 should be kept for use in G5–M5–Lesson 18's Debrief as well.

Student Debrief (15 minutes)

Lesson Objective: Draw parallelograms to clarify their attributes, and define parallelograms based on those attributes.

The Student Debrief is intended to invite reflection and active processing of the total lesson experience.

Invite students to review their solutions for the Problem Set. They should check work by comparing answers with a partner before going over answers as a class. Look for misconceptions or misunderstandings that can be addressed in the Debrief. Guide students in a conversation to debrief the Problem Set and process the lesson.

You may choose to use any combination of the questions below to lead the discussion.

- Allow students to share all the different parallelograms that are produced in Problem 1 of the Problem Set. Consolidate the lists of attributes students generated for parallelograms in Problem 4. What attributes do all parallelograms share? Where do these pairs seem to occur consistently? Is this true for all quadrilaterals? Trapezoids? Parallelograms?

- Use the parallelograms that students produce in Problem 1 to articulate the formal definition of a parallelogram. Continue posting these definitions in the classroom for reference as the topic proceeds.

A parallelogram:

- Is a quadrilateral in which both pairs of opposite sides are parallel.

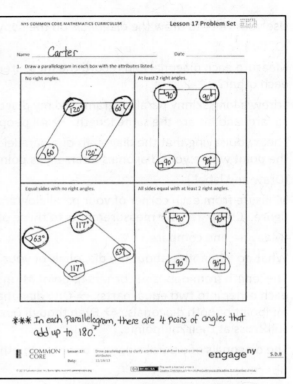

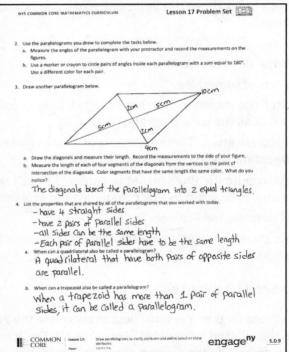

Lesson 17:   Draw parallelograms to clarify their attributes, and define
Date: parallelograms based on those attributes.
                     1/10/14

5.D.2

© 2014 Common Core, Inc. All rights reserved. **commoncore.org**

- When can a quadrilateral also be called a parallelogram? When can a trapezoid also be called a parallelogram? Respond to the following statements with *true* or *false*. Explain your reasoning.
  - All parallelograms are trapezoids.
  - All trapezoids are parallelograms.
  - All parallelograms are quadrilaterals.
  - All quadrilaterals are parallelograms.
- Continue the construction of the hierarchy diagram from G5–M5–Lesson 16. Students might draw or glue examples of parallelograms and/or list attributes within the diagram. Encourage them to explain their placement of the figures in the hierarchy.
- Continue exploring the formal definition of a quadrilateral (see the boxed text on the right) through the examination of counter-examples.

  A quadrilateral:

  - Consists of four different points A, B, C, D in the plane and four segments, $\overline{AB}, \overline{BC}, \overline{CD}, \overline{DA}$,
  - Is arranged so that the segments intersect only at their endpoints, and
  - Has no two adjacent segments that are collinear.

  Step 1: Begin by asking students to tell what they know about a quadrilateral. Today's response should be a polygon with four straight sides that *lie in the same plane.*

  Step 2: Follow the first bullet in the definition verbatim to draw four straight segments in the same plane, but have the segments intersect as shown to the right.

  Ask: "Is this figure also a quadrilateral? What must we add to our definition to eliminate the possibility of this figure?"

  Step 3: Lead students to see that a four-sided figure is only a quadrilateral if all four segments lie in the same plane *and the segments intersect only at their endpoints*. Then add the second bullet of the definition to that written in G5–M5–Lesson 16.

Exit Ticket (3 minutes)

After the Student Debrief, instruct students to complete the Exit Ticket. A review of their work will help you assess the students' understanding of the concepts that were presented in the lesson today and plan more effectively for future lessons. You may read the questions aloud to the students.

Lesson 17:   Draw parallelograms to clarify their attributes, and define
parallelograms based on those attributes.

Date: 1/10/14

5.D.24

© 2014 Common Core, Inc. All rights reserved. commoncore.org

Name _____   Date _____

1. Draw a parallelogram in each box with the attributes listed.

No right angles.	At least 2 right angles.
Equal sides with no right angles.	All sides equal with at least 2 right angles.

2. Use the parallelograms you drew to complete the tasks below.

   a. Measure the angles of the parallelogram with your protractor, and record the measurements on the figures.

   b. Use a marker or crayon to circle pairs of angles inside each parallelogram with a sum equal to 180°. Use a different color for each pair.

3. Draw another parallelogram below.

   a. Draw the diagonals and measure their length. Record the measurements to the side of your figure.

   b. Measure the length of each of four segments of the diagonals from the vertices to the point of intersection of the diagonals. Color segments that have the same length the same color. What do you notice?

4. List the properties that are shared by all of the parallelograms that you worked with today.

   a. When can a quadrilateral also be called a parallelogram?

   b. When can a trapezoid also be called a parallelogram?

| Lesson 17: | Draw parallelograms to clarify their attributes, and define parallelograms based on those attributes. |
| Date: | 1/10/14 |

5.D.26

© 2014 Common Core, Inc. All rights reserved. commoncore.org

Name _____ Date _____

1. Draw a parallelogram.

2. When is a trapezoid also called a parallelogram?

Lesson 17:   Draw parallelograms to clarify their attributes, and define
                   parallelograms based on those attributes.
Date: 1/10/14

5.D.

© 2014 Common Core, Inc. All rights reserved. **commoncore.org**

Name _____   Date _____

1. ∠A measures 60°. Extend the rays of ∠A and draw parallelogram ABCD on the grid paper.

    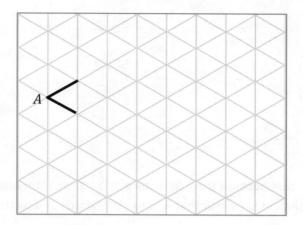

    a. What are the measures of ∠B, ∠C, and ∠D?

2. WXYZ is a parallelogram not drawn to scale.
    a. Using what you know about parallelograms, give the measure of sides XY and YZ.

    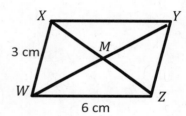

    b. ∠WXY = 113°. Use what you know about angles in a parallelogram to find the measure of the other angles.

∠XYZ = _____°   ∠YZW = _____°   ∠ZWX = _____°

3. Jack measured some segments in Problem 2. He found that WY = 4 cm and MZ = 3 cm.
    Give the lengths of the following segments:

    WM = _____ cm   MY = _____ cm

    XM = _____ cm   XZ = _____ cm

Lesson 17:	Draw parallelograms to clarify their attributes, and define parallelograms based on those attributes.	
Date:	1/10/14	**5.D.28**

© 2014 Common Core, Inc. All rights reserved. commoncore.org

4. Using the properties of the shapes, explain why all parallelograms are trapezoids.

5. Teresa says that because the diagonals of a parallelogram bisect each other, if one diagonal is 4.2 cm, the other diagonal must be half that length. Use words and pictures to explain Teresa's error.

COMMON CORE

Lesson 17: Draw parallelograms to clarify their attributes, and define parallelograms based on those attributes.

Date: 1/10/14

5.D.1

© 2014 Common Core, Inc. All rights reserved. **commoncore.org**

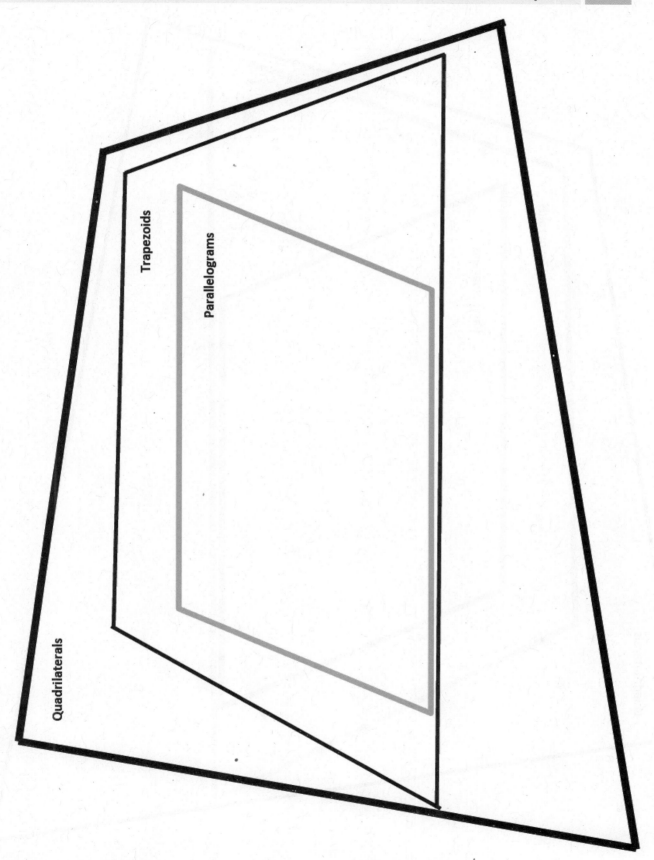

Quadrilaterals

Trapezoids

Parallelograms

 | Lesson 17:   Draw parallelograms to clarify their attributes, and define
parallelograms based on those attributes.
Date: 1/10/14   5.D.30

© 2014 Common Core, Inc. All rights reserved. **commoncore.org**

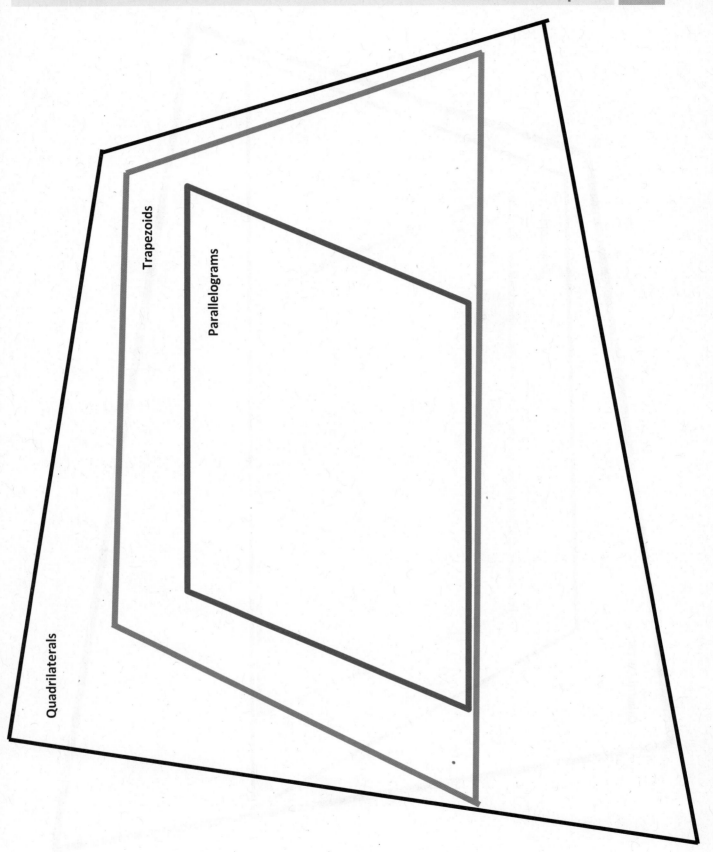

Quadrilaterals

Trapezoids

Parallelograms

Lesson 17: Draw parallelograms to clarify their attributes, and define
parallelograms based on those attributes.

Date: 1/10/14

5.D.3

© 2014 Common Core, Inc. All rights reserved. **commoncore.org**

Lesson 18

Objective: Draw rectangles and rhombuses to clarify their attributes, and define rectangles and rhombuses based on those attributes.

Suggested Lesson Structure

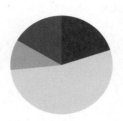

■ Fluency Practice   (12 minutes)
■ Application Problem   (6 minutes)
■ Concept Development   (32 minutes)
■ Student Debrief   (10 minutes)
  Total Time   **(60 minutes)**

Fluency Practice (12 minutes)

Sprint: Divide Whole Numbers by Fractions and Fractions by Whole Numbers **5.NBT.7**   (9 minutes)

Multiply by Multiples of 10 and 100 **5.NBT.2**   (3 minutes)

Sprint: Divide Whole Numbers by Fractions and Fractions by Whole Numbers (9 minutes)

Materials: (S) Divide Whole Numbers by Fractions and Fractions by Whole Numbers Sprint

Note: This fluency reviews G5–Module 4.

Multiply by Multiples of 10 and 100 (3 minutes)

Note: This fluency reviews G5–Modules 1–2.

  T: (Write $42 \times 10 =$ _____.) Say the multiplication sentence.
  S: $42 \times 10 = 420$.
  T: (Write $42 \times 10 = 420$. Below it, write $420 \times 2 =$ _____.) Say the multiplication sentence.
  S: $420 \times 2 = 840$.
  T: (Write $420 \times 2 = 840$. Below it, write $42 \times 20 = 42 \times \_\_ \times \_\_ =$ _____.) Say 42×20 as a three-factor multiplication sentence with 10 as one of the factors.
  S: $42 \times 10 \times 2 = 840$.

Follow the same process for 23×30.

  T: (Write $213 \times 30 = 213 \times \_\_ \times \_\_ =$ _____.) Write 213×30 as a three-step multiplication sentence, and solve.
  S: (Write $213 \times 30 = 213 \times 10 \times 3 = 6,390$.)

Lesson 18:   Draw rectangles and rhombuses to clarify their attributes, and define
             rectangles and rhombuses based on those attributes.   5.D.32
Date: 1/10/14

© 2014 Common Core, Inc. All rights reserved. commoncore.org

Repeat the process for 4,213 x 20.

T: (Write 21 × 100 = _____.) Say the multiplication sentence.

S: 31 × 100 = 2,100.

T: (Write 31 × 100 = 3,100. Below it, write 3,100 × 3 = _____.) Say the multiplication sentence.

S: 3,100 × 3 = 9,300.

T: (Write 3,100 x 3 = 9,300. Below it, write 21 × 300 = _____.) Say 21 × 300 as a three-factor multiplication sentence with 100 as one of the factors.

S: 21 × 100 × 3 = 6,300.

T: (Write 21 × 300 = 6,300.)

Direct students to solve using the same method for 43 × 300.

Application Problem (6 minutes)

How many 2-inch cubes are needed to build a rectangular prism that measures 10 inches by 6 inches by 14 inches?

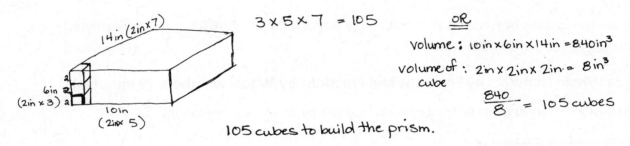

$3 \times 5 \times 7 = 105$

OR

Volume: $10\,in \times 6\,in \times 14\,in = 840\,in^3$

Volume of cube: $2\,in \times 2\,in \times 2\,in = 8\,in^3$

$\dfrac{840}{8} = 105\ cubes$

105 cubes to build the prism.

Note: Today's Application Problem requires students to reason about volume concepts from earlier in this module.

Concept Development (32 minutes)

Materials: (S) Ruler, set square or square template, protractor

Problem 1

a. Draw a rhombus, and articulate the definition.

b. Measure and label its angles to explore their relationships.

c. Fold and measure to explore diagonals of rhombuses.

T: Give the least specific name for all the shapes we've drawn so far.

Lesson 18:   Draw rectangles and rhombuses to clarify their attributes, and define
rectangles and rhombuses based on those attributes.

Date: 1/10/14

5.D.3

© 2014 Common Core, Inc. All rights reserved. commoncore.org

S: Quadrilaterals.

T: Tell your partner a more specific name for a shape we've drawn and explain what property is has that gives it that name.

S: Trapezoids, because we've drawn shapes with at least one pair of parallel sides. → All of the quadrilaterals could be called trapezoids and parallelograms. They had two pairs of parallel sides.

T: How did we start drawing the trapezoids and parallelograms?

S: By drawing a pair of parallel sides.

T: If we wanted to draw a parallelogram that is also a rhombus, what would I need to think about?

S: It would need to have four sides the same length. → It would need another pair of parallel sides, but we'd need to measure to be sure we drew the sides the same length.

T: Draw an angle with sides that are equal length. Then label the vertex as B and the endpoints of the sides as A and C.

S: (Draw an angle.)

T: Draw a line parallel to one of the sides through the endpoint of the other side.

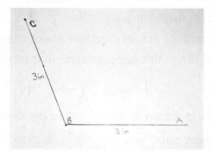

S: (Draw a parallel line.)

T: Now do the same for the second side.

S: (Draw a second parallel line.)

T: Label the last angle as D.

S: (Label the angle.)

T: Measure the sides and compare your figure with your partner's. What is the most specific name for this shape? How do you know?

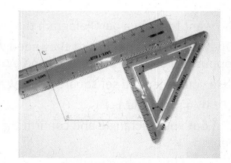

S: My sides were two inches long. My partner's were three inches long, but they both have two sets of parallel sides and the sides are all the same length. So we both drew a rhombus. → It's a parallelogram with four equal sides. → Mine is a parallelogram with equal sides, but my partner's is a square. We both drew a rhombus with four equal sides, but I drew my angles as 60 degrees and he drew right angles.

T: Measure the angles and mark them inside the rhombus.

S: (Measure and mark the angles.)

T: What do you notice? Turn and talk.

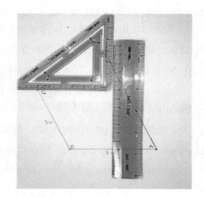

S: The angles that are beside each other all add up to a straight angle. → There are four pairs of angles that add up to 180°. → Angles between parallel lines equal 180°. → The opposite angles are almost exactly the same size.

T: Use your ruler to draw the diagonals of your rhombus. Then measure them and the distance from each corner to the point where they intersect. Tell your partner what you notice.

| Lesson 18: | Draw rectangles and rhombuses to clarify their attributes, and define rectangles and rhombuses based on those attributes. |
| Date: | 1/10/14 |

5.D.34

© 2014 Common Core, Inc. All rights reserved. commoncore.org

S: These diagonals are equal. → The diagonals bisect each other.

T: Now measure the angles formed by the diagonals. What is the measure?

S: They are right angles. → The angles are all 90°.

T: Do the diagonals of a rhombus bisect one another? How do you know?

S: Yes because the point where they cross is the midpoint of both diagonals.

T: What is the name for lines that intersect at a right angle?

S: Perpendicular lines.

T: Because they bisect each other at a 90° angle, we call these diagonals **perpendicular bisectors**.

T: From our drawing, what attribute be present to call this parallelogram a rhombus?

S: All four sides are equal.

T: What else did we discover about the diagonals of a rhombus?

S: The diagonals are perpendicular bisectors.

Problem 2

a. Draw a rectangle according to the definition of a rectangle.

b. Measure and label its angles to explore their relationships.

c. Fold and measure to explore diagonals of rectangles.

T: If I want to draw a parallelogram that is also a rectangle, what must I include in my drawing?

S: They are parallelograms so they need two sets of parallel sides. → Rectangles have right angles and opposite sides that are parallel and equal.

T: Use your ruler and set square to draw a rectangle.

S: (Draw a rectangle.)

T: Cut out your rectangle and confirm that the angles are all 90° and the opposite sides are the same length.

S: (Cut and fold the rectangle.)

T: Now measure the diagonals, the segments of the diagonals, and the angles around the intersection point. Record your measurements on the figure.

S: (Measure and record the figure.)

T: What do you notice? Turn and talk.

S: The diagonals are equal length. → The segments of the diagonals are equal. → The angles between the parallel lines equal 180°. → The diagonals are equal and bisect each other.

T: Are the diagonals perpendicular bisectors? How do you know?

S: They are not perpendicular bisectors because they don't form right angles.

T: What properties must be present for a parallelogram to also be a rectangle?

Lesson 18:   Draw rectangles and rhombuses to clarify their attributes, and define rectangles and rhombuses based on those attributes.

Date: 1/10/14

5.D.3

© 2014 Common Core, Inc. All rights reserved. **commoncore.org**

S: The sides across from each other have to be the same length. → All angles are 90°. → Diagonals bisect each other.

T: (Distribute the Problem Set to students.) Let's practice drawing more rhombuses and rectangles and thinking about their attributes by completing the Problem Set.

S: (Complete the Problem Set.)

Please note the extended time designated for the Debrief of today's lesson.

Problem Set

Students should do their personal best to complete the Problem Set within the allotted 10 minutes. For some classes, it may be appropriate to modify the assignment by specifying which problems they work on first. All problems do not specify a method for solving. Students solve these problems using the RDW approach used for Application Problems..

Note: Problem Sets from G5–M5–Lessons 16–17 should be kept for use in G5–M5–Lesson 18's Debrief as well.

Student Debrief (10 minutes)

Lesson Objective: Draw rectangles and rhombuses to clarify their attributes, and define rectangles and rhombuses based on those attributes.

The Student Debrief is intended to invite reflection and active processing of the total lesson experience.

Invite students to review their solutions for the Problem Set. They should check work by comparing answers with a partner before going over answers as a class. Look for misconceptions or misunderstandings that can be addressed in the Debrief. Guide students in a conversation to debrief the Problem Set and process the lesson.

You may choose to use any combination of the questions below to lead the discussion.

- Allow students to share all the different rhombuses and rectangles that are produced in Problem 1 of the Problem Set. What attributes do all rhombuses share? What attributes appear on

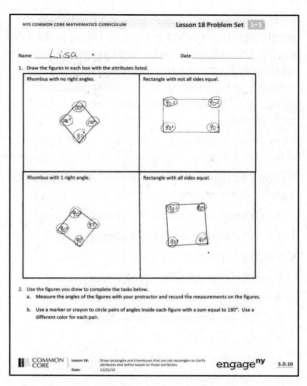

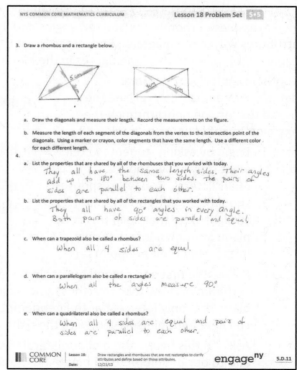

Lesson 18:   Draw rectangles and rhombuses to clarify their attributes, and define
Date: 1/10/14   rectangles and rhombuses based on those attributes.

5.D.36

© 2014 Common Core, Inc. All rights reserved. commoncore.org

the rhombus list that were not on the list for parallelograms? What attributes do all rectangles share? Is this true for all quadrilaterals? Rhombuses? Rectangles? Use the rhombuses and rectangles produced in Problem 1 to articulate the formal definitions. Continue posting definitions for comparisons.

- When can a quadrilateral also be called a rhombus? When can a quadrilateral also be called a rectangle?

- Respond to the following statements with *true* or *false*. Explain your reasoning.

  - All parallelograms are rhombuses.
  - All rhombuses are parallelograms.
  - All parallelograms are rectangles.
  - All rectangles are parallelograms.
  - All trapezoids are rhombuses.
  - All rhombuses are trapezoids.
  - All trapezoids are rectangles.
  - All rectangles are trapezoids.

- Continue the construction of the hierarchy diagram from G5–M5–Lessons 16–17. Students might draw or glue examples of rhombuses and rectangles and list attributes within the diagram. Encourage them to explain their placement of the figures in the hierarchy.

- Continue exploring the formal definition of a quadrilateral (see the boxed text on the right) through the examination of counter-examples.

  Step 1: Begin by asking students to tell what they know about a quadrilateral. Today's response should be a polygon with four straight sides that lie in the same plane and segments that only intersect at their endpoints.

  Step 2: Follow the first and second bullets in the definition verbatim to draw four straight segments in the same plane that only intersect at their endpoints but have collinear endpoints as shown to the right.

  Ask: "Is this figure also a quadrilateral? What must we add to our definition to eliminate the possibility of this figure?"

A rhombus:

- Is a quadrilateral with all sides of equal length.

A rectangle:

- Is a quadrilateral with four right angles.

NOTES ON
MULTIPLE MEANS OF
ENGAGEMENT:

If students are confused about the segments of a quadrilateral lying in the same plane or intersecting only at their endpoints, use the straws from G5–M5–Lessons 16–17 to demonstrate counter-examples.

A quadrilateral:

- Consists of four different points, A, B, C, D, in the plane and four segments, $\overline{AB}, \overline{BC}, \overline{CD}, \overline{DA}$,
- Is arranged so that the segments intersect only at their endpoints, and
- Has no two adjacent segments that are collinear.

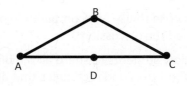

Lesson 18:   Draw rectangles and rhombuses to clarify their attributes, and define rectangles and rhombuses based on those attributes.

Date: 1/10/14

5.D.3

© 2014 Common Core, Inc. All rights reserved. **commoncore.org**

Step 3: Lead students to see that a four-sided figure is only a quadrilateral if all four segments lie in the same plane, the segments intersect only at their endpoints, *and no two segments are collinear*. Then add the third bullet of the definition to that written in G5–M5–Lesson 17.

Exit Ticket (3 minutes)

After the Student Debrief, instruct students to complete the Exit Ticket. A review of their work will help you assess the students' understanding of the concepts that were presented in the lesson today and plan more effectively for future lessons. You may read the questions aloud to the students.

Lesson 18:   Draw rectangles and rhombuses to clarify their attributes, and define
rectangles and rhombuses based on those attributes.

Date: 1/10/14

5.D.38

© 2014 Common Core, Inc. All rights reserved. **commoncore.org**

A

Correct _____

Divide.

1	$\frac{1}{2} \div 2 =$		23	$4 \div \frac{1}{4} =$	
2	$\frac{1}{2} \div 3 =$		24	$\frac{1}{3} \div 3 =$	
3	$\frac{1}{2} \div 4 =$		25	$\frac{2}{3} \div 3 =$	
4	$\frac{1}{2} \div 7 =$		26	$\frac{1}{4} \div 2 =$	
5	$7 \div \frac{1}{2} =$		27	$\frac{3}{4} \div 2 =$	
6	$6 \div \frac{1}{2} =$		28	$\frac{1}{5} \div 2 =$	
7	$5 \div \frac{1}{2} =$		29	$\frac{3}{5} \div 2 =$	
8	$3 \div \frac{1}{2} =$		30	$\frac{1}{6} \div 2 =$	
9	$2 \div \frac{1}{5} =$		31	$\frac{5}{6} \div 2 =$	
10	$3 \div \frac{1}{5} =$		32	$\frac{5}{6} \div 3 =$	
11	$4 \div \frac{1}{5} =$		33	$\frac{1}{6} \div 3 =$	
12	$7 \div \frac{1}{5} =$		34	$3 \div \frac{1}{6} =$	
13	$\frac{1}{5} \div 7 =$		35	$6 \div \frac{1}{6} =$	
14	$\frac{1}{3} \div 2 =$		36	$7 \div \frac{1}{7} =$	
15	$2 \div \frac{1}{3} =$		37	$8 \div \frac{1}{8} =$	
16	$\frac{1}{4} \div 2 =$		38	$9 \div \frac{1}{9} =$	
17	$2 \div \frac{1}{4} =$		39	$\frac{1}{8} \div 7 =$	
18	$\frac{1}{5} \div 2 =$		40	$9 \div \frac{1}{8} =$	
19	$2 \div \frac{1}{5} =$		41	$\frac{1}{8} \div 7 =$	
20	$3 \div \frac{1}{4} =$		42	$7 \div \frac{1}{6} =$	
21	$\frac{1}{4} \div 3 =$		43	$9 \div \frac{1}{7} =$	
22	$\frac{1}{4} \div 4 =$		44	$\frac{1}{8} \div 9 =$	

Lesson 18: Draw rectangles and rhombuses to clarify their attributes, and define
rectangles and rhombuses based on those attributes.

Date: 1/10/14

5.D.3

© 2014 Common Core, Inc. All rights reserved. commoncore.org

B

Divide.

Improvement _____   # Correct _____

1	$\frac{1}{2} \div 2 =$		23	$3 \div \frac{1}{3} =$
2	$\frac{1}{5} \div 3 =$		24	$\frac{1}{4} \div 4 =$
3	$\frac{1}{5} \div 4 =$		25	$\frac{3}{4} \div 4 =$
4	$\frac{1}{5} \div 7 =$		26	$\frac{1}{3} \div 3 =$
5	$7 \div \frac{1}{5} =$		27	$\frac{2}{3} \div 3 =$
6	$6 \div \frac{1}{5} =$		28	$\frac{1}{6} \div 2 =$
7	$5 \div \frac{1}{5} =$		29	$\frac{5}{6} \div 2 =$
8	$3 \div \frac{1}{5} =$		30	$\frac{1}{5} \div 5 =$
9	$2 \div \frac{1}{2} =$		31	$\frac{3}{5} \div 5 =$
10	$3 \div \frac{1}{2} =$		32	$\frac{3}{5} \div 4 =$
11	$4 \div \frac{1}{2} =$		33	$\frac{1}{5} \div 6 =$
12	$7 \div \frac{1}{2} =$		34	$6 \div \frac{1}{5} =$
13	$\frac{1}{2} \div 7 =$		35	$6 \div \frac{1}{4} =$
14	$\frac{1}{4} \div 2 =$		36	$7 \div \frac{1}{6} =$
15	$2 \div \frac{1}{4} =$		37	$8 \div \frac{1}{7} =$
16	$\frac{1}{3} \div 2 =$		38	$9 \div \frac{1}{8} =$
17	$2 \div \frac{1}{3} =$		39	$\frac{1}{8} \div 8 =$
18	$\frac{1}{2} \div 2 =$		40	$9 \div \frac{1}{9} =$
19	$2 \div \frac{1}{2} =$		41	$\frac{1}{9} \div 8 =$
20	$4 \div \frac{1}{3} =$		42	$7 \div \frac{1}{7} =$
21	$\frac{1}{3} \div 4 =$		43	$9 \div \frac{1}{6} =$
22	$\frac{1}{3} \div 3 =$		44	$\frac{1}{8} \div 6 =$

Lesson 18:   Draw rectangles and rhombuses to clarify their attributes, and define
rectangles and rhombuses based on those attributes.

Date: 1/10/14

5.D.40

© 2014 Common Core, Inc. All rights reserved. commoncore.org

Name _____   Date _____

1. Draw the figures in each box with the attributes listed.

Rhombus with no right angles.	Rectangle with not all sides equal.
Rhombus with 1 right angle.	Rectangle with all sides equal.

2. Use the figures you drew to complete the tasks below.

    a. Measure the angles of the figures with your protractor and record the measurements on the figures.

    b. Use a marker or crayon to circle pairs of angles inside each figure with a sum equal to 180°. Use a different color for each pair.

Lesson 18:   * Draw rectangles and rhombuses to clarify their attributes, and define
             rectangles and rhombuses based on those attributes.
Date: 1/10/14

5.D.4

© 2014 Common Core, Inc. All rights reserved. **commoncore.org**

3. Draw a rhombus and a rectangle below.

    a. Draw the diagonals and measure their length. Record the measurements on the figure.

    b. Measure the length of each segment of the diagonals from the vertex to the intersection point of the diagonals. Using a marker or crayon, color segments that have the same length. Use a different color for each different length.

4.

    a. List the properties that are shared by all of the rhombuses that you worked with today.

    b. List the properties that are shared by all of the rectangles that you worked with today.

    c. When can a trapezoid also be called a rhombus?

    d. When can a parallelogram also be called a rectangle?

    e. When can a quadrilateral also be called a rhombus?

Date: 1/10/14

© 2014 Common Core, Inc. All rights reserved. **commoncore.org**

Name _____ Date _____

1. Draw a rhombus.

2. Draw a rectangle.

Lesson 18: Draw rectangles and rhombuses to clarify their attributes, and define rectangles and rhombuses based on those attributes.

Date: 1/10/14

5.D.4

© 2014 Common Core, Inc. All rights reserved. **commoncore.org**

Name _____   Date _____

1. Use the grid paper to draw.

a. A rhombus with no right angles.   b. A rhombus with 4 right angles.

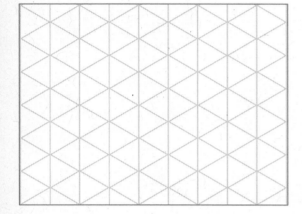   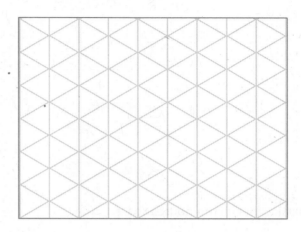

c. A rectangle with not all sides equal.   d. A rectangle with all sides equal.

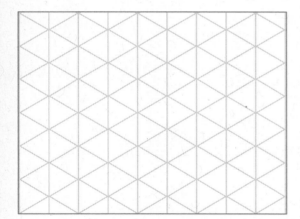   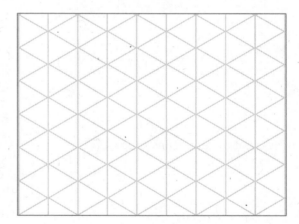

COMMON CORE

Lesson 18:   Draw rectangles and rhombuses to clarify their attributes, and define
               rectangles and rhombuses based on those attributes.

Date: 1/10/14

5.D.44

© 2014 Common Core, Inc. All rights reserved. commoncore.org

2.   A rhombus has a perimeter of 217 cm. What is the length of each side of the rhombus?

3.   List the properties that all rhombuses share.

4.   List the properties that all rectangles share.

Lesson 18:   Draw rectangles and rhombuses to clarify their attributes, and define
               rectangles and rhombuses based on those attributes.
Date: 1/10/14

5.D.4

© 2014 Common Core, Inc. All rights reserved. **commoncore.org**

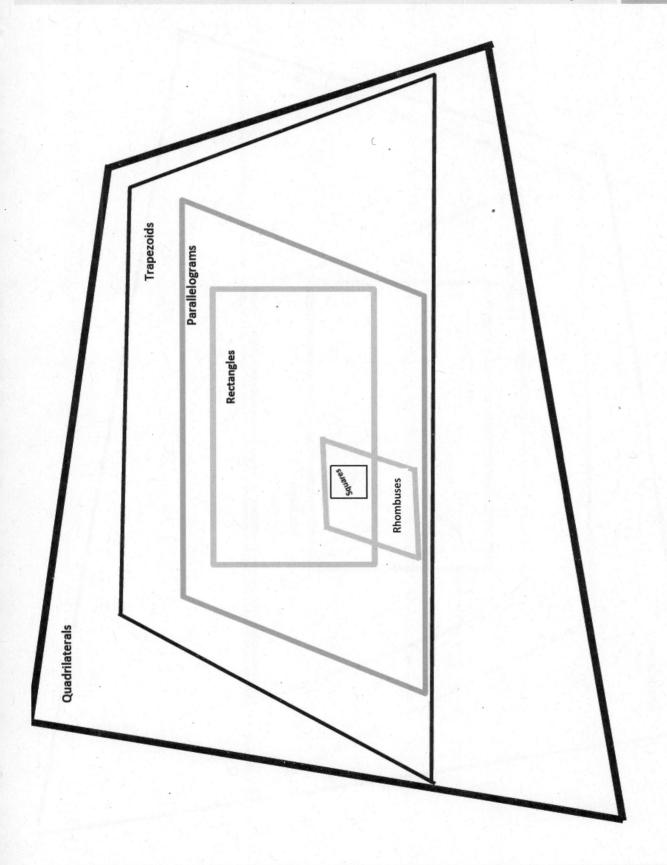

Quadrilaterals

Trapezoids

Parallelograms

Rectangles

Squares

Rhombuses

Lesson 18:   Draw rectangles and rhombuses to clarify their attributes, and define
rectangles and rhombuses based on those attributes.

Date: 1/10/14

5.D.46

© 2014 Common Core, Inc. All rights reserved. **commoncore.org**

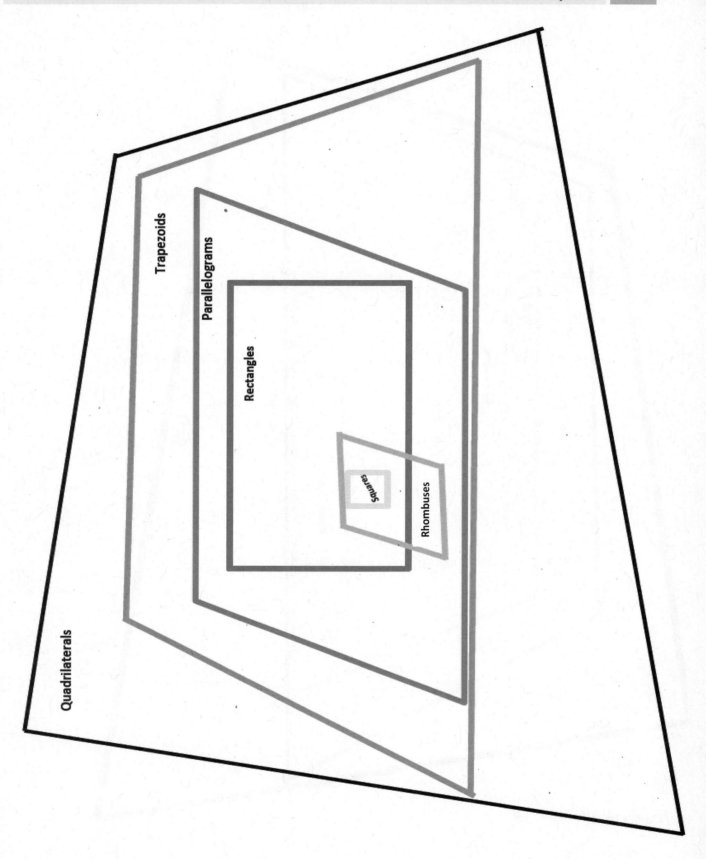

Lesson 18: Draw rectangles and rhombuses to clarify their attributes, and define
rectangles and rhombuses based on those attributes.

Date: 1/10/14

5.D.4

© 2014 Common Core, Inc. All rights reserved. **commoncore.org**

Lesson 19

Objective: Draw kites and squares to clarify their attributes, and define kites and squares based on those attributes.

Suggested Lesson Structure

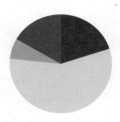

■ Fluency Practice   (12 minutes)
■ Application Problem   (4 minutes)
  Concept Development   (34 minutes)
■ Student Debrief   (10 minutes)
  Total Time   **(60 minutes)**

Fluency Practice (12 minutes)

- Sprint: Multiply by Multiples of 10 and 100 **5.NBT.2**   (8 minutes)
- Divide by Multiples of 10 and 100 **5.NBT.2**   (4 minutes)

Sprint: Multiply by Multiples of 10 and 100 (8 minutes)

Materials: (S) Multiply by Multiples of 10 and 100 Sprint

Note: This fluency reviews G5–Module 2.

Divide by Multiples of 10 and 100 (4 minutes)

Materials: (S) Personal white boards

Note: This fluency reviews G5–Module 2.

   T: (Write $240 \div 10 =$ _____.) Say the division sentence.
   S: $240 \div 10 = 24$.
   T: (Write $240 \div 10 = 24$. To the right, write $24 \div 2 =$ _____.) Say the division sentence.
   S: $24 \div 2 = 12$.
   T: (Write $24 \div 2 = 12$. Below it, write $240 \div 20 =$ _____.) Say $420 \div 20$ as a division sentence, but divide first by 10 and then by 2 rather than by 20.
   S: $240 \div 10 \div 2 = 12$.
   T: (Write $240 \div 20 = 12$.)

$240 \div 10 = 24$ $24 \div 2 = 12$

$240 \div 20 = 12$

10   ×   2

Lesson 19:   Draw kites and squares to clarify their attributes, and define kites and
             squares based on those attributes.
Date: 1/10/14

5.D.48

© 2014 Common Core, Inc. All rights reserved. commoncore.org

Continue the process for the following possible sequence: 690 ÷ 30, 8,600 ÷ 20, 4,800 ÷ 400, and 9,600 ÷ 300.

Application Problem (4 minutes)

The teacher asked her class to draw parallelograms that are rectangles. Kylie drew Figure 1, and Zach drew Figure 2. Zach agrees that Kylie has drawn a parallelogram but says that it's not a rectangle. Is he correct? Use properties to justify your answer.

Note: Today's Application Problem gives students another opportunity to verbalize the hierarchical nature of the relationships between types of quadrilaterals.

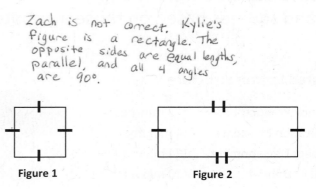

Zach is not correct. Kylie's figure is a rectangle. The opposite sides are equal lengths, parallel, and all 4 angles are 90°.

Figure 1   **Figure 2**

Concept Development (34 minutes)

Materials: (S) Ruler, set square or square template, protractor

Problem 1

   a. Draw a square and articulate the definition.

   b. Measure and label its angles to explore their relationships.

   c. Measure to explore diagonals of squares.

   T: What shapes have we drawn so far?

   S: Quadrilaterals. → Rhombuses and rectangles. → Trapezoids and parallelograms, but in a rhombus all sides are the same length.

   T: Can a rectangle ever be a rhombus? Can a rhombus ever be a rectangle? Turn and talk.

   S: Well, a rectangle and a rhombus are both parallelograms, but a rectangle has right angles and a rhombus doesn't. → Rhombuses have four equal sides, but rectangles don't. I'm not sure if a rhombus can be a rectangle. → A square is a rhombus and a rectangle at the same time.

   T: Let's see if we can answer this question by drawing.

   T: Draw a segment 3 inches long on your blank paper and label the endpoints A and B.

MP.7   S: (Draw segment.)

   T: (Demonstrate.) Now using your set square, draw three-inch segments from both point A and point B at a 90° angle to AB.

   S: (Draw additional segments.)

   T: Label the endpoints as C and D. Are AC and BD parallel? How do you know?

   S: I checked with my set square. They are parallel. → They must be parallel because we drew them both as right angles to the same segment.

Lesson 19:   Draw kites and squares to clarify their attributes, and define kites and squares based on those attributes.
Date: 1/10/14

5.D.4

© 2014 Common Core, Inc. All rights reserved. commoncore.org

T: Use your straightedge to connect points C and D.

T: Measure segment CD. What is its length?

S: CD is also 3 inches.

T: What have we drawn? How do you know?

S: A square. It has four right angles and four equal sides.

T: Based on the properties of parallel sides, tell your partner another name for this shape and justify your choice.

S: It's a trapezoid. It has one pair of parallel sides. → I can call this a parallelogram because there are two sets of parallel sides.

T: Use your protractor to measure angles C and D. What are their measures?

S: 90°. → All of the angles are 90°.

T: Since this is a parallelogram with four right angles and two sets of opposite equal sides, what can we call it?

S: A rectangle.

T: Since this is a parallelogram with four equal sides, what can we call it?

S: A rhombus.

T: Let's return to our question, can a rhombus ever be a rectangle? Can a rectangle ever be a rhombus? Why or why not?

S: Yes. A square is a rhombus and a rectangle at the same time. → A rectangle can be a rhombus if it is a square. → A rhombus can be a rectangle if it is a square.

T: Using what you just drew, list the attributes of a square with your partner.

S: A square has four sides that are equal and four right angles. → A square has opposite sides parallel and four right angles, and the sides are all equal. → A square is a rectangle with four sides that are equal length. → A square is a rhombus with four right angles.

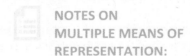

NOTES ON
MULTIPLE MEANS OF
REPRESENTATION:

English language learners and others may feel overwhelmed distinguishing terms in this lesson. To support understanding, point to a picture or make gestures to clarify the meaning of *parallel, rhombus, attribute,* etc., each time they are mentioned. Building additional checks for understanding into instruction may also prove helpful, as might recording student observations of shape attributes and definitions in a list, table, or graphic organizer.

T: Draw the diagonals of the square. Before we measure them, predict whether the diagonals will bisect each other and justify your predictions using properties. Turn and talk.

S: The parallelograms we drew had bisecting diagonals, and this is definitely a parallelogram. I think the diagonals will bisect. → I think they will bisect each other because a square is a rectangle and all the rectangles' diagonals we measured bisected each other. → We drew rhombuses yesterday, and all those diagonals bisected each other. A square is a rhombus so that should be true in a square too.

T: Measure the length of the diagonals. Then measure the distance from each corner to the point where they intersect to test your prediction.

	Lesson 19:	Draw kites and squares to clarify their attributes, and define kites and squares based on those attributes.	
	Date:	1/10/14	

5.D.50

© 2014 Common Core, Inc. All rights reserved. commoncore.org

S: (Draw and measure.)

T: What did you find?

S: The diagonals do bisect each other.

T: Now, measure the angles where the diagonals intersect with your protractor.

S: (Measure the intersecting angles.)

T: What did you find?

S: They intersect at right angles. → All the angles are 90°. → The diagonals are perpendicular to each other.

T: When the diagonals of a quadrilateral bisect each other at a 90° angle, we say the diagonals are **perpendicular bisectors**.

Problem 2

a.   Draw a kite, and articulate the definition.

b.   Measure and label its sides and angles to explore their relationships.

c.   Measure to explore diagonals of kites.

T: We have one more quadrilateral to explore. Let's see if you can guess the figure if I give you some real world clues. It works best outside on windy days, and it's flown with a string. (Give clues until the figure is named.)

S: A kite.

T: Sketch a kite.

S: (Sketch.)

T: Compare your kite to your neighbor's. How are they alike? How are they different? Turn and talk.

S: Mine is narrow, and my partner's is wider. → Mine is taller, and my partner's is shorter. → They all have four sides.

T: Let's draw a kite using our tools. Draw an angle of any measure with two sides that are the same length but at least two inches long. Mark the vertex as I and the endpoints of the segments as K and T.

S: (Draw a kite.)

T: Use your scissors to cut along the rays of your angle.

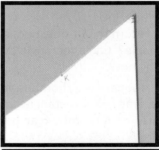

S: (Cut along the rays.)

T: Fold your angle in half matching points K and T. (See image.) Open it, and mark a point on the fold and label it E.

S: (Fold and label.)

T: Use your ruler to connect your point to the ends of the other segments. Then cut out your kite.

S: (Cut out the kite.)

Lesson 19: Draw kites and squares to clarify their attributes, and define kites and squares based on those attributes.

Date: 1/10/14

5.D.

© 2014 Common Core, Inc. All rights reserved. **commoncore.org**

T: Measure the two sides that you just drew. What do you notice about the sides? How are they different from parallelograms?

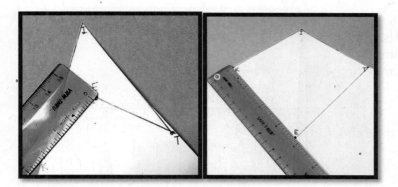

S: There are two sets of sides that are equal to each other, but they are next to each other, not across from each other. → Opposite sides are not equal on mine, but adjacent sides are. → None of these sides are parallel to each other.

T: Use your protractor to measure the angles of your kite, and record the measurements on your figure.

S: (Measure and record the angles of the kite.)

T: What do you notice? Turn and talk. (Allow students to time share with a partner.)

T: Now, draw the diagonals of the kite. Measure the length of the diagonals, the segments of the diagonals, and the angles where the diagonals intersect.

S: (Draw and measure the diagonals, segments, and angles.)

T: What can you say about the diagonals of a kite? Turn and talk.

S: My diagonals cross outside my kite, but they are still perpendicular. → The diagonals are not the same length. → The diagonals meet at 90° angles, they are perpendicular. → One diagonal bisects the other, but they are not both bisected.

T: Tell your partner the attributes of a kite.

S: A quadrilateral with adjacent sides equal. → A quadrilateral with at least one pair of adjacent sides equal.

T: A kite is a quadrilateral that has adjacent sides, or sides next to each other, that are equal. Can a kite ever be a parallelogram? Can a parallelogram ever be a kite? Why or why not? Turn and talk.

S: A square and a rhombus have diagonals that are perpendicular to each other. I wonder if they could be kites. → Squares and rhombuses have sides

NOTES ON KITES:

If no student produces a concave kite (an arrowhead) through the process of drawing in the lesson, draw one for students to consider. It is important to note that although the diagonals do not intersect within the kite, the same relationships hold true. The lines containing the diagonals will intersect at a right angle and only one will bisect the other. Students who produce such a kite may need help drawing the diagonals.

Lesson 19:   Draw kites and squares to clarify their attributes, and define kites and squares based on those attributes.

Date: 1/10/14

5.D.52

© 2014 Common Core, Inc. All rights reserved. commoncore.org

next to each other that are equal. They are the only parallelograms that could also be called kites. → Any quadrilateral with all sides equal would have adjacent sides equal, so a rhombus and a square could be kites.

T: (Distribute the Problem Set to students.) Let's practice drawing more squares and kites and thinking about their attributes by completing the Problem Set.

S: (Complete the Problem Set.)

Please note the extended time designated for the Debrief of today's lesson.

Problem Set

Students should do their personal best to complete the Problem Set within the allotted 10 minutes. For some classes, it may be appropriate to modify the assignment by specifying which problems they work on first. All problems do not specify a method for solving. Students solve these problems using the RDW approach used for Application Problems.

Student Debrief (10 minutes)

Lesson Objective: Draw kites and squares to clarify their attributes, and define kites and squares based on those attributes.

The Student Debrief is intended to invite reflection and active processing of the total lesson experience.

Invite students to review their solutions for the Problem Set. They should check work by comparing answers with a partner before going over answers as a class. Look for misconceptions or misunderstandings that can be addressed in the Debrief. Guide students in a conversation to debrief the Problem Set and process the lesson.

You may choose to use any combination of the questions below to lead the discussion.

- Allow students to share the myriad squares and kites that are produced in Problem 1 of the Problem Set. Compare and contrast these

---

NYS COMMON CORE MATHEMATICS CURRICULUM   Lesson 19 Problem Set 5•5

Name _Lisa_____   Date _____

1. Draw the figures in each box with the attributes listed. If your figure has more than one name, write it in the box.

Rhombus with 2 right angles.	Kite with all sides equal.
Rhombus, rectangle, square, parallelogram, trapezoid, quadrilateral	Kite, quadrilateral, rhombus, parallelogram, trapezoid
Kite with 4 right angles.	**Kite with 2 pairs of adjacent sides equal (but the pairs are not equal to each other.)**
Kite, rectangle, square, parallelogram, trapezoid, quadrilateral, rhombus	Kite, quadrilateral

2. Use the figures you drew to complete the tasks below.
    a. Measure the angles of the figures with your protractor and record the measurements on the figures.
    b. Use a marker or crayon to circle pairs of angles inside each figure with a sum equal to 180°. Use a different color for each pair.

COMMON CORE | Lesson 19: Draw kites and squares to clarify their attributes and define based on those attributes. | engage^ny •5.D.10
Date: 12/21/13

NYS COMMON CORE MATHEMATICS CURRICULUM   Lesson 19 Problem Set 5•5

3.
a. List the properties shared by all of the squares that you worked with today.
    4 equal sides, all 90° angles, both pairs of sides parallel.

b. List the properties shared by all of the kites that you worked with today.
    4 sides, pairs of angles add up to 180°, 2 sets of adjacent equal sides.

c. When can a rhombus also be called a square?
    When all 4 angles measure 90°

d. When can a kite also be called a square?
    When all 4 sides are equal and at 90° to each other.

e. When can a trapezoid also be called a kite?
    When all 4 sides or all 4 angles are equal, if it's a square or rhombus.

COMMON CORE | Lesson 19: Draw kites and squares to clarify their attributes and define based on those attributes. | engage^ny 5.D.11
Date: 12/21/13

Lesson 19:   Draw kites and squares to clarify their attributes, and define kites and squares based on those attributes.

Date: 1/10/14

© 2014 Common Core, Inc. All rights reserved. commoncore.org

quadrilaterals.

- Use the figures produced in Problem 1 to articulate the formal definitions of both squares and kites. Continue to post the definitions.

- Consolidate the lists of attributes students generated for squares and kites in Problem 4. What attributes do all squares share? What attributes do all kites share? When is a quadrilateral a kite, but not a square or rhombus?

- When can a quadrilateral also be called a square?

- Respond to the following statements with *true* or *false*. Explain your reasoning.
  - All squares are quadrilaterals.
  - All quadrilaterals are squares.
  - All rhombuses are squares.
  - All squares are rhombuses.
  - All rectangles are squares.
  - All squares are rectangles.
  - All squares are parallelograms.
  - All parallelograms are squares.
  - All kites are quadrilaterals.
  - All quadrilaterals are kites.
  - All kites are squares.
  - All squares are kites.

- Finish the construction of the hierarchy diagram. (See the template at the end of the lesson.) Students might draw or glue examples of squares and kites or list attributes within the diagram. Encourage them to explain their placement of the figures in the hierarchy.

A square:
- Is a rhombus with four right angles.
- Is a rectangle with four equal sides.

A kite:
- Is a quadrilateral in which two consecutive sides have equal length, and
- Has two remaining sides of equal length.

Exit Ticket (3 minutes)

After the Student Debrief, instruct students to complete the Exit Ticket. A review of their work will help you assess the students' understanding of the concepts that were presented in the lesson today and plan more effectively for future lessons. You may read the questions aloud to the students.

COMMON CORE

Lesson 19:   Draw kites and squares to clarify their attributes, and define kites and
              squares based on those attributes.
Date: 1/10/14

5.D.54

© 2014 Common Core, Inc. All rights reserved. commoncore.org

A   # Correct _____

Multiply.

1	2 x 10 =		23	33 x 20 =	
2	12 x 10 =		24	33 x 200 =	
3	12 x 100 =		25	24 x 10 =	
4	4 x 10 =		26	24 x 20 =	
5	34 x 10 =		27	24 x 100 =	
6	34 x 100 =		28	24 x 200 =	
7	7 x 10 =		29	23 x 30 =	
8	27 x 10 =		30	23 x 300 =	
9	27 x 100 =		31	71 x 2 =	
10	3 x 10 =		32	71 x 20 =	
11	3 x 2 =		33	14 x 2 =	
12	3 x 20 =		34	14 x 3 =	
13	13 x 10 =		35	14 x 30 =	
14	13 x 2 =		36	14 x 300 =	
15	13 x 20 =		37	82 x 20 =	
16	13 x 100 =		38	15 x 300 =	
17	13 x 200 =		39	71 x 600 =	
18	2 x 4 =		40	18 x 40 =	
19	22 x 4 =		41	75 x 30 =	
20	22 x 40 =		42	84 x 300 =	
21	22 x 400 =		43	87 x 60 =	
22	33 x 2 =		44	79 x 800 =	

Lesson 19:	Draw kites and squares to clarify their attributes, and define kites and squares based on those attributes.
Date:	1/10/14

5.D.5

© 2014 Common Core, Inc. All rights reserved. **commoncore.org**

B

Improvement _____ · · · · · · · · # Correct _____

Multiply.

1	3 x 10 =		23	44 x 20 =	
2	13 x 10 =		24	44 x 200 =	
3	13 x 100 =		25	42 x 10 =	
4	5 x 10 =		26	42 x 20 =	
5	35 x 10 =		27	42 x 100 =	
6	35 x 100 =		28	42 x 200 =	
7	8 x 10 =		29	32 x 30 =	
8	28 x 10 =		30	32 x 300 =	
9	28 x 100 =		31	81 x 2 =	
10	4 x 10 =		32	81 x 20 =	
11	4 x 2 =		33	13 x 3 =	
12	4 x 20 =		34	13 x 4 =	
13	14 x 10 =		35	13 x 40 =	
14	14 x 2 =		36	13 x 400 =	
15	14 x 20 =		37	72 x 30 =	
16	14 x 100 =		38	15 x 300 =	
17	14 x 200 =		39	81 x 600 =	
18	2 x 3 =		40	16 x 40 =	
19	22 x 3 =		41	65 x 30 =	
20	22 x 30 =		42	48 x 300 =	
21	22 x 300 =		43	89 x 60 =	
22	44 x 2 =		44	76 x 800 =	

Lesson 19: Draw kites and squares to clarify their attributes, and define kites and squares based on those attributes.

Date: 1/10/14

5.D.56

© 2014 Common Core, Inc. All rights reserved. commoncore.org

Name _____   Date _____

1. Draw the figures in each box with the attributes listed. If your figure has more than one name, write it in the box.

Rhombus with 2 right angles.	Kite with all sides equal.
Kite with 4 right angles.	Kite with 2 pairs of adjacent sides equal. (The pairs are not equal to each other.)

2. Use the figures you drew to complete the tasks below.

   a. Measure the angles of the figures with your protractor, and record the measurements on the figures.

   b. Use a marker or crayon to circle pairs of angles inside each figure with a sum equal to 180°. Use a different color for each pair.

Lesson 19:   Draw kites and squares to clarify their attributes, and define kites and squares based on those attributes.

Date: 1/10/14

5.D.

© 2014 Common Core, Inc. All rights reserved. **commoncore.org**

3.

a. List the properties shared by all of the squares that you worked with today.

b. List the properties shared by all of the kites that you worked with today.

c. When can a rhombus also be called a square?

d. When can a kite also be called a square?

e. When can a trapezoid also be called a kite?

Lesson 19:   Draw kites and squares to clarify their attributes, and define kites and
            squares based on those attributes.
Date: 1/10/14

5.D.58

© 2014 Common Core, Inc. All rights reserved. **commoncore.org**

Name _____   Date _____

1. List the property that must be present to call a rectangle a square.

2. Excluding rhombuses and squares, explain the difference between parallelograms and kites.

Lesson 19:   Draw kites and squares to clarify their attributes, and define kites and
squares based on those attributes.
Date: 1/10/14

5.D.5

© 2014 Common Core, Inc. All rights reserved. **commoncore.org**

Name _____   Date _____

1.

    a. Draw a kite that is not a parallelogram on the grid paper.

    b. List all the properties of a kite.

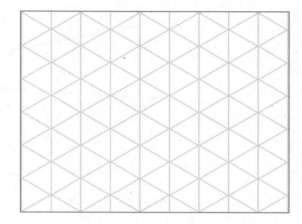

    c. When can a parallelogram also be a kite?

2. If rectangles must have right angles, explain how a rhombus could also be called a rectangle.

3. Draw a rhombus that is also a rectangle on the grid paper.

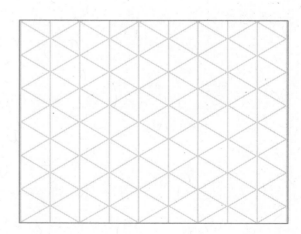

COMMON CORE

Lesson 19:   Draw kites and squares to clarify their attributes, and define kites and squares based on those attributes.

Date: 1/10/14

5.D.60

© 2014 Common Core, Inc. All rights reserved. commoncore.org

4. Kirkland says that figure $EFGH$ below is a quadrilateral because it has four points in the same plane and four segments with no three endpoints collinear. Explain his error.

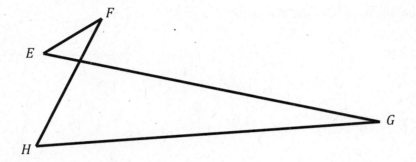

COMMON CORE

Lesson 19: Draw kites and squares to clarify their attributes, and define kites and squares based on those attributes.

Date: 1/10/14

5.D.

© 2014 Common Core, Inc. All rights reserved. **commoncore.org**

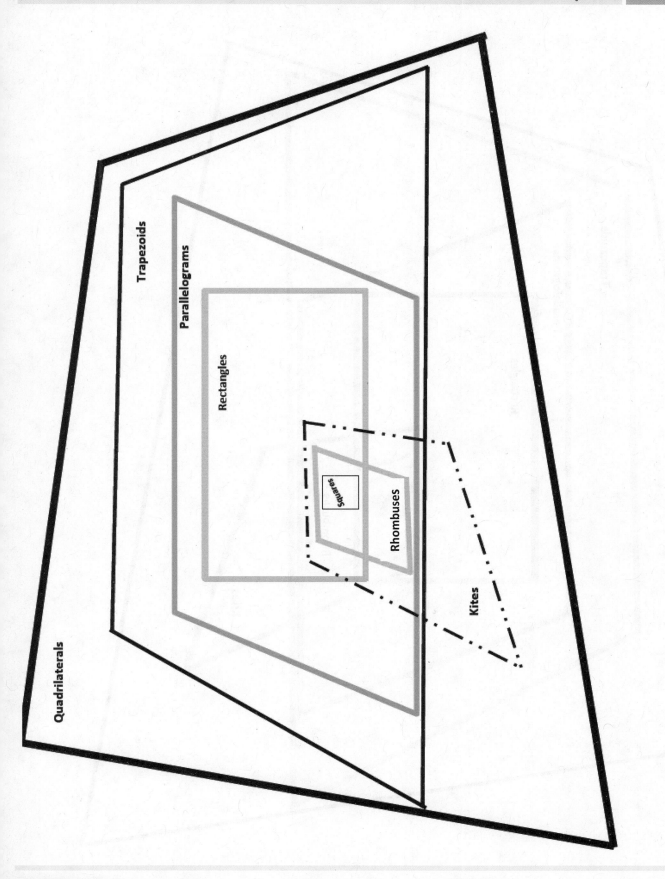

Quadrilaterals

Trapezoids

Parallelograms

Rectangles

Rhombuses

Squares

Kites

COMMON CORE

Lesson 19: Draw kites and squares to clarify their attributes, and define kites and squares based on those attributes.

Date: 1/10/14

5.D.62

© 2014 Common Core, Inc. All rights reserved. **commoncore.org**

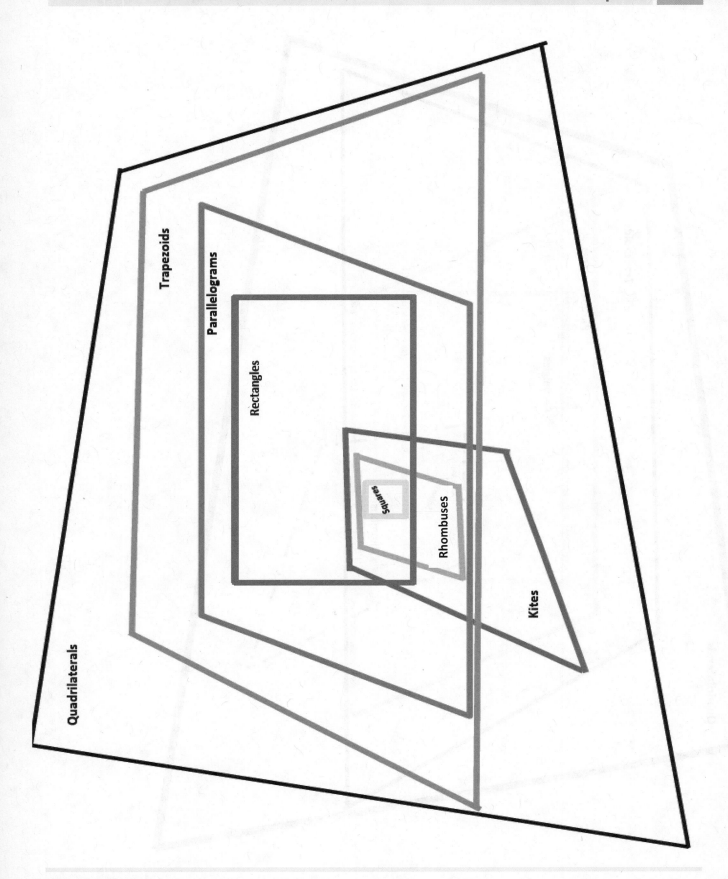

COMMON CORE

Lesson 19: Draw kites and squares to clarify their attributes, and define kites and squares based on those attributes.

Date: 1/10/14

5.D.6

© 2014 Common Core, Inc. All rights reserved. **commoncore.org**

Lesson 20

Objective: Classify two-dimensional figures in a hierarchy based on properties.

Suggested Lesson Structure

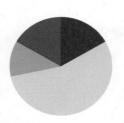

- ■ Fluency Practice   (10 minutes)
- ■ Application Problem   (7 minutes)
- ■ Concept Development   (33 minutes)
- ■ Student Debrief   (10 minutes)

   Total Time   **(60 minutes)**

Fluency Practice (10 minutes)

- Divide by Multiples of 10 and 100 **5.NBT.2**   (4 minutes)
- Find the Volume **5.MD.5**   (6 minutes)

Divide by Multiples of 10 and 100 (4 minutes)

Materials: (S) Personal white boards

Note: This fluency reviews G5–Module 2.

T: (Write 930 ÷ 10 = _____.) Say the division sentence.
S: 930 ÷ 10 = 93.
T: (Write 930 ÷ 10 = _____. To the right, write 93 ÷ 3 = _____.) Say the division sentence.
S: 93 ÷ 3 = 31.
T: (Write 93 ÷ 3 = 31. Below it, write 930 ÷ 30 = _____.) Say 930 ÷ 30 as a division sentence, but divide first by 10 and then by 3.
S: 930 ÷ 10 ÷ 3 = 31.
T: (Write 930 ÷ 30 = 31.)

$930 \div 10 = 93 \qquad 93 \div 3 = 31$

$930 \div 30 = 31$

$10 \quad \times \quad 3$

Continue the process for the following possible sequence: 420 ÷ 20, 4,800 ÷ 40, 8,400 ÷ 400, and 6,900 ÷ 300.

Lesson 20:	Classify two-dimensional figures in a hierarchy based on properties.
Date:	1/10/14

5.D.64

© 2014 Common Core, Inc. All rights reserved. commoncore.org

Find the Volume (6 minutes)

Materials: (S) Personal white boards

Note: This fluency reviews G5–M5–Topic B.

- T: Say the formula for finding the volume of a rectangular prism.
- S: Length times width times height.
- T: Visualize a line that breaks the figure into two rectangular prisms.

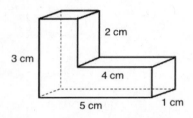

NOTES ON MULTIPLE MEANS OF ACTION AND EXPRESSION:

All students may benefit from building the composite three-dimensional figures for the Find the Volume fluency. Consider offering cubic units and then have them re-analyze the drawing once having built the figure.

- T: Find the volume of the composite figure by adding the volumes of each rectangular prism.
- S: (Write 3 cm × 1 cm × 1 cm = 3 cubic cm. 4 cm × 1 cm × 1 cm = 4 cubic cm. 3 cubic cm + 4 cubic cm = 7 cubic cm.)

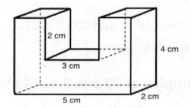

Continue process for the other composite figure.

Application Problem (7 minutes)

Nita buys a rug that is $10\frac{3}{4}$ feet × $12\frac{1}{2}$ feet. What is the area of the rug? Show your thinking with an area model and a multiplication sentence.

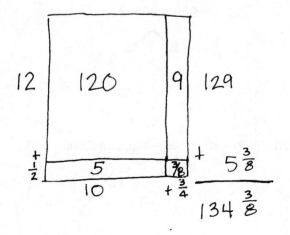

$$10\frac{3}{4} \times 12\frac{1}{2}$$
$$= (10 \times 12) + \left(10 \times \frac{1}{2}\right) + \left(\frac{3}{4} \times 12\right) + \left(\frac{3}{4} \times \frac{1}{2}\right)$$
$$= 120 + 5 + 9 + \frac{3}{8}$$
$$= 134\frac{3}{8}$$

The area of the rug is $134\frac{3}{8}$ ft².

Lesson 20:   Classify two-dimensional figures in a hierarchy based on properties.
Date: 1/10/14

5.D.6

© 2014 Common Core, Inc. All rights reserved. commoncore.org

Note: Today's Application Problem reviews areas of regions with fractional sides from earlier in this module.

Concept Development (33 minutes)

Materials: (S) Personal white board, figure name cards (see template), shapes sheet for sorting, protractor, ruler, set square, hierarchy blank

Part 1

Justify responses to true or false statements about quadrilaterals based on properties.

   a. Trapezoids are always quadrilaterals.

   b. Quadrilaterals are always trapezoids.

NOTES ON MULTIPLE MEANS OF REPRESENTATION:

Depending on the English proficiency level of English language learners, it might be helpful to demonstrate how to justify responses to true or false statements, give extra response time, or provide sentence frames or starters, such as the following:

- The statement is true or false because….
- I disagree because….

IP.3

T: (Project Sentence (a) on the board.) Talk to your partner about whether the statement is true or false. Justify your answer using properties of the shapes.

S: This is true because all trapezoids have the properties of quadrilaterals. They just have an extra property. They have at least one set of parallel sides. → Look at this trapezoid I drew. It has four segments in the same plane that only intersect at their endpoints. You can't draw a trapezoid without these properties of quadrilaterals. It is true that trapezoids are always quadrilaterals.

T: (Project Sentence (b) on the board.) What about this statement? Trapezoids are always quadrilaterals. Are quadrilaterals always trapezoids? Why or why not? Turn and talk.

S: This isn't true. There are lots of quadrilaterals that don't have any parallel sides. → If a quadrilateral doesn't have parallel sides, it can't be a trapezoid. This statement is false.

T: (Write on the board: _____ *are always* _____. Give pairs of students a set of shape name cards.) Write this sentence frame on your personal board, and turn all your cards face down on your table.

S: (Write the sentence frame.)

T: Each partner should choose a shape name card and place it in one of the blanks in the sentence frame. Work together to decide whether your statement is true or false, and use the properties of the figures to justify your answer. Then, switch the cards in the frame, and repeat the sequence. Finally, put the cards back on the table facedown. (Allow students time to work.)

Part 2

Classify two-dimensional figures in a hierarchy using tools to confirm properties.

T: (Project the image of a trapezoid and the hierarchy diagram from G5–M5–Lesson 19.) What does this shape look like?

Lesson 20:   Classify two-dimensional figures in a hierarchy based on properties.
Date: 1/10/14

5.D.66

© 2014 Common Core, Inc. All rights reserved. **commoncore.org**

S: Quadrilateral. → A trapezoid.

T: How could I use my tools to be sure of these classifications? What properties would I need to confirm in order to classify this shape as a trapezoid. Turn and talk.

S: It's two-dimensional, and it has four sides, so we know it's a quadrilateral. → I can see it's a quadrilateral, but to be sure it's a trapezoid, I could use my set square to check if it had at least one pair of parallel sides.

T: I'll confirm for you that this figure does have four segments in the same plane and they only intersect at their endpoints. None of the endpoints are collinear, and it has one pair of parallel sides. With that information, could I place this figure inside the quadrilateral on the hierarchy diagram? Why or why not?

S: Yes. It is a quadrilateral.

T: (Place the figure on the diagram inside the quadrilateral only.) Could I place it inside the trapezoid on the hierarchy diagram? Why or why not?

S: Yes, because it has one set of parallel sides, it can go there.

T: Can I place it inside the parallelogram on the hierarchy? Why or why not?

S: No, it doesn't have two sets of parallel sides, so it can't go inside the parallelogram.

T: This figure is inside the quadrilateral ring and the trapezoid ring. What does that mean for its properties?

S: It has all the properties of a quadrilateral and all the properties of a trapezoid.

T: (Give one shape sheet and a copy of the hierarchy diagram from G5–M5–Lesson 19 to each pair of students.) Work with your partner to classify the shapes on your sheet. Use your tools to confirm their properties. Then cut them out and glue them on the hierarchy diagram. Be prepared to defend their placement.

S: (Work.)

Circulate and ask questions of students as they confirm properties and sort. Encourage students to verbalize that attributes belonging to a category of figures also belong to all subcategories of the figure. The following sentence frame might be used: *Because a _____ is a _____ it must have _____.* (For example: Because a <u>rhombus</u> is a <u>trapezoid</u> it must have <u>at least one set of parallel sides</u>.)

Problem Set (10 minutes)

Students should do their personal best to complete the Problem Set within the allotted 10 minutes. For some classes, it may be appropriate to modify the assignment by specifying which problems they work on first. All problems do not specify a method for solving. Students solve these problems using the RDW approach used for Application Problems.

Student Debrief (10 minutes)

Lesson Objective: Classify two-dimensional figures in a hierarchy based on properties.

The Student Debrief is intended to invite reflection and active processing of the total lesson experience.

Lesson 20:   Classify two-dimensional figures in a hierarchy based on properties.

Date: 1/10/14   5.D.6

© 2014 Common Core, Inc. All rights reserved. **commoncore.org**

Invite students to review their solutions for the Problem Set. They should check work by comparing answers with a partner before going over answers as a class. Look for misconceptions or misunderstandings that can be addressed in the Debrief. Guide students in a conversation to debrief the Problem Set and process the lesson.

You may choose to use any combination of the questions below to lead the discussion.

- The false statements in Problem 1 may be corrected in many ways. Allow students opportunity to share approaches.

- Students might be challenged to draw a counter example for false statements in Problem 1.

- Ask students to draw other quadrilaterals with the same attributes as those in Problem 2. What is the most specific name for the shape? What's the least specific name?

- Review the formal definitions of all the quadrilaterals from the topic. Compare them with a view toward noticing the hierarchical nature. For example, a rhombus is a parallelogram with four equal sides. Point out that because a rhombus *is* a parallelogram, it has all the attributes of a parallelogram *and* four equal sides.

- As the most specific quadrilateral that we've explored, a square can be correctly classified as any of the quadrilaterals on the hierarchy. (Making a list of all of a square's attributes using sides, angles, and diagonals, then specifying which more general quadrilateral contributes the property, can help drive home the understanding of the hierarchy.)

Exit Ticket (3 minutes)

After the Student Debrief, instruct students to complete the Exit Ticket. A review of their work will help you assess the students' understanding of the concepts that were presented in the lesson today and plan more effectively for future lessons. You may read the questions aloud to the students.

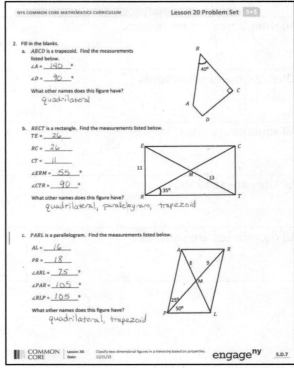

COMMON CORE™

Lesson 20:   Classify two-dimensional figures in a hierarchy based on properties.
Date: 1/10/14

5.D.68

© 2014 Common Core, Inc. All rights reserved. commoncore.org

Name _____   Date _____

1. True or false. If the statement is false, rewrite it to make it true.

		T	F
a.	All trapezoids are quadrilaterals.		
b.	All parallelograms are rhombuses.		
c.	All squares are trapezoids.		
d.	All rectangles are squares.		
e.	Rectangles are always parallelograms.		
f.	All parallelograms are trapezoids.		
g.	All rhombuses are rectangles.		
h.	Kites are never rhombuses.		
i.	All squares are kites.		
j.	All kites are squares.		
k.	All rhombuses are squares.		

Lesson 20:   Classify two-dimensional figures in a hierarchy based on properties.
Date: 1/10/14

5.D.6

© 2014 Common Core, Inc. All rights reserved. **commoncore.org**

2. Fill in the blanks.

a. *ABCD* is a trapezoid. Find the measurements listed below.

∠A = _____°

∠D = _____°

What other names does this figure have?

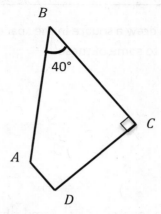

b. *RECT* is a rectangle. Find the measurements listed below.

TE = _____

RC = _____

CT = _____

∠ERM = _____°

∠CTR = _____°

What other names does this figure have?

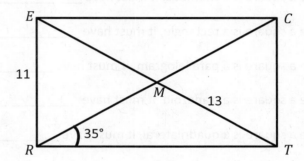

c. *PARL* is a parallelogram. Find the measurements listed below.

AL = _____

PR = _____

∠ARL = _____°

∠PAR = _____°

∠RLP = _____°

What other names does this figure have?

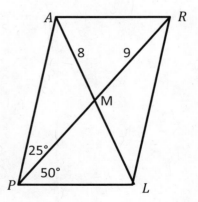

Lesson 20: Classify two-dimensional figures in a hierarchy based on properties.
Date: 1/10/14

5.D.70

© 2014 Common Core, Inc. All rights reserved. commoncore.org

Name _____   Date _____

Use your tools to draw a square in the space below. Then fill in the blanks with an attribute. There is more than one answer to some of these.

a. Because a square is a kite, it must have _____.

b. Because a square is a rhombus, it must have _____.

c. Because a square is a rectangle, it must have _____.

d. Because a square is a parallelogram, it must have _____.

e. Because a square is a trapezoid, it must have _____.

f. Because a square is a quadrilateral, it must have _____.

© 2014 Common Core, Inc. All rights reserved. commoncore.org

Name _____ Date _____

1. Follow the flow chart and put the name of the figure in the boxes.

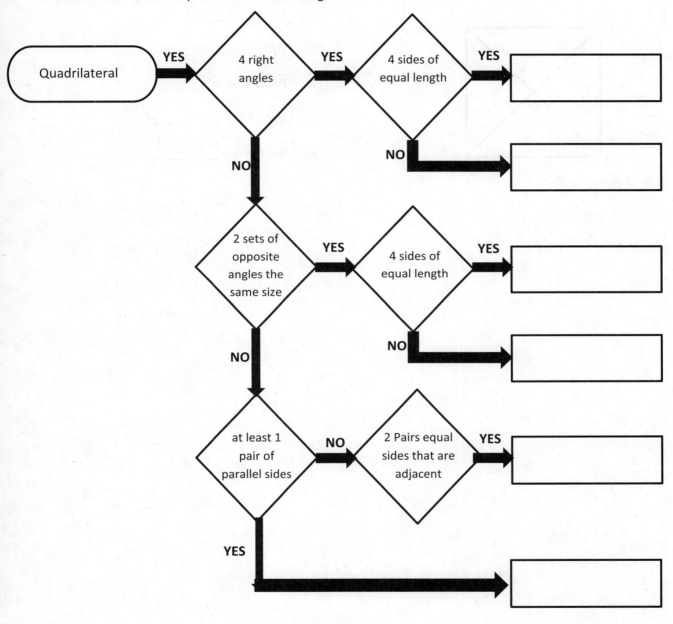

Lesson 20:   Classify two-dimensional figures in a hierarchy based on properties.
Date: 1/10/14

5.D.72

© 2014 Common Core, Inc. All rights reserved. **commoncore.org**

2. *SQRE* is a square with area 49 cm² and *RM* = 4.95 cm. Find the measurements using what you know about the properties of squares.

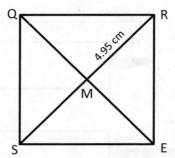

a. *RS* = _____ cm

b. *QE* = _____ cm

c. Perimeter = _____ cm

d. $m\angle QRE$ = _____ °

e. $m\angle RMQ$ = _____ °

COMMON CORE™

Lesson 20:   Classify two-dimensional figures in a hierarchy based on properties.
Date: 1/10/14

5.D.7.

© 2014 Common Core, Inc. All rights reserved. **commoncore.org**

Quadrilaterals	**Trapezoids**
Parallelograms	**Rectangles**
Rhombuses	**Kites**
Squares	**Polygons**

© 2014 Common Core, Inc. All rights reserved. **commoncore.org**

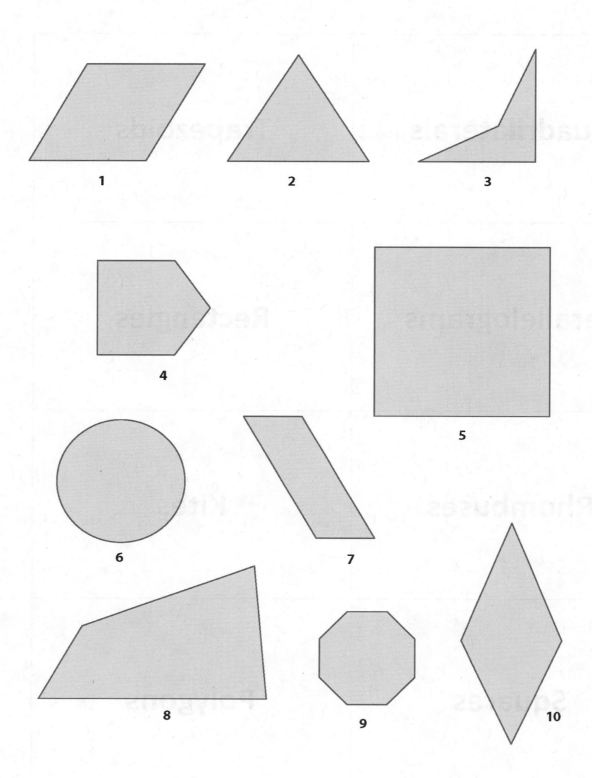

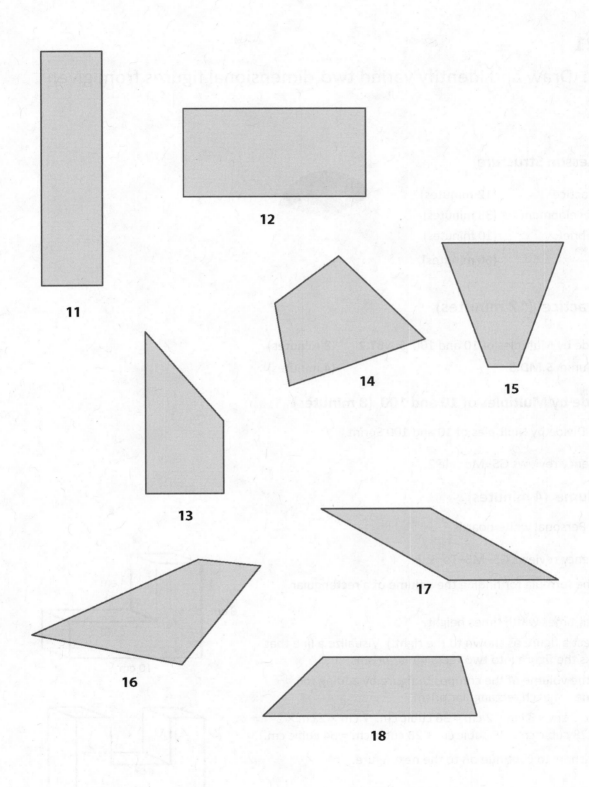

11

12

13

14

15

16

17

18

Lesson 20:   Classify two-dimensional figures in a hierarchy based on properties.
Date: 1/10/14

5.D.76

© 2014 Common Core, Inc. All rights reserved. commoncore.org

Lesson 21

Objective: Draw and identify varied two-dimensional figures from given attributes.

Suggested Lesson Structure

■ Fluency Practice   (12 minutes)
  Concept Development   (38 minutes)
■ Student Debrief   (10 minutes)
  Total Time   **(60 minutes)**

Fluency Practice (12 minutes)

▪ Sprint: Divide by Multiples of 10 and 100 **5.NBT.2**   (8 minutes)
▪ Find the Volume **5.MD.5**   (4 minutes)

Sprint: Divide by Multiples of 10 and 100 (8 minutes)

Materials: (S) Divide by Multiples of 10 and 100 Sprint

Note: This fluency reviews G5–Module 2.

Find the Volume (4 minutes)

Materials: (S) Personal white boards

Note: This fluency reviews G5–M5–Topic B.

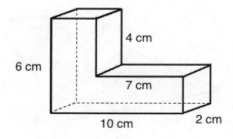

T: Say the formula for finding the volume of a rectangular prism.
S: Length times width times height.
T: (Project a figure as shown to the right.) Visualize a line that breaks the figure into two rectangular prisms.
T: Find the volume of the composite figure by adding the volumes of each rectangular prism.
S: (Write 6 cm × 3 cm × 2 cm = 36 cubic cm. 7 cm × 2 cm × 2 cm = 28 cubic cm. 36 cubic cm + 28 cubic cm = 64 cubic cm.)

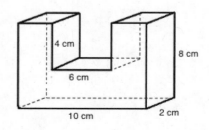

Allow early finishers to continue on to the next figure.

Lesson 21:   Draw and identify varied two-dimensional figures from given attributes.
Date: 1/10/14

5.D.7

© 2014 Common Core, Inc. All rights reserved. commoncore.org

Concept Development (38 minutes)

Materials: (S) Task cards, ruler, set square, protractor, Problem Set (or blank paper)

Note: The drawing tasks in the Concept Development are time consuming. In order to give students ample time, no Application Problem is included in today's lesson.

Note: Today's Concept Development asks students to apply the nested relationships among quadrilaterals that have been explored throughout the topic. It should be conducted following a protocol similar to that of a problem-solving lesson involving word problems. Allow students to wrestle with the drawing tasks and then share the work during the Debrief. Allow students to re-draw as necessary after the Debrief discussion. Task cards (24 per set) should be copied in sufficient quantity that pairs of students can share six cards.

MP.3

T: (Project on the board: *Draw a quadrilateral that has two pair of equal sides. Tell as many names as you can for this shape. Circle the most specific name.*) What shape could you draw to satisfy the attributes on this task card? Turn and talk. Then draw your shape.

S: I could draw a parallelogram. It has two sets of equal sides. → A rectangle would work because it has two pairs of equal sides. → It says two pair of equal sides. I would draw a square. It has two sets of equal sides. The two sets also happen to be equal to each other. → A rhombus would work, too, because it's like a square. It has two sets of equal sides. → I could draw a kite. It has two pairs of equal sides. The sides that are equal are just next to each other rather than across from each other.

T: Compare your shape with your neighbor's. Did we all draw the same shape? Is there only one shape that would be correct for this task?

S: (Share work with partner.)

T: This is the shape I drew. (Project a rectangle.) Name this shape.

S: Rectangle. → Parallelogram. → Quadrilateral. → Polygon. → Trapezoid.

T: (Record student responses.) Which of the names we listed is the most specific?

S: Rectangle.

T: (Circle *rectangle* on board.) Is there a quadrilateral that we shouldn't construct for this card? Why not?

S: A trapezoid that isn't a parallelogram, because it wouldn't have two pairs of equal sides. → An isosceles trapezoid would not work for this task card because there would only be one set of equal sides.

T: Pull six task cards from the envelope on your table. Record the number of the task and a brief summary of the task in the boxes on your Problem Set. Follow the directions on the cards to draw the shapes in the boxes.

NOTES ON
MULTIPLE MEANS OF
ENGAGEMENT:

The task cards for today's lesson are numbered from simplest to most complex. Differentiate instruction by assigning tasks based on student need.

NOTES ON
MULTIPLE MEANS OF
ENGAGEMENT:

The relationships between sides and angles in quadrilaterals can serve as an interesting extension. Students can explore the effects of changing side lengths on angle size and vice versa with online tools like Interactive Quadrilaterals at:
http://www.mathsisfun.com/geometry/quadrilaterals-interactive.html.

Lesson 21:	Draw and identify varied two-dimensional figures from given attributes.
Date:	1/10/14

5.D.78

© 2014 Common Core, Inc. All rights reserved. commoncore.org

S: (Work.)

The Problem Set serves as a recording sheet for the drawing in the lesson. Time should be given for students to share their approaches to constructing the figures on the task cards.

Student Debrief (10 minutes)

Lesson Objective: Draw and identify varied two-dimensional figures from given attributes.

The Student Debrief is intended to invite reflection and active processing of the total lesson experience.

Invite students to review their solutions for the Problem Set. They should check work by comparing answers with a partner before going over answers as a class. Look for misconceptions or misunderstandings that can be addressed in the Debrief. Guide students in a conversation to debrief the Problem Set and process the lesson.

You may choose to use any combination of the questions below to lead the discussion.

- Find someone who completed two of the same tasks you did. Compare the shapes that you drew. Must they be the same shape to correctly follow the directions on the card? Why or why not?

- Which tasks produced quadrilaterals with the same specific name on everyone's Problem Set? Which tasks produced the most varied quadrilaterals?

- Choose three of your quadrilaterals and paste them in the correct part of the hierarchy diagram. Explain why they belong there.

- Explain to your partner how you corrected John's error in Problem 2.

- What part of a kite's definition did Jack not understand in Problem 3? How did you correct his thinking?

- How do all the shapes that were drawn today fit the definition of a quadrilateral?

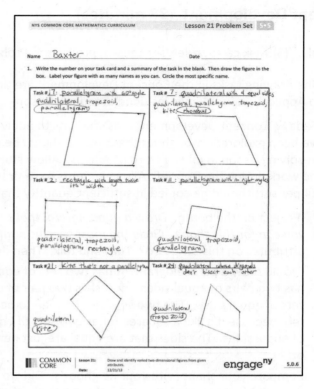

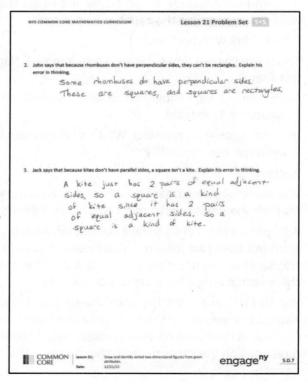

© 2014 Common Core, Inc. All rights reserved. commoncore.org

Exit Ticket (3 minutes)

After the Student Debrief, instruct students to complete the Exit Ticket. A review of their work will help you assess the students' understanding of the concepts that were presented in the lesson today and plan more effectively for future lessons. You may read the questions aloud to the students.

© 2014 Common Core, Inc. All rights reserved. commoncore.org

A

Correct _____

Divide.

1	$30 \div 10 =$	23	$480 \div 4 =$
2	$430 \div 10 =$	24	$480 \div 40 =$
3	$4,300 \div 10 =$	25	$6,300 \div 3 =$
4	$4,300 \div 100 =$	26	$6,300 \div 30 =$
5	$43,000 \div 100 =$	27	$6,300 \div 300 =$
6	$50 \div 10 =$	28	$8,400 \div 2 =$
7	$850 \div 10 =$	29	$8,400 \div 20 =$
8	$8,500 \div 10 =$	30	$8,400 \div 200 =$
9	$8,500 \div 100 =$	31	$96,000 \div 3 =$
10	$85,000 \div 100 =$	32	$96,000 \div 300 =$
11	$600 \div 10 =$	33	$96,000 \div 30 =$
12	$60 \div 3 =$	34	$900 \div 30 =$
13	$600 \div 30 =$	35	$1,200 \div 30 =$
14	$4,000 \div 100 =$	36	$1,290 \div 30 =$
15	$40 \div 2 =$	37	$1,800 \div 300 =$
16	$4,000 \div 200 =$	38	$8,000 \div 200 =$
17	$240 \div 10 =$	39	$12,000 \div 200 =$
18	$24 \div 2 =$	40	$12,800 \div 200 =$
19	$240 \div 20 =$	41	$2,240 \div 70 =$
20	$3,600 \div 100 =$	42	$18,400 \div 800 =$
21	$36 \div 3 =$	43	$21,600 \div 90 =$
22	$3,600 \div 300 =$	44	$25,200 \div 600 =$

COMMON CORE | **Lesson 21:** Draw and identify varied two-dimensional figures from given attributes.
| **Date:** 1/10/14

5.D.81

© 2014 Common Core, Inc. All rights reserved. commoncore.org

B

Improvement _____   # Correct _____

Divide.

1	20 ÷ 10 =	23	840 ÷ 4 =
2	420 ÷ 10 =	24	840 ÷ 40 =
3	4,200 ÷ 10 =	25	3,600 ÷ 3 =
4	4,200 ÷ 100 =	26	3,600 ÷ 30 =
5	42,000 ÷ 100 =	27	3,600 ÷ 300 =
6	40 ÷ 10 =	28	4,800 ÷ 2 =
7	840 ÷ 10 =	29	4,800 ÷ 20 =
8	8,400 ÷ 10 =	30	4,800 ÷ 200 =
9	8,400 ÷ 100 =	31	69,000 ÷ 3 =
10	84,000 ÷ 100 =	32	69,000 ÷ 300 =
11	900 ÷ 10 =	33	69,000 ÷ 30 =
12	90 ÷ 3 =	34	800 ÷ 40 =
13	900 ÷ 30 =	35	1,200 ÷ 40 =
14	6,000 ÷ 100 =	36	1,280 ÷ 40 =
15	60 ÷ 2 =	37	1,600 ÷ 400 =
16	6,000 ÷ 200 =	38	8,000 ÷ 200 =
17	240 ÷ 10 =	39	14,000 ÷ 200 =
18	24 ÷ 2 =	40	14,600 ÷ 200 =
19	240 ÷ 20 =	41	2,560 ÷ 80 =
20	6,300 ÷ 100 =	42	16,100 ÷ 700 =
21	63 ÷ 3 =	43	14,400 ÷ 60 =
22	6,300 ÷ 300 =	44	37,800 ÷ 900 =

Lesson 21:	Draw and identify varied two-dimensional figures from given attributes.	5.D.82
Date:	1/10/14	

© 2014 Common Core, Inc. All rights reserved. commoncore.org

Name _____   Date _____

1. Write the number on your task card and a summary of the task in the blank. Then draw the figure in the box. Label your figure with as many names as you can. Circle the most specific name.

Task #___: _____

Task #___: _____

Task #___: _____

Task #___: _____

Task #___: _____

Task #___: _____

© 2014 Common Core, Inc. All rights reserved. commoncore.org

2. John says that because rhombuses do not have perpendicular sides, they cannot be rectangles. Explain his error in thinking.

3. Jack says that because kites don't have parallel sides, a square is not a kite. Explain his error in thinking.

 **Lesson 21:**   Draw and identify varied two-dimensional figures from given attributes.

Date: 1/10/14   5.D.84

© 2014 Common Core, Inc. All rights reserved. commoncore.org

Name _____   Date _____

1.   Use the word bank to fill in the blanks.   ╔══════════════════════════╗
                                                 ║ **trapezoids   parallelograms** ║
                                                 ╚══════════════════════════╝

   All _____ are _____, but not all _____ are _____.

2.   Use the word bank to fill in the blanks.   ╔════════════════════╗
                                                 ║ **kites   rhombuses** ║
                                                 ╚════════════════════╝

   All _____ are _____, but not all _____ are _____.

Lesson 21:   Draw and identify varied two-dimensional figures from given
Date: attributes.
          1/10/14

5.D.85

© 2014 Common Core, Inc. All rights reserved. commoncore.org

Name _____   Date _____

1. Answer the questions by checking the box.

	Alltimes	Always
a. Is a square a rectangle?		
b. Is a rectangle a kite?		
c. Is a rectangle a parallelogram?		
d. Is a square a trapezoid?		
e. Is a parallelogram a trapezoid?		
f. Is a trapezoid a parallelogram?		
g. Is a kite a parallelogram?		

   h. For each statement that you answered with "sometimes," draw and label an example that justifies your answer.

2. Use what you know about quadrilaterals to answer each question below
   a. Explain when a trapezoid is not a parallelogram. Sketch an example.

   b. Explain when a kite is not a parallelogram. Sketch an example.

 **Lesson 21:** Draw and identify varied two-dimensional figures from given attributes.

Date: 1/10/14

5.D.86

© 2014 Common Core, Inc. All rights reserved. commoncore.org

Task 1: Draw a trapezoid with a right angle.	**Task 2:** Draw a rectangle with a length that is twice its width.
Task 4: Draw a rhombus with right angles.	**Task 3:** Draw a quadrilateral with 2 pairs of equal sides and no parallel sides.
Task 5: Draw a parallelogram with two pairs of perpendicular sides.	**Task 6:** Draw a rhombus with 4 equal angles.

COMMON CORE

Lesson 21:   Draw and identify varied two-dimensional figures from given attributes.

Date: 1/10/14

5.D.87

© 2014 Common Core, Inc. All rights reserved. **commoncore.org**

Task 7: Draw a quadrilateral with four equal sides.	**Task 8:** Draw a parallelogram with right angles.	**Task 9:** Draw a parallelogram with a side of 4 cm and a side of 6 cm.
Task 10: Draw an isosceles trapezoid.	**Task 11:** Draw a parallelogram with no right angles.	**Task 12:** Draw a rectangle that is also a rhombus.

Lesson 21:   Draw and identify varied two-dimensional figures from given attributes.

Date: 1/10/14

5.D.88

© 2014 Common Core, Inc. All rights reserved. commoncore.org

Task 13: Draw a quadrilateral that has at least one pair of equal opposite angles.	Task 14: Draw a quadrilateral that has only one pair of equal opposite angles.	Task 15: Draw a trapezoid with four right angles.
Task 16: Draw a kite that is also a parallelogram.	Task 17: Draw a parallelogram with a 60° angle.	Task 18: Draw a rectangle that is not a rhombus.

Lesson 21: Draw and identify varied two-dimensional figures from given attributes.
Date: 1/10/14

5.D.89

© 2014 Common Core, Inc. All rights reserved. commoncore.org

Task 19: Draw a rhombus that is not a rectangle.	**Task 20:** Draw a parallelogram that is not a rectangle.	**Task 21:** Draw a kite that is not a parallelogram.
Task 22: Draw a quadrilateral whose diagonals bisect each other at a right angle.	**Task 23:** Draw a trapezoid that is not a parallelogram.	**Task 24:** Draw a quadrilateral whose diagonals do not bisect each other.

COMMON CORE | Lesson 21: | Draw and identify varied two-dimensional figures from given attributes.
| | Date: | 1/10/14

5.D.90

© 2014 Common Core, Inc. All rights reserved. **commoncore.org**

Name _____ Date _____

1. Tell the volume of each solid figure made of 1-inch cubes. Specify the correct unit of measure.

a.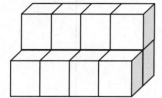

b.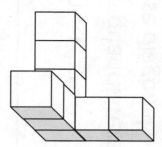

2. Jack found the volume of the prism pictured to the right by multiplying 5 × 8 and then adding: 40 + 40 + 40 = 120. He says the volume is 120 cubic inches.

   a. Jill says he did it wrong. He should have multiplied the bottom first (3 × 5) and then multiplied by the height. Explain to Jill why Jack's method works and is equivalent to her method.

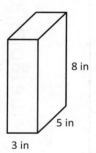

8 in

5 in

3 in

   b. Use Jack's method to find the volume of this right rectangular prism.

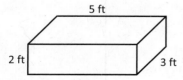

5 ft

2 ft

3 ft

© 2014 Common Core, Inc. All rights reserved. **commoncore.org**

3. If the figure below is made of cubes with 2-cm side lengths, what is its volume? Explain your thinking.

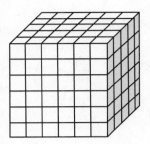

4. The volume of a rectangular prism is 840 in^3. If the area of the base is 60 in^2, find its height. Draw and label a model to show your thinking.

5. The following structure is composed of two right rectangular prisms that each measure 12 inches by 10 inches by 5 inches, and one right rectangular prism that measures 10 inches by 8 inches by 36 inches. What is the total volume of the structure? Explain your thinking.

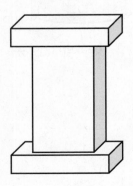

© 2014 Common Core, Inc. All rights reserved. **commoncore.org**

6. a. Find the volume of the rectangular fish tank. Explain your thinking.

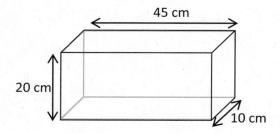

   b. If the fish tank is completely filled with water, and then 900 cubic centimeters are poured out, how high will the water be? Give your answer in centimeters, and show your work.

7. Juliet wants to know if the chicken broth in this beaker will fit into this rectangular food storage container. Explain how you would figure it out without pouring the contents in. If it will fit, how much more broth could the storage container hold? If it will not fit, how much broth would be left over? **(Remember 1 cm³ = 1 mL.)**

beaker

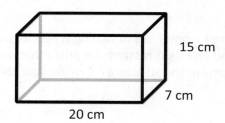

storage container

© 2014 Common Core, Inc. All rights reserved. commoncore.org

Mid-Module Assessment Task	Topics A–B
Standards Addressed	

Geometric measurement: understand concepts of volume and relate volume to multiplication and to addition.

5.MD.3   Recognize volume as an attribute of solid figures and understand concepts of volume measurement.

        a.   A cube with side length 1 unit, called a "unit cube," is said to have "one cubic unit" of volume, and can be used to measure volume.

        b.   A solid figure which can be packed without gaps or overlaps using n unit cubes is said to have a volume of n cubic units.

5.MD.4   Measure volumes by counting unit cubes, using cubic cm, cubic in, cubic ft, and improvised units.

5.MD.5   Relate volume to the operations of multiplication and addition and solve real world and mathematical problems involving volume.

        a.   Find the volume of a right rectangular prism with whole-number side lengths by packing it with unit cubes, and show that the volume is the same as would be found by multiplying the edge lengths, equivalently by multiplying the height by the area of the base. Represent threefold whole-number products as volumes, e.g., to represent the associative property of multiplication.

        b.   Apply the formulas $V = l \times w \times h$ and $V = b \times h$ for rectangular prisms to find volumes of right rectangular prisms with whole-number edge lengths in the context of solving real world and mathematical problems.

        c.   Recognize volume as additive. Find volumes of solid figures composed of two non-overlapping right rectangular prisms by adding the volumes of the non-overlapping parts, applying this technique to solve real world problems.

Evaluating Student Learning Outcomes

A Progression Toward Mastery is provided to describe steps that illuminate the gradually increasing understandings that students develop *on their way to proficiency*. In this chart, this progress is presented from left (Step 1) to right (Step 4). The learning goal for each student is to achieve Step 4 mastery. These steps are meant to help teachers and students identify and celebrate what the student CAN do now and what they need to work on next.

© 2014 Common Core, Inc. All rights reserved. **commoncore.org**

A Progression Toward Mastery

Assessment Task Item and Standards Assessed	STEP 1 Little evidence of reasoning without a correct answer. (1 Point)	STEP 2 Evidence of some reasoning without a correct answer. (2 Points)	STEP 3 Evidence of some reasoning with a correct answer or evidence of solid reasoning with an incorrect answer. (3 Points)	STEP 4 Evidence of solid reasoning with a correct answer. (4 Points)
1 **5.MD.3** **5.MD.4**	The student has neither the correct volume nor the correct unit of measure for either figure.	The student calculates the volume incorrectly for both figures but uses the correct unit of measure.	The student calculates the volume for one figure correctly and uses the correct unit of measure for both.	The student correctly calculates the volume and uses the correct unit of measure for both: a. 12 in^3 b. 8 in^3
2 **5.MD.5a** **5.MD.5b**	The student is unable to explain the equivalence of the two approaches and is unable to find the volume of the prism in Part (b) using Jack's method.	The student makes an attempt to explain the equivalence of the two approaches, but uses faulty logic and is unable to find the volume of the prism in Part (b) using Jack's method.	The student explains the equivalence between the two approaches by explaining the sides may be multiplied in any order because any face can be used as the base of the figure, but is unable to use Jack's method to calculate the volume of the prism in Part (b).	The student correctly explains the equivalence between the two approaches by explaining the sides may be multiplied in any order because any face can be used as the base of the figure, and uses Jack's method to correctly calculate the area of the prism in Part (b) as $(3 \times 2) \times 5 = 30$ ft^3.
3 **5.MD.5a**	The student is neither able to calculate the volume of the figure nor explain the reasoning used.	The student uses a correct method for finding the volume of the cube, but does not take into account the size of the cubes (2-cm side lengths) and does not explain the reasoning used.	The student uses a correct method for finding the volume of the cube and is able to explain the reasoning used, but does not take into account the size of the cubes (2-cm side lengths).	The student correctly answers 1,440 cm^3 and is able to explain the reasoning used.

© 2014 Common Core, Inc. All rights reserved. **commoncore.org**

A Progression Toward Mastery

4 **5.MD.5**	The student is neither able to calculate the height of the prism nor able to draw and label a model.	The student is able to either find the missing height or draws an unlabeled model.	The student draws a labeled model, but makes a calculation error when finding the height of the prism.	The student clearly: • Draws a three-dimensional rectangular prism as a model. • Labels the model. • Calculates the height of the prism as 14 in.
5 **5.MD.5c**	The student is able to calculate the volume of one part of the figure, but is unable to explain the reasoning used.	The student explains the reasoning used, but makes more than one calculation error.	The student explains the reasoning used, but makes one calculation error.	The student: • Correctly calculates the volume of the prism as 4,080 in^3. • Clearly explains the reasoning used.
6 **5.MD.5b**	The student is unable to correctly answer any part of the task.	The student correctly answers either Part (a) or Part (b), but does not explain the reasoning used.	The student calculates either Part (a) or Part (b) correctly and explains the reasoning used.	The student correctly: a. Calculates 9,000 cm^3 and clearly explains the reasoning used. b. Calculates 18 cm and shows correct work and reasoning.
7 **5.MD.3**	The student attempts a calculation, but does not achieve an answer or explain her thinking.	The student attempts part of the answer, but miscalculates or does not explain her thinking.	The student explains her thinking and correctly calculates either the volume in the beaker or the volume of the container, but makes a mistake in the other, leading to incorrect answers.	The student: • Clearly explains a method for determining if the contents will fit without pouring 2,400 mL = 2,400 cm^3. • Correctly answers that the broth will not fit. • Correctly answers that Juliet needs 300 more mL (or cm^3), or 0.3 L, of volume.

Module 5:   Addition and Multiplication with Volume and Area
Date: 1/10/14

5.S.6

© 2014 Common Core, Inc. All rights reserved. **commoncore.org**

Name _____Jean_____ Date _____

1. Tell the volume of each solid figure made of 1-inch cubes. Specify the correct unit of measure.

a.

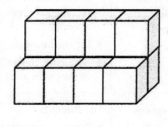

12 in^3

b.

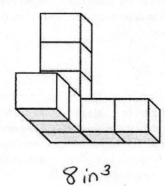

8 in^3

2. Jack found the volume of the prism pictured to the right by multiplying 5 × 8 and
then adding: 40 + 40 + 40 = 120. He says the volume is 120 cubic inches.

a. Jill says he did it wrong. He should have multiplied the bottom first (3 × 5) and
then multiplied by the height. Explain to Jill why Jack's method works and is
equivalent to her method.

Jack thought about it like layers.
He figured out the area of the side
(8 × 5) and imagined there were 3 of them,
so he added those up. That's how he got
120, which is the same as (3×5) × 8.

8 in

5 in

3 in

b. Use Jack's method to find the volume of this right rectangular prism.

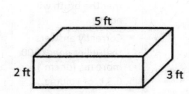

5 ft

2 ft

3 ft

$5 \times 3 = 15$

$15 + 15 = 30$

30 ft^2

© 2014 Common Core, Inc. All rights reserved. **commoncore.org**

3. If the figure below is made of cubes with 2 cm side lengths, what is its volume? Explain your thinking.

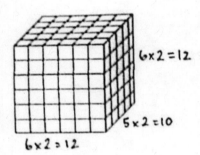

6×2=12

5×2=10

6×2=12

$12 \times 12 \times 10 = 144 \times 10 = 1,440 \text{ cm}^3$

First I counted the cubes, and since they are worth 2 cm each, I doubled the number on each side. Then I could have added layers, but multiplying was faster.

4. The volume of a rectangular prism is 840 in³. If the area of the base is 60 in², find its height. Draw and label a model to show your thinking.

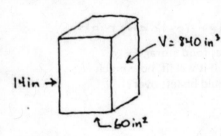

V = 840 in³

14 in →

60 in²

$\dfrac{84\emptyset}{6\emptyset} = \dfrac{84}{6} = 14$

14 inches

5. The following structure is composed of two right rectangular prisms that each measure 12 inches by 10 inches by 5 inches, and one right rectangular prism that measures 10 inches by 8 inches by 36 inches. What is the total volume of the structure? Explain your thinking.

$12 \text{ in} \times 10 \text{ in} \times 5 \text{ in} = 120 \text{ in}^2 \times 5 \text{ in} = 600 \text{ in}^3$

$600 \text{ in}^3 \times 2 = 1,200 \text{ in}^3$

$10 \text{ in} \times 8 \text{ in} \times 36 \text{ in} = 360 \text{ in}^2 \times 8 \text{ in}$

$= 2,880 \text{ in}^3$

The volume is 4,080 in³

360
× 8
———
2,880

2,880
+ 1,200
———
4,080

I found the volume of the top piece, then doubled it.
Then I added that to the volume of the middle piece.

12 in

10 in
5 in

36 in

8 in

10 in

© 2014 Common Core, Inc. All rights reserved. commoncore.org

6. a. Find the volume of the rectangular fish tank.. Explain your thinking.

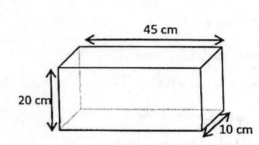

$45\,cm \times 20\,cm \times 10\,cm = 900\,cm^2 \times 10\,cm = 9{,}000\,cm^3$

I multiplied all the sides to get the volume.

b. If the fish tank is completely filled with water, and then 900 cubic centimeters are poured out, how high will the water be? Give your answer in centimeters and show your work.

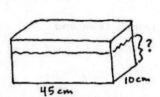

$$9{,}000\,cm^3$$
$$-\ \ 900\,cm^3$$
$$8{,}100\,cm^3$$

Base: $45 \times 10 = 450$

$$\begin{array}{r} 18 \\ 450\overline{)8{,}100} \\ -450 \\ \hline 3600 \end{array}$$

The water is 18 cm high.

$$\begin{array}{r} 450 \\ \times\ \ 8 \\ \hline 3{,}600 \end{array}$$

7. Juliet wants to know if the chicken broth in this beaker will fit into this rectangular food storage container. Explain how you would figure it out without pouring the contents in. If it will fit, how much more broth could the storage container hold? If it won't fit, how much broth would be left over? (Remember 1 cm³ = 1 mL.)

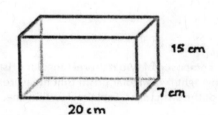

First, I have to find the volume of the storage container.

$20\,cm \times 15\,cm \times 7\,cm = 300\,cm^2 \times 7\,cm = 2{,}100\,cm^3 = 2.1\,L$

Since each line on the beaker is 400 mL, the beaker holds 2.4 L

It won't fit in the storage container. $2.4\,L - 2.1\,L = 0.3\,L$

Juliet will have 0.3 L or 300 mL left over.

© 2014 Common Core, Inc. All rights reserved. commoncore.org

Name _____   Date _____

1. Use your ruler to draw a rectangle that measures $4\frac{1}{2}$ by $2\frac{3}{4}$ inches, and find its area.

2. Heather has a rectangular yard. She measures it and finds out it is $24\frac{1}{2}$ feet long by $12\frac{4}{5}$ feet wide.

   a. She wants to know how many square feet of sod she will need to completely cover the yard. Draw the yard and label the measurements.

   b. How much sod will Heather need to cover the yard?

   c. If each square foot of sod costs 65 cents, how much will she have to pay to cover her yard?

© 2014 Common Core, Inc. All rights reserved. **commoncore.org**

3. A rectangular container that has a length of 30 cm, a width of 20 cm, and a height of 24 cm is filled with water to a depth of 15 cm. When an additional 6.5 liters of water is poured into the container, some water overflows. How many liters of water overflow the container? Use words, pictures, and numbers to explain your answer. **(Remember 1 cm³ = 1 mL.)**

4. Jim says that a $2\frac{1}{2}$ inch by $3\frac{1}{4}$ inch rectangle has a section that is 2 inches × 3 inches and a section that is $\frac{1}{2}$ inch × $\frac{1}{4}$ inches. That means the total area is just the sum of these two smaller areas, or $6\frac{1}{8}$ in². Why is Jim incorrect? Use an area model to explain your thinking. Then give the correct area of the rectangle.

5. Miguel and Jacqui built towers out of craft sticks. Miguel's tower had a 4-inch square base. Jacqui's tower had a 6-inch square base. If Miguel's tower had a volume of 128 cubic inches, and Jacqui's had a volume of 288 cubic inches, whose tower was taller? Explain your reasoning.

© 2014 Common Core, Inc. All rights reserved. **commoncore.org**

6. Read the statements. Circle "True" or "False." Explain your choice for each using words and/or pictures.

    a. All parallelograms are quadrilaterals.   True   False

    b. All squares are rhombuses.   True   False

    c. Squares are rhombuses, but not rectangles.   True   False

    d. The opposite angles in a parallelogram have the same measure.   True   False

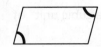

    e. Because the angles in a rectangle are 90°, it is not a parallelogram.   True   False

    f. The sum of the angle measures of any trapezoid is greater than the sum of the angle measures of any parallelogram.   True   False

    g. The following figure is a parallelogram.   True   False

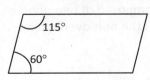

© 2014 Common Core, Inc. All rights reserved. **commoncore.org**

End-of-Module Assessment Task	Topics A–D
Standards Addressed	

Apply and extend previous understandings of multiplication and division to multiply and divide fractions.

5.NF.4   Apply and extend previous understandings of multiplication to multiply a fraction or whole number by a fraction.

     b.   Find the area of a rectangle with fractional side lengths by tiling it with unit squares of the appropriate unit fraction side lengths, and show that the area is the same as would be found by multiplying the side lengths. Multiply fractional side lengths to find areas of rectangles, and represent fraction products as rectangular areas.

5.NF.6   Solve real world problems involving multiplication of fractions and mixed numbers, e.g., by using visual fraction models or equations to represent the problem.

Geometric measurement: understand concepts of volume and relate volume to multiplication and to addition.

5.MD.3   Recognize volume as an attribute of solid figures and understand concepts of volume measurement.

     a.   A cube with side length 1 unit, called a "unit cube," is said to have "one cubic unit" of volume, and can be used to measure volume.

     b.   A solid figure which can be packed without gaps or overlaps using n unit cubes is said to have a volume of n cubic units.

5.MD.4   Measure volumes by counting unit cubes, using cubic cm, cubic in, cubic ft, and improvised units.

5.MD.5   Relate volume to the operations of multiplication and addition and solve real world and mathematical problems involving volume.

     a.   Find the volume of a right rectangular prism with whole-number side lengths by packing it with unit cubes, and show that the volume is the same as would be found by multiplying the edge lengths, equivalently by multiplying the height by the area of the base. Represent threefold whole-number products as volumes, e.g., to represent the associative property of multiplication.

     b.   Apply the formulas $V = l \times w \times h$ and $V = b \times h$ for rectangular prisms to find volumes of right rectangular prisms with whole-number edge lengths in the context of solving real world and mathematical problems.

     c.   Recognize volume as additive. Find volumes of solid figures composed of two non-overlapping right rectangular prisms by adding the volumes of the non-overlapping parts, applying this technique to solve real world problems.

© 2014 Common Core, Inc. All rights reserved. **commoncore.org**

Classify two-dimensional figures into categories based on their properties.

5.G.3   Understand that attributes belonging to a category of two-dimensional figures also belong to all subcategories of that category. *For example, all rectangles have four right angles and squares are rectangles, so all squares have four right angles.*

5.G.4   Classify two-dimensional figures in a hierarchy based on properties.

Evaluating Student Learning Outcomes

A Progression Toward Mastery is provided to describe steps that illuminate the gradually increasing understandings that students develop *on their way to proficiency.* In this chart, this progress is presented from left (Step 1) to right (Step 4). The learning goal for each student is to achieve Step 4 mastery. These steps are meant to help teachers and students identify and celebrate what the student CAN do now and what they need to work on next.

© 2014 Common Core, Inc. All rights reserved. **commoncore.org**

A Progression Toward Mastery

Assessment Task Item and Standards Assessed	STEP 1 Little evidence of reasoning without a correct answer. (1 Point)	STEP 2 Evidence of some reasoning without a correct answer. (2 Points)	STEP 3 Evidence of some reasoning with a correct answer or evidence of solid reasoning with an incorrect answer. (3 Points)	STEP 4 Evidence of solid reasoning with a correct answer. (4 Points)
1 5.NF.4b	The student is unable to draw the rectangle and unable to find the area.	The student draws one dimension accurately, but is unable to find the area.	The student accurately draws both dimensions of the rectangle, but makes a calculation error when finding the area.	The student correctly: • Draws the rectangle. • Calculates the area as 12 3/8 in^2.
2 5.NF.4b 5.NF.6	The student is unable to draw the yard, calculate the area using appropriate units, or calculate the cost of the sod.	The student does one of the following: • Draws and labels the yard. • Calculates the area of the yard. • Uses the correct units (square feet). • Finds the cost of the sod.	The student is able to correctly perform two of the following actions in any combination: • Draws and labels the yard. • Calculates the area of the yard. • Uses the correct units (square feet). • Finds the cost of the sod.	The student correctly: • Draws the yard and labels correctly with the length as 24 1/2 ft and the width as 12 4/5 ft. • Calculates the area of the yard using appropriate units as 313 6/10 ft^2 or 313 3/5 ft^2. • Finds the cost of the sod to be $203.84.
3 5.MD.3 5.MD.5	The student is unable to find the volume of the water that has overflowed and is unable to explain the reasoning used.	The student finds the volume of the water that has overflowed, but is unable to explain the reasoning used.	The student makes a calculation error in finding the volume of the water that has overflowed, but is able to clearly explain the reasoning used.	The student finds the volume of the water that has overflowed to be 1.1 L and uses words, numbers, and pictures to clearly explain the reasoning used.
4 5.NF.4b 5.NF.6	The student is not able to draw an area model, provide an explanation of Jim's error, or give the correct area.	The student does one of the following: • Accurately partitions the area model in both dimensions. • Provides a clear	The student does two of the following: • Accurately partitions the area model in both dimensions. • Provides a clear	The student: • Accurately partitions the area model in both dimensions. • Provides a clear explanation of Jim's

© 2014 Common Core, Inc. All rights reserved. commoncore.org

A Progression Toward Mastery

		explanation of Jim's error. ■ Calculates the correct area of the rectangle.	explanation of Jim's error. ■ Calculates the correct area of the rectangle.	error. ■ Calculates the correct area of the rectangle as 8 1/8 in^2.
5 **5.MD.5**	The student is neither able to find the heights of the towers, nor able to answer which tower is the taller.	The student makes an attempt to calculate the towers' heights, but makes errors in both calculations. Explanation of reasoning used is unclear.	The student calculates the heights of towers, but makes a calculation error which causes an error in the determination of the taller tower. However, the explanation of the reasoning used is clear.	The student: ■ Accurately calculates the heights of both towers (8 inches). ■ Explains clearly that the towers are equal in height.
6 **5.G.3** **5.G.4**	The student provides a combination of at least three correct true or false responses and/or explanations.	The student provides a combination of at least six correct true or false responses and/or explanations.	The student provides a combination of at least seven correct true or false responses and/or explanations.	The student provides seven correct true or false responses and clear explanations for all seven items. a. True b. True c. False d. True e. False f. False g. False

© 2014 Common Core, Inc. All rights reserved. **commoncore.org**

Name ___Jean_____   Date _____

1. Use your ruler to draw a rectangle that measures $4\frac{1}{2}$ by $2\frac{3}{4}$ inches, and find its area.

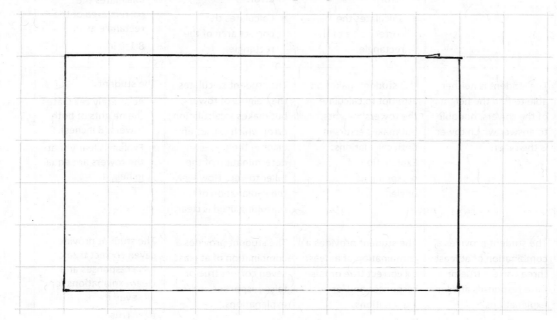

$$\frac{9}{2} \times \frac{11}{4} = \frac{99}{8} =$$

$$12\frac{3}{8} \text{ in}^2$$

2.

   a. Heather has a rectangular yard. She measures it and finds out it is $24\frac{1}{2}$ feet long by $12\frac{4}{5}$ feet wide.
She wants to know how many square feet of sod she will need to completely cover the yard.
Draw the yard and label the measurements.

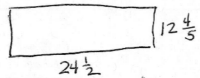

$12\frac{4}{5}$

$24\frac{1}{2}$

   b. How much sod will Heather need to cover the yard?

$\boxed{313\frac{3}{5} \text{ ft}^2}$ $12\frac{4}{5} \times 24\frac{1}{2} = \frac{64}{5} \times \frac{49}{2} = \frac{3136}{10} = \frac{1568}{5} = 313\frac{3}{5}$

$\begin{array}{r} 313 \\ 5\overline{)1568}\ r3 \end{array}$

$\begin{array}{r} 1568 \\ 2\overline{)3136} \end{array}$

$\begin{array}{r} 64 \\ \times 49 \\ \hline 576 \\ 256 \\ \hline 3136 \end{array}$

   c. If each square foot of sod costs 65 cents, how much will she have to pay to cover her yard?

$313\frac{3}{5} = 313.6$ $\$203.84$

$\begin{array}{r} 313.6 \\ \times .65 \\ \hline 15680 \\ 18816 \\ \hline 203.840 \end{array}$

© 2014 Common Core, Inc. All rights reserved. commoncore.org

3. A rectangular container that has a length of 30 cm, a width of 20 cm and a height of 24 cm is filled with water to a depth of 15 cm. When an additional 6.5 liters of water are poured into the container, some water overflows. How many liters of water overflow the container? Use words, pictures and numbers to explain your answer.

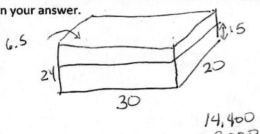

$$\begin{array}{r} 14,400 \\ -9000 \\ \hline 5,400 \end{array}$$

Volume of Container:

$30 \times 20 \times 24 = 720 \times 20 = 14,400 \text{cm}^3$

Volume of water:

$30 \times 20 \times 15 = 450 \times 20 = 9000 \text{ cm}^3$

$5,400 \text{ cm}^3$ left, or 5.4 L

6.5 L $- 5.4$ L $= 1.1$ L

$\underline{1.1 \text{ L overflow.}}$

4. Jim says that a $2\frac{1}{2}$ inch by $3\frac{1}{4}$ inch rectangle has a section that is 2 inches × 3 inches and a section that is $\frac{1}{2}$ inch × $\frac{1}{4}$ inches. That means the total area is just the sum of these two smaller areas, or $6\frac{1}{8}$ in². Why is Jim incorrect? Use an area model to explain your thinking. Then give the correct area of the rectangle.

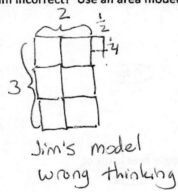

Jim's model
wrong thinking

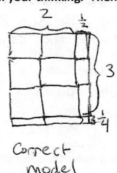

Correct
model

If you add up all the parts, you get $2+2+2 = 6$ whole and $\frac{1}{2}+\frac{1}{2}+\frac{1}{2}+\frac{1}{4}+\frac{1}{4} = 2$ plus one little $\frac{1}{2} \times \frac{1}{4}$ piece $= \frac{1}{8}$ so $8\frac{1}{8}$. Same as $2\frac{1}{2} \times 3\frac{1}{4} = \frac{5}{2} \times \frac{13}{4} = \frac{65}{8} = \boxed{8\frac{1}{8} \text{ in}^2}$

5. Miguel and Jacqui built towers out of craft sticks. Miguel's tower had a 4-inch square base. Jacqui's tower had a 6-inch square base. If Miguel's tower had a volume of 128 cubic inches, and Jacqui's had a volume of 288 cubic inches, whose tower was taller? Explain your reasoning.

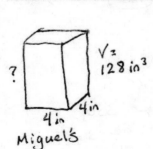

Miguel's

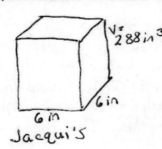

Jacqui's

$$16\overline{)128} \\ \underline{-128} \\ 0$$

$$30\overline{)288} \\ \underline{-288} \\ 0$$

$$\begin{array}{r} 36 \\ \times8 \\ \hline 288 \end{array}$$

$$\begin{array}{r} 16 \\ \times8 \\ \hline 128 \end{array}$$

They are both the same height, 8 in! When I divided both volumes by the area of the bases, I got 8 for both.

© 2014 Common Core, Inc. All rights reserved. **commoncore.org**

6. Read the statements. Circle "True" or "False." Explain your choice for each using words and/or pictures.

a. All parallelograms are quadrilaterals.   (True)   False

A parallelogram is a kind of quadrilateral with 2 sets of parallel sides.

b. All squares are rhombuses.   (True)   False

A rhombus has 4 equal sides, and so does a square. But not all rhombuses are squares.

c. Squares are rhombuses, but not rectangles.   True   (False)

Squares are both, because they also have 4 right angles.

d. The opposite angles in a parallelogram have the same measure.   (True)   False

It's because the sides are parallel to each other and they all have to add to 360, so both pairs have to be the same.

e. Because the angles in a rectangle are 90°, it is not a parallelogram.   True   (False)

The sides are still parallel pairs, so it's a parallelogram.

f. The sum of the angle measures of any trapezoid is greater than the sum of the angle measures of any parallelogram.   True   (False)

The angle measures of any quadrilateral, including Trapezoids and parallelograms, is always 360°.

g. The following figure is a parallelogram   True   (False)

115°
60°

It's not because the angles would have to add up to 180, but they only make 175. This would mean all the angles together would make 350, which is impossible. They have to be 360.

© 2014 Common Core, Inc. All rights reserved. commoncore.org